I Only Know
Who I Am When I
Am Somebody Else

I Only Know Who I Am When I Am Somebody Else

My Life on the Street, on the Stage, and in the Movies

DANNY AIELLO

WITH GIL REAVILL

GALLERY BOOKS

New York   London   Toronto   Sydney   New Delhi

G

Gallery Books
A Division of Simon & Schuster, Inc.
1230 Avenue of the Americas
New York, NY 10020

First Gallery Books hardcover edition October 2014

GALLERY BOOKS and colophon are registered trademarks
of Simon & Schuster, Inc.

For information about special discounts for bulk purchases,
please contact Simon & Schuster Special Sales at 1-866-506-1949
or business@simonandschuster.com.

The Simon & Schuster Speakers Bureau can bring authors
to your live event. For more information or to book an event,
contact the Simon & Schuster Speakers Bureau at 1-866-248-3049
or visit our website at www.simonspeakers.com.

Interior design by Jill Putorti
Jacket design by Laywan Kwan
Jacket photographs by Brian Hamill

Manufactured in the United States of America

10 9 8 7 6 5 4 3 2 1

Library of Congress Cataloging-in-Publication Data is available.

ISBN 978-1-4767-5190-0
ISBN 978-1-4767-5192-4 (ebook)

To my wife, Sandra,
and my children, Rick, Danny III, Jaime, and Stacey,
for getting me through the toughest times of my life;
and to the memory of my mother, Frances,
who represents the good in me.

DANNY / WHO LOVES YOU? xxx Paul Mazursky

My hope was that Paul Mazursky would write the foreword to this book. Sadly, he passed away during the writing, so I decided not to have one.

Paul/"Who loves you?"/Danny Aiello

I Only Know
Who I Am When I
Am Somebody Else

Chapter One

Searching for Me

In March 1990, I was sitting in the audience at L.A.'s Dorothy Chandler Pavilion, waiting for the winners to be announced at the sixty-second Academy Awards ceremony. All around me were gorgeous women and handsome men. The Oscars were the kind of event that showed this New York City kid just how far he had come from his beginnings on the streets of the West Side of Manhattan and the South Bronx.

My stomach was tied in knots. That year, I was nominated as Best Actor in a Supporting Role for my performance as Sal Frangione in Spike Lee's controversial film *Do the Right Thing*.

The nomination was so important to me. It told me, *You're not only a working actor, but you've been accepted by your peers.* For a guy who never set foot in an acting class and who only started his career in his mid-thirties, this was a supreme validation.

I recall clearly what else I felt that night, with all the glitter and glamour flowing around me like a river.

No matter where I was, I was an outsider. Even with an Oscar nomination and everybody talking about my performance, I still had a nagging sense that somehow I didn't belong.

It's a feeling that I've always had. At something like this major awards event, the sense of being an outsider was especially sharp. *What am I doing here?* I kept thinking. I wasn't a member of the Hollywood inner circle. I grew up working-class, not privileged. I'm street. And here I was, surrounded by people who were more like avenues, landscaped boulevards, private drives.

The thing about being an actor, though, is that you're never alone. With me that evening were all the characters I had ever portrayed in the movies and on the stage. They whispered in my ear, telling me that while winning isn't everything, losing doesn't have a hell of a lot to say for itself. Those voices are always present.

Throughout my life, I've always been searching for me. Creating characters is part of that search. At the Oscars that night, the truth was both simple and complicated.

I only know who I am when I am somebody else.

It sounds like a riddle, but it's the reality of my life. When I'm playing a character, only then do I know who I am, only then am I complete.

I've experienced dark times in my life when I've been an outsider even to myself. I've been so depressed and confused that I've experienced a loss of self. Acting helped save me.

Geena Davis, who was presenting the Best Actor in a Supporting Role award that evening, stepped up to the podium onstage. She introduced all the contenders, my name among them. I was up against some heavy hitters: Marlon Brando, Denzel Washington, Martin Landau, and Dan Aykroyd.

"The Academy Award for this year's best supporting actor goes to . . ." She struggled opening up the envelope.

The moment hung in the balance for me. In a lot of ways, it represented a culmination of the journey I was on, leading me to great heights and devastating lows, transporting me to places like the Dorothy Chandler Pavilion in Los Angeles.

I want to invite you, the reader, on this journey in search of self. It's my hope that this personal journey of mine might help you on yours.

Come on along.

Chapter Two

My Very Own West Side Story

Memories of my childhood emerge from a warm, golden glow of family, especially the devotion of my dear mother, Frances Pietrocova Aiello.

Mom was my rock. She made me the man I am today. My father, Daniel Aiello Sr., took a hike early on, before I was born. Throughout my childhood, he was absent more often than not. It was up to my mother to keep our family together. Her example taught me that the real heroes aren't the ones who win gold medals or Nobel Prizes (or Academy Awards).

As a kid, I never knew how poor we were because all my friends were from hard-luck families. I came into a world that was far away from the one we live in now. Some of this book was written by speaking to a virtual woman named Siri. I travel in a car that has a navigation system guided by a satellite that orbits sixteen thousand miles above the planet. If I have a factual question, the answer is immediate, at my fingertips.

When I was born in June 1933, we weren't in the modern age quite yet. The Aiellos still had one foot in the last century. That golden glow around my family that I remember from my childhood came from kerosene lamps. Electricity was dirt cheap, and Thomas Edison's incandescent bulbs could have lit our rooms for nickels a week, but kerosene was cheaper than dirt.

City planner Robert Moses and the rest of the bigwigs of New York City had called our West Side neighborhood "blighted." Pretty soon they would come in with bulldozers and flatten it for redevelopment. When I look at a map of modern Manhattan, I can't find the blocks where I grew up. They've been erased and built over.

If you want to catch a glimpse of what my old neighborhood was like, just see the movie *West Side Story*. Director Robert Wise shot that film in the condemned city blocks that would become the site of Lincoln Center for the Performing Arts. As for me, I might as well have been born a Jet all the way, as the song goes. Those were my childhood haunts, right there on the big screen. Preserved in shot after shot of that classic movie were the streets and ramshackle tenements that thousands of families like mine called home.

By the time *West Side Story* was released in 1961, almost everything depicted was already in the process of being destroyed. But for nearly a decade, from the time I was born until we moved to the Bronx, a small ten-block-square slice of Manhattan's West Side was my childhood turf.

An unofficial line existed in that area of Manhattan, separating the haves and the have-nots. In my neighborhood, the line was West End Avenue. Nowadays, the closer you get to the Hudson River, the higher the rent. It was the direct opposite back then. The Aiellos lived on the west side of West End Avenue. To the east of West End, the residents weren't rich, but there was some money there—not much, but some. Farther east, past the dividing line of Broadway, there lay another land, a land of giants. That's where the real money was.

You would have thought our West Side neighborhood was something out of a Charles Dickens novel. In the 1930s, there were still horse-drawn carts traveling the streets. A stone trough for watering horses sat on the corner of Seventy-Second Street and Broadway, and an actual stable was on our block. Just to indicate the kind of transition period America was enjoying back then, the stable sold automobile tires, too.

Merchants would travel down West End Avenue every day, hawking their wares with their wagons and mules. One actually called out, "Rags! We sell rags!" but why the hell anyone would want to buy a rag is a mystery to me that's gotten lost in time.

To give you another idea of the time and place: early every morning, the iceman cometh, straight out of the Eugene O'Neill play. If the iceman made a sale, he'd drape a burlap sack over his back and grab a suitcase-sized block of ice with a huge pair of metal tongs. He'd sling the heavy block onto his back and trudge up the stairs to the customer's apartment. The block would then slide right into a compartment in an old-fashioned icebox, not an electric refrigerator. After a day or two, the ice would melt and the whole process would start over again.

My mother's family, the Pietrocovas, came from the Naples

and Sorrento areas of Italy. Both Mom and Dad were born in the United States. The West Side neighborhood where I grew up was home to many immigrant Italians. But I was as American as a kid could get.

Home for me, baby "Junior" Aiello, was a basement railroad apartment on West Sixty-Eighth Street, just off West End Avenue. They called them railroad apartments because the rooms were laid out in a straight line. You could stand at one end of our place and look all the way through to the other side.

There were four rooms for eight of us—me; my mother; my four sisters, Helen, Gloria, Rosebud, and Annabelle; my brother Joey; and my grandfather Raphael, who went by the Americanized name of "Ralph." The toilet was in the hallway, and other tenants in the building had access to it, as well.

Our apartment wasn't wired for electricity. Instead of a shower, we had a tub in the kitchen area. Baths were a once-a-week occasion. Heat came from a wood-burning stove in the parlor. My mother cooked on a cast-iron stove. The smell of wood smoke and kerosene still sucks me right back into those early days of childhood.

The amazing thing is that we preserved our privacy in that apartment. Never do I remember seeing any member of my family in a state of undress. In our home, "respect" was the most important word. If there was a closed door anywhere, you were to knock before entering. My mother didn't preach this. Instead, she set the example by doing it every day.

My father showed up at most a couple times a month. At my young age, I didn't understand that a dad could be anything other than someone who dropped by every once in a while. All I heard were vague excuses for his absence. He was "traveling," Mom said. I would see the man for a few hours one evening and then he would be gone, leaving behind a faint smell of cigar smoke in his wake. I didn't know him well enough to miss him.

As a kid I didn't have much to do with my older siblings, either. I was the second youngest of the six surviving Aiello children. Helen, Gloria, and Rosebud were all leading their teenage lives, as was my older brother Joey. That left me spending a lot of time with my sister Annabelle.

When the teenagers did bother to notice us, it often wasn't pretty. I recall a memorable beating I took from my brother Joey. He would have been around twelve or thirteen at the time, while I was only seven or eight. Joey kept a pistol hidden in his clothes drawer. I found the handgun, took it to school, and promptly lost it. I can't remember if it was confiscated by a teacher or by an older schoolmate. But I do remember Joey's anger. He was much bigger than me. When he started to hit me, I had no other choice but to sit there and take it until he felt bad about doing it.

Helen, as the oldest sister, acted as a second mother in the family. She worked, earned money for the family, and had a boyfriend. The only resentment I felt around home about my absentee father came not from Mom but from Helen. She and my father didn't get along at all. She was old enough to have spent time with him as a child and old enough to grasp the enormity of his deserting us.

Back in those days of the 1930s, old-fashioned traditions held on. My family and most of those around us didn't use funeral homes. We dressed our dead by ourselves. This practice left me with one of my enduring memories of childhood, the night I slept with an open casket. My grandmother on my mother's side passed away, and her wake was held right there in our apartment. There was Grandmother that night, resting in peace in her coffin, and there was I, little five-year-old Junior Aiello, trying to sleep only a few feet away.

My childhood was death-haunted in another way, too. A mystery hung in the air when I was growing up, one that still plagues me to this day. My mother and father had seven children together, four girls and three boys. One of those boys, Ralphie, who was named after my grandfather Raphael, died as an infant before I was born.

Old memories float up whenever I think about my brother's death. He was like a phantom that haunted my youth. I would bother my mother about him. What was he like? How did he die? Would I see him in heaven?

"When he fell sick, the doctors told me it would be bad for him to drink water," Mom recalled, sadness in her eyes from the memory. "I would take a wet cloth and dab his lips, but that's all I could do. 'Wa-wa,' Ralphie kept saying. He was begging for water, but I couldn't let him drink any."

Wa-wa. Wa-wa. Whenever she told me the story, both of us would wind up in tears.

I've searched through birth records and hospital documents since then. The death certificate I obtained states that Ralph Aiello passed away on August 3, 1932, at Riverside Hospital on North Brother Island in the Bronx.

Family legend had it that Ralphie was first buried in a potter's field on Hart Island. Later, supposedly a Catholic charity linked to the St. Patrick's diocese paid to exhume the little body and have it formally placed in a proper grave. The burial records claim he was interred in Calvary Cemetery in Queens. But I honestly believe that it never happened. I think Ralphie still rests in that potter's field.

There's nothing I can say that conclusively proves this. There are only inferences I make from what my mother told me. I have the text of a letter from Calvary Cemetery:

> *Please be advised that Ralph Aiello was interred in section 39 on August 6th, 1932 at the age of 7 months. Ralph Aiello was interred in an untitled grave. This grave holding is for indigent burials only. There are no markers allowed on this grave holding.*

North Brother Island, where my brother died, is sometimes identified in city records as a "leper colony." That meant it was a place of quarantine. In those days before antibiotics, contagious diseases were much feared. My brother's death certificate listed an infectious disease, pertussis, as the cause of death. Whooping cough.

Mary Mallon, the notorious cook known better as Typhoid Mary, was quarantined on North Brother Island during the time my brother was in the hospital there. Because she was an asymptomatic carrier of typhoid fever bacteria, Typhoid Mary caused the deaths of dozens of people for whom she prepared meals.

My brother was born days before Christmas in 1931. When he was just seven months and fourteen days old, he fell sick. On Friday, July 29, 1932, city health authorities transported the feverish baby to North Brother Island. By the following Wednesday, Ralphie Aiello was dead.

My mother often told me of a close call she had in her life. "I was going to visit your brother Ralphie," she said. "I was waiting at the dock, but your father was late to come, so I didn't go on the boat."

The ferry, a steamer called *Observation*, exploded and sank in the East River. Seventy-two people were killed in the disaster. It happened at a little past eight o'clock on the morning of September 9, 1932—*five weeks after my brother passed away*. Mom must have intended to take the ferry in order to visit his grave in the potter's field. If that's the case, then the reinterment of my brother's remains on August 6, 1932, doesn't make sense.

The family story was that the Catholic charities placed my brother's body in a cemetery plot. No one had the money back then for individual grave plots. Did a St. Patrick's charity pay to reinter him? The story could have all been just a comforting tale to make everyone feel better.

Ralphie was blood to me. I am a part of this boy. In the scheme of things, his death and burial might be just a minor mystery, important only to the family. If I can ever locate his remains to a certainty, I want to give Ralphie a proper headstone. It's the least I can do to honor the brother I never knew.

My West Side neighborhood might have been a constant, but as a family we moved a lot, both before and after I was born. There were two moves during my first ten years, once out of that first basement railroad apartment to the fourth floor of a tenement, then back into another basement. All three places were on the same block of West Sixty-Eighth Street. The reason was always the same, too: a lack of rent money. We needed to start over with a new landlord.

This wasn't a rare practice on the West Side of Manhattan. A lot of families did the same thing. The building superintendents were making a small fortune off the constant upheaval in the neighborhood. They would earn a payment by turning the lodgings over. When the Aiellos moved out, the next day someone else would move in. The new tenants had to pay a fee to the super in order to take possession. The landlords might not even have known about the constant turnover. It was musical chairs, only with apartments.

In those days the family dog, Bessie—a big blond collie—served as my constant companion. She ate what we did, namely our table scraps—we didn't know from dog food back then. I was a scrawny kid, able to take occasional rides on the dog's back. My mother sent me and Bessie out together to pick up items at the local grocery. I'd let her carry the bag on the way back home. Bessie was such a good dog that she would never run off with the groceries to make a meal for herself.

Given that we never had much money, the Aiello kids existed on a steady diet of peanut butter sandwiches, which we loved. When we could get bananas, we'd add slices to the sandwiches. Another staple was potato-and-egg sandwiches. And oatmeal, which I hated, but my mother fed it to us until it came out of our ears. We also ate the traditional peasant foods of my mother's Italian heritage: beans, lentils, and pastafazool (pasta and beans).

Meat was a rarity in our household. At most, it was a once-a-week thing. Sunday dinner meant a special meal of wonderful freshly made spaghetti and meatballs. We dined without wine—we were the only Italian-American family in the universe that didn't have it on the table during dinner. The reason might have been that we couldn't afford it, but the lasting effect was that not one member of my family ever became a big drinker.

To this day, I don't know how my mother did it. She fed, clothed, and sheltered six children and my grandfather. She once told me she had pared the family food budget down to thirteen cents a day!

Mom had a hard-and-fast rule: "If you go out and they're serving dinner at the home of a friend, you tell them that you aren't hungry." When I'd ask why, she wouldn't explain. She would just shake her head and say to just do what she said. Only as an adult did I realize that it was simply a point of pride for her. She didn't want anybody in the neighborhood to think her children were hungry. And I did what I was told, too, even though there were plenty of times I would have gladly accepted a free meal.

Even with the Aiello family living as close to the bone as we did, I was still a problem child when it came to food. I was fussy. Often I refused to eat what was put in front of me. The worst were the onions, and any dish that had come near them would be immediately pushed away.

Mom would say, "I removed all the onions."

"Not the smell, Mama," I'd protest. "You didn't remove the smell!"

There was no chance I would eat any kind of seafood. If it looked "ugly" to my young eyes, that was that. My friends and I used to go to the docks on the Hudson River and watch people fish from the shoreline. I still remember the eels—they made me feel sick just looking at them.

"I'd never put anything that ugly in my mouth!" To this day, I have an aversion to eating anything that swims.

Chapter Three

Mothers and Fathers and Sons

I was a very sickly child. I was anemic and had a touch of asthma. From age six to when I was eight or nine, I was hospitalized several times for eczema, scratching myself bloody. It got so bad that I had to put gloves on at school to keep my fingernails from digging big red gouges into my flesh. At night, when I went to bed, my mother would transfer my socks from my feet to my hands for the same reason.

I was small and should have been sitting up in the front of the class. Instead, because of embarrassment over my incessant scratching, I chose to sit in the back row. It was excruciating. I could see my classmates stealing glances at me, giving taunting smiles, giggling. I was a sensitive kid, so of course I imagined that I was disgusting to them.

The tragedy was that I really liked some aspects of school. Definitely not math, but I couldn't wait to read whenever teachers called on me. I simply loved reading out loud. If they ever asked me to get up and speak without a book in my hands, I was too shy. Whenever I was reading another person's words, I didn't stammer or lose my place.

Though eczema practically overwhelmed my young life, I tried to hide from my mother how it affected my time in class. I didn't want her to be upset. She already had too much to worry about. I didn't have many friends at school. It wasn't because I didn't want them. I thought they didn't want me.

In school, I might have been relatively friendless, but on the street, it was different. The best times I had as a kid were when I played outdoors. Then I didn't have the time to worry about scratching and bleeding. I was too busy having fun.

I was a hell of a stickball player. I was always out on the block in front of whatever apartment we lived in at the time. We didn't have yards, we had the street. The asphalt made a long, narrow field for playing ball. Traffic wasn't as vicious back then as it is today.

Using a broom handle for a bat and a pink rubber Spaldeen ball, we played the West Side version of the game, with a pitcher who delivered a one-bounce pitch. First base was that fire hydrant there, second base was sixty feet down the block, third base was that old battered Ford over there. On the pavements of New York City, I began to develop the baseball skills that would pay off later in my life in unexpected ways.

My friends and I played other games, too, traditional street contests that had been passed down by our older siblings. I would take newspapers and roll them up extra tight, then wrap twine around them until I had something that resembled an oval shape. That served for our football, as heavy as a brick. A real inflatable pigskin was wishful thinking, of course beyond our means.

Punchball was played in a square, with the goal being to "punch" the ball out through the line of opposing players. Johnny on the Pony was a pile-on contest that resembled the offensive line action in the NFL.

Sometimes, we found other, more dangerous ways to amuse ourselves. The freight railroad tracks ran along the Hudson River, just a few blocks away. A neighborhood kid got his hands on some .22 rimfire bullets, I guess from a supply his father kept. My friends and I used to put the shells on the railroad tracks and wait for the trains to run over them. The sharp reports sounded like strings of firecrackers going off. We'd laugh like maniacs. Looking back, we were lucky that a stray round didn't kill anybody.

Our street games didn't end until dark. I still remember the sound of mothers calling children home as evening shadows fell, the calls echoing between the tenement buildings of Sixty-Eighth Street.

Every night before bedtime, the entire family would gather around the radio. Our Philco was like a piece of furniture, with a cabinet of varnished wood and a dial that glowed orange. All over the West Side and all over America, households would be doing the same thing, listening to the radio as a popular evening pastime. Our favorite shows had headlining comics such as Fred Allen, Jack Benny, and Edgar Bergen. There were also crime serials and mysteries like *The Shadow*, *Mr. District Attorney*, *Inner Sanctum*, and *The Green Hornet*.

The holidays were another time of great family togetherness. One of my clearest childhood memories centers around what I've always considered to be my first Christmas. The year was 1939, and I was six years old.

On Christmas Eve, I lay in my bed listening to a conversation that my little sister, Annabelle, was having with my mom in the next room. "Is Santa Claus bringing us presents this Christmas?" Annabelle asked.

"I bet he comes this year," Mom replied.

Last year, he didn't come, I thought, mentally joining in on the conversation. *We don't have a tree. Where will Santa put the presents?*

"How will he get in?" Annabelle asked. "There's no chimney for him to climb down."

"Maybe the window," Mom said.

My six-year-old mind didn't think Santa could fit through the window. And I didn't think kids could get presents if the family didn't have a tree. I was all torn up with worry.

Through a crack in the door, I could see my mom smiling and giving my little sister a hug. "Santa is amazing," she said. "Magical things can happen at Christmastime."

On Christmas Day, Grandpa Ralph woke me at six a.m. He was already dressed. He didn't have a job but always looked as though he was heading out to one, wearing a crisp white shirt and a suit jacket.

"Ju-ju," he said—my name was Junior at the time—"this is for you, a good boy."

My eyes were still full of sleep. I rubbed them clear. I opened my hand and saw a nickel. I was so excited. Grandfather kissed me on the cheek and went out the door.

The whole morning was enchanted. I looked up from my bed, out the window, and through the basement grating, and saw snow falling. Then I turned toward the parlor and saw a tree. Not a very big one, but it was a tree nonetheless. Our first Christmas tree! I thought I was dreaming.

Understand that this was not a privileged person's holiday. It wasn't even a reasonably well-off family's Christmas. I found out later that my older sister Helen had actually pinched the tree from a street merchant. That morning, its boughs were decorated not with store-bought lights and ornaments, but with bottle caps tied to different-colored shoestrings. The Christmas stockings were used socks that we kids had actually worn, now repurposed and filled with tiny candies.

But to my young eyes, it was a perfect Christmas morning. It was just as Mom said to Annabelle, *magical*. Underneath the tree, there was at least one gift for each of us. My first real Christmas present was a pair of boxing gloves. Maybe I should have seen those gloves as a sign of the struggles ahead.

I didn't think about any of that on this, my first *real* Christmas. I was too happy. I was in the warm embrace of my family, and nothing else mattered.

In my early days, my mother acted as both parents. I used to tell my friends that Dad was in Cleveland on business, making up the fairy tale that he worked as a police detective, "chasing prisoners."

Why a detective? I'm not sure, but I think it was because I had seen my father wearing a fedora and a raincoat, and detectives in the movies and comic strips always wore the same, so my young mind simply made the connection. And why Cleveland? Perhaps I thought of it as a faraway land, at least far enough removed that my friends could never check up on the white lie I was telling.

The strange thing about my mother was that no matter how my father would treat her, Mom would never bad-mouth him. Her husband might disappear for half a year at a time, but she would say absolutely nothing against the man. And because my mother loved him, we children did, too.

My father was nineteen when he married my mother in 1921. Frances was only fifteen. Even though Dad and Mom had met at formal, chaperoned events in the West Side neighborhood where they both lived, his family didn't want the marriage to take place. Frances was too young to make a suitable match.

What was my father doing when he wasn't with us? "He's a trucker," Mom would say. "He's away a lot."

It took a long time before the real picture finally came into focus. My father held jobs as a teamster and a moving man. But those weren't the only ways he earned a living. Back then, they had a name for what my father was: a knock-around guy. That meant he wasn't a mobster himself, but he consorted with them.

Within weeks of the wedding, he took a job with the infamous bootlegger Dutch Schultz. He drove trucks for the beer baron. In the early days of Prohibition, mob rivalries were still being sorted out. For a while, my father called himself "Dan Dillon" to be able to pass for Irish. This was when he worked for Roger Touhy, the Irish-American gangster who was a rival of Al Capone.

A story Mom told me about those days used to fascinate me as a child. In the 1920s, during the height of Prohibition, my mother was at home in the family apartment when there came a knock on the door. My father realized what was happening and immediately hid under the bed. A trio of wiseguys confronted Mom, demanding to know where her husband was.

My mother didn't know what it was all about. She was pregnant with my brother Joey at the time. "I just kept repeating that he wasn't at home," she told me. The wiseguys finally relented. As they were leaving, Mom said they gave her a parting tribute.

"We know he's here," one of the mobsters told her. "You just saved your man's life."

She never could find out what my father had done to warrant a visit from mob enforcers. But the image of my mother fending off gangsters while my father hid under the bed made a lasting impression on me. It told me how things were with my parents in the period before I was born.

"He's away a lot" was really code for my father's being in prison. A hijacking scam he was involved with got busted and he wound up doing a two-year stretch in New York City's Rikers Island.

One of my earliest memories of my father is visiting him in jail. He was getting processed in downtown Manhattan at the Tombs, a.k.a. the City Prison. My mother brought me down to see him. They would not allow me into the prison, as I was too young. Mom left me with a policeman in the vestibule while she went upstairs to visit Dad.

When my mother returned, she took me by the hand. We walked out into the street in front of the jail.

"Look up," she said.

I peered upward at the dirty façade of the Tombs. In a barred window on the fourth floor I saw a small light, a shaky, wavering flame. It was my father. He held a cigarette lighter, a signal to his little boy.

I definitely don't want to make it seem like my spotty relationship with my father was some monstrous hardship. It wasn't that way at all. Whatever my dad was doing outside the home didn't much matter to me during that first decade of my young life. What *did* matter was that the man who gave me his name was never around.

As a kid I started working in 1942, at the ripe old age of nine. I was a skinny child but tough. Plus I was willing to do anything that would bring in a few nickels to the family. I ended up shining shoes in Grand Central Terminal.

That year, the mobilization for World War II hit New York City in a big way. Servicemen poured through town, transferring to their respective deployments. The trains in and out of the city were jammed. Everywhere you looked was a uniform. And if you looked hard enough, you would have seen a pint-sized me sidling up to my prospective customers.

"Shine, soldier? Shine?"

Man, those boots! The tall, government-issued combat boots were heavy as hell and made to wear like iron. But I loved them because I got to charge extra to work on them. A regular shine was a dime, but the combat boots brought in a quarter.

A sergeant would breathe fire on any soldier who didn't have his boots shined to a high gloss. That's where I came in. I buffed those boots until I could see my reflection in them. I used to pop that rag, making music with my buffing cloth. The better the show I put on, the bigger the tips I got. I was like a frantic bee buzzing around the soldiers.

What I remember most is how the boots always seemed to be in mint condition. They were a light, yellowish tan, not even broken in yet and still smelling of new leather. I would be giving them their first shine.

The boots were worn by boys maybe ten years older than me. Where were they headed? To the beaches of Normandy or Guadalcanal. I didn't think about it then, but those fresh, clean boots shined in Grand Central Terminal marched through Europe or the Pacific theater, through mud and snow and blood. A lot of those boots never came back.

Every day before I set up, I would buy a stack of newspapers. This was during the golden age of New York City journalism. I brought the tabloids to my shoe-shine spot, and my patrons liked them because they were easy to page through while I got to work. I would end up selling copies of the *Daily News*, the *Daily Mirror*, and the *New York Journal-American*, doubling the cover price. But my customers would happily pay the premium because they saw me as a determined little kid working his ass off to make a living.

On a good day, I cleared a couple of dollars. With a few first-rate tips, I might even bring home five dollars. I never kept any money for myself. I wouldn't have known what to do with it if I did. Every member of the Aiello family pitched in.

It wasn't enough. Nothing was ever enough. "Rent is due" is a terrifying phrase I remember hearing constantly throughout my childhood. With the war in Europe raging, it almost seemed like our family troubles were mirroring the turmoil in the world as a whole. Everything was in flux. The modern world was being born right before my eyes.

I would return again and again to a furniture shop on Broadway and Seventieth Street, a few blocks from where we lived. Displayed in a window was a strange glowing device that must have been the first television ever produced. Animated images danced on a screen.

But TV couldn't hold a candle to my real passion, which was sneaking into the big movie palaces on Broadway. I rarely had the dime it cost for admission. A family friend, Al Vironi, worked as an usher and would slip us kids into the theater for free.

The movies had an irresistible attraction for me. Penniless as I was, I simply had to see them as often as I could. The male stars of the day were everything that I desperately yearned to find—the father figures to replace the one who was missing in my life. Wallace Beery, the great MGM star of the 1930s, was my first favorite, along with Fredric March, Broderick Crawford, Spencer Tracy. These were stars who allowed me to dream of what life could be like.

Around this time my childhood nightmares started, and a lot of those began in the movie theaters, too. Boris Karloff as Frankenstein's monster and Lon Chaney Jr. as the Wolfman scared the hell out of me, to the degree that I had to go to sleep with the bedcovers pulled up over my head as they worked their way into my dreams, disturbing my sleep.

It didn't help my nightmares any when we moved for the summer to a free place a relative provided for us in Coney Island, Brooklyn. It was 1942. We were in a second-floor apartment above a wax museum on the boardwalk. Lilly's World in Wax Musee featured gory tableaus of famous crimes. The one that burned itself into my nightmares was of a madman from the 1920s named William "the Fox" Hickman. In the museum, Hickman's wax figure was posed dismembering his victim Marion Parker in a bathtub. My dreams were haunted back then.

When we left Brooklyn that summer, we didn't return to our old neighborhood. Our wayward journeys from apartment to apartment weren't over yet. The West Side may have been blighted and poverty stricken, but it had been my home for almost a decade. Smack in the middle of the chaotic war years, rent worries forced us to move yet again. This time we didn't just change addresses. We moved to a whole new world.

Chapter Four

Fists, Don't Fail Me Now

No one welcomed us when the Aiellos landed on the streets of the South Bronx. We were on our own, strangers in a strange land.

We left a few members of the family behind when we moved. Our new apartment in the Bronx did not accept pets, so our collie, Bessie, stayed behind with Jonesie, a black man who was a family friend. I was heartbroken to have to leave her.

After we moved to the Bronx, I never saw my grandfather again, either. Apparently there had been a secret reason Raphael was getting dressed up every day in sharp clothes. He wasn't headed out to look for work. He was meeting women-friends. My grandfather married again and moved to Plainview, Long Island. He outlived that second wife and another one besides, living until he was well into his eighties.

So I first showed up in the Bronx minus a dog and minus a grandfather. I had to find my own way. All the neighborhoods I grew up in were scrappy, physical places. My friends and I fought constantly. We used to have fistfights in the hallways of the tenements where we lived. In those close quarters, it was like fighting in an alley. Your back was always to some wall.

There were two kinds of fights in my younger years. The first was clearly anger related. We played the dozens. Somebody went too far with the insults and pretty soon fists were flying. The second was more about entertainment—real punches landed, but we were fighting just to see who was the quickest, the strongest, the most unrelenting. Our heroes were the boxers who made headlines: Joe Louis, Billy Conn, Willie Pep, and Beau Jack.

In the Bronx, I was the new kid on the block, so I had to prove myself. I was battling on the streets of an ethnically mixed neighborhood. Officially, it was called Crotona Park East, but I don't remember any of the locals calling it that. The majority of the population was Jewish, but there were Italians, Irish, Germans, Puerto Ricans, and black people. We lived in the middle of it all, in a series of cheap apartments along Stebbins Avenue, Boston Road, Hoe Avenue, Home Street, Southern Boulevard, and Freeman Street.

The Aiellos were on Home Relief, a welfare program that President Franklin Roosevelt had pushed through during the Great Depression. Government spending on the war effort had started to lift the economy, but it took a while before the good times reached the Bronx.

All through the war years, my mother did piecework, either as a seamstress or stuffing envelopes for mail-order campaigns. Our kitchen table was always piled high with stacks of advertising in-serts. At the time, there were still manufacturing jobs in New York City. Most of the men were away overseas, so my mother was fi-nally able to land a job, working as a supervisor in the Sid Spindel toy factory on Southern Boulevard. She still did her piecework to make ends meet.

I attended PS 54 on Intervale Avenue, five blocks away. After school, Annabelle and I would walk over to the factory and yell up to the window. "Mom! Hey, Mom!" She'd appear at the window and toss us money for an after-school snack, coins wrapped in a napkin or a piece of paper—a quarter, sometimes a little bit more, whatever she could spare.

My mother constantly juggled her day to make things work for her children. The older Aiello kids were off on their own. Mom would prepare breakfast for Annabelle and me before we left for school. We would have our lunch at Jack's Restaurant, at Free-man Street and Southern Boulevard. We'd always order the same thing: mashed potatoes with brown gravy. We didn't have to pay ourselves, since my mother ran a tab, paying for our lunches at the end of every week.

Mom finished work at five p.m. and came straight home to prepare supper for us. She sometimes had a second job in the eve-ning, cooking at a local restaurant. The woman was tireless, and all her efforts flowed from her love and devotion to her children. I used to take it for granted back then. Now I recall what she did with reverence.

I don't know if it was the family's relocation to a new neighbor-hood or just normal growing pains, but during this period, around age thirteen, I began to act the rebellious teenager. My oldest sister, Helen, wasn't around at home much anymore, so Mom was the only one who was there to discipline me. I played hooky a lot, disappearing from PS 98, Herman Ridder Junior High on Boston Road. My teachers reached out to my mother, begging her to get me to school.

"He's so sweet, I love him," my teacher Mrs. Rossellini would say. "Why doesn't he come to class?"

When my mother confronted me about my excessive absences, I'd swear to her that I really had been attending school. Of course, there'd be hell to pay for my lies. She got so angry that she would come after me with a broom. I dove under my bed, the only place to get away from her. I used the bedsprings to pull myself up off the floor, as Mom would be swatting and sweeping under the bed. But she could never reach me, and in my heart I know that she really didn't want to.

I was wild outside the home, too. When you're uneducated, there are always people around who are verbally quicker. They're able to use words to put you down. When they got to me, I didn't talk back but just used my fists. That's how I settled my differences with people. Throughout my Bronx years, I was always nursing bruises and scrapes. Part of my ear got torn off in a fight. I got stabbed. That was just the way of the streets.

At times it seemed that nobody got out of the South Bronx unscathed. I can still trace the wounds I got during those days. I received the scar that is the most attractive part of my face when a guy ripped my eye open. I also have a scar on my thigh from when I got shot by a bullet fired from a zip gun.

Constructing zip guns was a popular pastime in the neighborhood. We got all the materials necessary from shop class at PS 98.

I took an L-shaped piece of wood, fitted it with a lamp pipe for a barrel, and used a nail for a firing pin with a rubber band to propel the nail into the bullet. Then I'd wrap the whole mess in white adhesive tape. I used a lot of tape, in the vain hope that the thing wouldn't explode in my face.

The first time I was taken into the local precinct house was when I was caught stealing a Hooton chocolate bar from the Woolworth's on Westchester Avenue near the Simpson Street el stop. The store manager called the police. Two officers arrived and took me to the "Four-One," the Forty-First Precinct stationhouse in the Bronx. There they handcuffed me to a radiator near the bullpen, right next to a holding cell crammed with people who definitely should not have been out on the street.

The cops wanted to scare me, trying to teach me a lesson. I learned two things that day: I never wanted to be in a bullpen again unless I was a relief pitcher with the Yankees, and I never wanted to be handcuffed to a radiator that was being used as a toilet.

The precinct house of the Four-One went by another nickname. Because of its embattled status in the middle of a high-crime zone, it came to be called "Fort Apache," after the old John Wayne cavalry movie. Thirty-five years after I sat chained to that urine-soaked radiator in the Four-One, I would return there to film *Fort Apache, the Bronx*, starring Paul Newman, with me acting the role of the psychopathic cop Morgan.

As a young teen, I ran with a group of neighborhood kids. We called ourselves the Kingsmen. Belonging to the Kingsmen was based more on which block you lived on than from what country your people had emigrated. Outsiders looked on us as a street gang, but really, we were just a stickball team.

The neighborhood had block parties that extended from day to night. In the evening there was music, bands, dancing. It was like a festival. The streets were closed off. The events were usually run by the PAL, the Police Athletic League. The PAL organizers would also cordon off a ring and allowed us kids to fight if we wanted to, only not bare fisted, the way we usually did. We had to wear boxing gloves.

Our stickball contests at times pitted neighborhood against neighborhood. Stebbins Avenue might play Boston Road, or Freeman Street would line up against Hoe Avenue. We played for money, a few dollars at most. In reality, the games were for boasting privileges.

Fights broke out all over the place. The stickball wars swept up not only the players but everybody from the whole neighborhood. Tenants from our blocks fought tenants from their blocks, pitched battles right there in the street. It was madness. Combatants employed bottles, fists, or garbage cans. The cops arrived, confiscated the broom handles that we used as bats, and settled everyone down.

Until the next game.

Crotona Park East might have been a wild ethnic mix back then, but like I said, the population was predominately Jewish. As a kid, I was hired as a Sabbath goy. I would go around to the Jewish homes on holy days and light stoves or turn on lamps. Observant Jews were not allowed to perform even the simplest task on the Sabbath—from driving a car to flipping a switch.

I was too young to drive, although I would have probably been delighted if I was ever asked. But the lights and stoves were easy, and the families I helped out were very appreciative. Since no one in that community could handle money on the holy days, I got paid in empty milk bottles worth two or three cents per deposit. Even though it wasn't much, I was grateful for it.

Just as we had when we lived on the West Side of Manhattan, the Aiello family kept moving. The rent was always due. Like my earlier days before we moved to the Bronx, I remained a working kid. I no longer journeyed down to Grand Central to shine shoes, but I delivered the *Saturday Evening Post*, canvas bag and everything, a real newsie.

I also used to deliver loads of wash from the local laundries to the customers. Wet wash was very heavy but cheaper. If customers wanted dry laundry, they paid a premium. They'd accept the heavy bundle from me and hang it out to dry themselves via clotheslines running from back windows to poles erected for that purpose in the back of each apartment building. The laundries never paid me a salary. I got paid only in tips.

At this point, I was hustling for any job I could get, working in downtown grocery stores like Gristedes and later at the fancier Charles & Company. I delivered messages for Western Union.

A few of my gigs actually furthered my informal education. Even though I was technically too young to be allowed inside Charley's Pool Hall on Boston Road, I learned my way around a billiards table when I got hired to sweep up at the joint. The same thing happened at Tremont Gym AC, one flight up off the street on East Tremont Avenue near the Elsmere Theatre. For a time I wielded a broom there, too, and picked up pointers on how to box, watching the French middleweight Marcel Cerdan train for his match with Jake LaMotta.

Eventually I entered into a little shadier style of work. I ran numbers for the local mob. The racketeers liked to use underage children to carry betting slips because they knew that police couldn't bust us. We were a gang of little snot-nosed kids running around to neighborhood street corners and candy stores. Along with the money, we collected the slips with the numbers scrawled on them.

Everything would eventually be delivered to the numbers "bank," a storefront operation at Fordham Road and Belmont Avenue, where the neighborhood controllers worked. But as runners, we rarely went up there. Instead, we would turn in our slips at the local diner, Fred's, located at Boston Road and Stebbins Avenue. A runner's pay was nothing, just a few nickels for every run.

I collected from a poverty-stricken betting public that had little money to spare but was always hoping for better days. Even the most down-and-out folks could find a nickel, dime, or quarter. Hitting a number was a common dream in the neighborhood, the odds being 500 to 1. On a quarter bet, the payoff was a hundred and twenty-five dollars. That sum represented the jackpot fantasy for the poor people of the Bronx.

During those days I was always hustling, always looking for ways to make bank. In 1946, the summer I turned thirteen, I somehow finagled a way to join the National Guard. This was the postwar period, when the guard was so starved for manpower that it would take anyone. I was short, five foot seven, and still looked as though I were nine. My mother had to sign permission papers to allow me to go.

The guard assigned me to the Forty-Second Infantry Division. As part of my enlistment, I had to go away to Pine Camp in upstate New York for two weeks out of the year. It was all for money.

I turned over to my mother the seventy-five-dollars-per-month National Guard compensation.

Other attempts at making something of myself were less successful. When I was fourteen years old, my mother brought me down to East Fifty-Second Street in Manhattan, where they were holding tryouts for the *Arthur Godfrey's Talent Scouts* radio show. All through the 1940s and beyond, the prime-time variety program was extremely popular and had a huge nationwide audience. The whole Aiello family listened to it, gathered around the radio in our apartment in the Bronx every Monday night at eight-thirty.

Mom always wanted me to sing. She thought I was a real Caruso. I definitely could not manage opera, but I had a good time singing at gatherings of friends and relatives.

For the audition, I planned to do "All of Me," the 1931 classic of all classics, written by Gerald Marks and Seymour Simons. While Mom and I were sitting in the vestibule of the *Talent Scouts* audition hall, waiting for my name to be called, nervousness overcame me. I asked if I could be excused to go to the bathroom. I fled that audition and never returned. I got on the subway and hightailed it back to the Bronx. The next time my mother saw me was at home.

I was too nervous to perform in public. All I could think about were the millions of people in Arthur Godfrey's audience, listening to the radio and hearing me screw up. My nervousness about singing stayed with me for a long time afterward.

During this time, we lived on Stebbins Avenue in the Bronx and I worked in a drugstore at East 170th Street, delivering prescriptions. My best friend was fifteen-year-old Bey Domini, a kid who could draw anything and had all the makings of a great artist. He and his mom lived in the same building we did, and that year I spent more time in his apartment than in my own.

Hanging around so much with Bey, I noticed something odd. Over time, there seemed to be fewer pieces of furniture in the apartment. It turned out that Bey was selling the family furnishings to support his heroin addiction.

His mother seemed unable to do anything to stop him. Bey began avoiding me, his best friend. I wasn't around when Bey Domini, a kid with everything going for him, died of a drug overdose at age fifteen. I believe it was this incident from my childhood, more than anything else, that created a hatred in me for drug use and a low tolerance for those who used that shit.

I was still just a kid, fooling around with street fights, zip guns, and shoplifting—pretty ordinary stuff for the South Bronx in those days. What dogged me more than anything was a nagging sense of searching for something. For a long time, I thought it might be my missing father.

I saw my dad more in my teens than when I was little. Now that I was older, I wanted the chance to get to know him better. When I was fifteen, my dad arranged for me to live with him in a boardinghouse for a couple months one summer in Astoria, Queens, near Steinway Street. My mother was all for it. She thought it was a good idea for father and son to mend fences.

Those two months turned out to be a lonely time for me. Unlike when I was living with Mom, I had a strict curfew. I had to be at the boardinghouse by nine every evening. It was embarrassing. I was going out with a girl named Joan Delaney back then, and she wound up walking me home at the early hour of nine o'clock.

I had no friends in the neighborhood, and I saw my dad only

briefly at night, when he was getting ready for sleep. He was always early to bed, early to rise. That summer, he would come back to the boardinghouse, smoke one of his trademark White Owl cigars, and then turn in, barely speaking to me at all.

The closest we ever came to an intimate father-son talk was one night he showed me a tackle box he kept beneath his bed. "There's money in it," he said. "If you ever need any, go ahead and take it."

"Okay, Dad."

A long, awkward silence followed. "How's your mother?" he asked me.

"Mom would feel a lot better if you were home," I said.

"I have to be out of town most of the time," he said.

For the period when we shared living quarters, he'd disappear for days at a stretch. I never knew where he went. I never saw him with any friends. I didn't know how he spent his days.

I found out one afternoon when I encountered my father walking down the street near our boardinghouse, accompanied by a woman. A few times over the course of that summer, I had seen them together before, but I didn't know who she was. This time he introduced us. Her name, he said, was Eileen. She nodded to me. We didn't shake hands. It was an awkward moment for both of us.

That was the last and only extended period of time I ever spent with my dad. I never told my mother about the other woman.

Chapter Five

How Baseball Saved My Life

In ninth grade my run-ins with the law turned a little more serious than a stolen candy bar. Due to constantly missing school because of my eczema attacks, I had been held back a year. I was older than the other kids in my class, sixteen instead of fifteen. In 1950, while I attended PS 98 on Boston Road in the Bronx, I was called into the principal's office one day.

Two plainclothes detectives from the NYPD waited for me there. With no questions, no ceremony, and certainly no reading of my rights, they marched me out to the street and loaded me into their unmarked car.

The detective who wasn't driving leaned over the seat toward me. "You know someone named Joe Ariargo, a Spanish kid?" he asked. "The one that got his ass kicked? You have anything to do with that?"

I knew what they were talking about. I had heard rumors around the neighborhood. The beating had happened the week before. But I sure as hell had had nothing to do with it, and I told the detectives that.

"You're Danny Aiello, right? They call you Junior?"

"Yes, sir," I said. "But it wasn't me."

"Well, we were given your name by a witness."

All the stories of false accusations and innocent men locked away for crimes they didn't commit suddenly occurred to me.

The cops took me thirty blocks south on Boston Road, then farther south on Third Avenue. I swear a pop song was on the car radio during that drive, repeating the lyrics "I have an alibi" over and over. I figured the detectives wouldn't appreciate it if I sang along.

The ride gave me plenty of time to think. The mind is a funny thing. The more I thought, the more doubts came to me. Even though I was innocent, I started to feel guilty. I was sure that the whole catalog of my petty crimes showed on my face. Maybe I really *had* attacked Joey Ariargo.

The bulls pulled up at Lincoln Hospital, on 149th Street just off Grand Concourse. I had visited the ER there many times before for various busted bones, scrapes, and wounds. But I'd never had the honor of being walked through the lobby by a pair of NYPD detectives.

We took the elevator to the fourth floor. The cops sat me down in a chair across the corridor from the injured kid's room. They didn't play good cop/bad cop. They were both bad.

"If he identifies you, you're going away for attempted murder," one of them said. The two of them disappeared into the room.

They must've let me sit there sweating for maybe five minutes, but to me it felt like hours. Then the door to Joey Ariargo's sick-room slowly swung open. I stared at a form lying in bed, his whole head swaddled in bandages like a character in a cartoon. Whoever had done the job on Joey had done it completely.

The door slammed back shut again. A few minutes later the detectives emerged. Without a word they lifted me out of the chair, one under each arm as if they were marching me off to prison. Down in the hospital elevator, through the lobby, and out to the street we went. They drove me back to school, still not giving a word of explanation.

The cop up front spat out a single sentence: "Get the fuck out of my car." It turned out that Joey Ariargo had not fingered me as his attacker.

I could see how my life was going. Trouble kept showing up at my door. The next time the police visited, or the next time a zip gun went off, maybe I wouldn't be so lucky.

In my neighborhood, if you weren't continuing on in school, or if you didn't have a good job, you went into the military. I had dropped out of high school, and I didn't have any employment prospects, so I bailed out of the Bronx and into the service. Two things happened almost at the same time in June 1950: I turned seventeen, and that same week, the Korean War started.

My mother didn't want to let me go. But she could read my future the same as I could. On January 5, 1951, I became the property of the U.S. Army. I didn't even shave yet. For the whole time I was in the service, I sent home my Class Q allotment dependency checks to my mother. In my mind, I remained what I always was: a working kid. The army was just another job.

My fight card was just as crowded in the service as it had been on the streets of the Bronx. The first tussle I had went down immediately after I enlisted, when I stood in a chow line at Fort Dix in New Jersey. We had just been processed and hadn't even been given uniforms yet. It was raining and I had an army-issued poncho on, with civilian clothes underneath.

A soldier tried to cut into the line in front of me. I reacted instantly and tried to throw a punch. It was a silly move. My arm got caught in the folds of the rain poncho and all I managed to do was twirl around like a dancer.

Our sergeant saw it all happen. "Hold up, hold up!" he yelled. "You two, get inside, both of you!" The whole platoon trooped into the barracks. There the sergeant had the two of us fight over our differences with bare fists.

My opponent's name was Jerry Gitling. He was built like a wrestler. He was so muscular that if he had grabbed me and squeezed, he probably could have killed me. Yet I knocked him down with one punch. I knew I had hurt him very badly. Jerry struggled back up onto his feet. It was clear that he wanted to fight me but didn't have a clue how to do it. I didn't have to hit him again.

That's how it was in this man's army. If you got into an argument with a fellow soldier, the sergeant made you fight it out. This was a regular occurrence for me in the service, but I was just doing what I had always done back home. Jerry Gitling, the husky guy I first faced off with, became one of my best buddies in basic training, though I lost track of him later.

I was sent home on furlough prior to doing two weeks of advanced combat training at Fort Benning, Georgia. While back in the Bronx, I said good-bye to a lot of people. There was a lot of hugging and crying from Mom, my sisters, my brother, and many of my friends.

When I returned to camp, my unit proceeded to Georgia and completed its combat training. I was summoned in front of the commanding officer with seven other soldiers from the regiment.

"Men, your eight names were drawn from a hat," the CO announced. "You are being cut from the mission."

I was stunned. In the course of training together, our troop had become very close. We knew we were going into firefights alongside each other. That kind of knowledge makes for deep friendships. Now those bonds were about to be broken.

The whole process seemed totally random. My name was drawn from a hat? What was that all about? I had no idea why the eight of us, from among thousands of soldiers in the regiment, were chosen not to go. I began to feel like a punk. I imagined that the other men were thinking that we'd chickened out and didn't want to go into combat, or that we'd gotten out of it because we had connections.

The unit was soon shipped to Korea, while the eight of us were sent on furlough once again. I didn't want to return home. I felt it would be embarrassing. What was I going to tell my friends and family? That I didn't go to Korea the last time, but I would be going the next time? Who the hell was going to believe me?

While on this second furlough, my father gave me one last keepsake memory before I was shipped out. The incident is imprinted so clearly in my mind. I was in uniform in Times Square, walking down Broadway at Fiftieth Street. I remember being able to see the marquee of Radio City Music Hall, all the way over at Sixth Avenue. The movie *The Great Caruso* was playing, starring Mario Lanza.

In one of those chance meetings that happen in New York, I saw my father coming up the crowded sidewalk. He accompanied a woman I didn't recognize. When he saw me, he reacted as if nothing at all was wrong. He introduced his companion to me as Marge Fontane, one of the Fontane Sisters, a popular singing group of the day. My father seemed proud of himself.

"She's the lead singer!" he crowed, as if that fact would somehow impress me. I went home, feeling guilty for not telling my mother about this new "other woman."

When I returned from furlough a second time, fate intervened once again. The day before being shipped out to Korea, we were lined up for roll call. Another eight names were called out, different ones this time, except that once more, one of them was mine. Again, the CO said that these eight names had been picked out of a hat, and the eight of us were cut out from the rest of the regiment. The odds against my being picked twice were astronomical.

Why was my name chosen, not once but twice? How could that be possible? I will never know. I also have no idea how many of those men I trained with wound up dying on the Korean peninsula.

The news came down from on high that I would be transferred with my new regiment to Germany. I wasn't too thrilled about that. I had thought I was going to Korea. That's what I had volunteered for. Of course, we could still ship out to the war from Europe. In October 1951, we embarked from Norfolk, Virginia, on the *General R. E. Callan*, an old beat-up transport ship.

The trip across the Atlantic to Germany was my first time at sea, and I immediately got sicker than a dog. Ten minutes out of port, I was ready to commit suicide. My bunk was on F-deck, the lowest part of the ship, which is actually below the waterline. All

I could think of was going to sleep. I staggered down to my bunk, slowly crawled in, and lay flat on my back. I still clutched my rifle, which was drenched in Cosmoline lubricant and wrapped in plastic. The oily smell sickened me further.

My CO, Captain Mitchell, came down to rouse me. "Private Aiello, get up on your feet!" he yelled.

"I can't," I moaned.

"Get your ass out of the rack or you'll be court-martialed!" Mitchell shouted. He was screaming, his face inches from mine.

I didn't move. "Sir, let me die," I said feebly. "You can shoot me. Feed me to the sharks."

"One last time, as your commanding officer I order you, Private Aiello—get on your feet!"

"Sir, I don't care if you're the president of the United States, I am going to die here, and I don't give a fuck!" I managed to further enrage Captain Mitchell when I tried to justify my actions, lying there in my bunk with my oily M1 carbine.

"What are you doing with that weapon, Aiello?"

"Sir, you told us if we didn't clean the rifle, we would have to sleep with it. I'm sleeping with it, sir!"

Mitchell never did have me court-martialed. He felt I was too sick to know what I was saying or doing. He was a good guy and I served under him throughout my time in Europe.

The voyage wasn't a leisure cruise, of course. As soldiers, we all had responsibilities to fulfill, the worst being KP—"kitchen patrol": washing dishes, mopping floors, everything but the cooking. When it came to making three square meals a day, the army had other soldiers doing that. They called them chefs. After experiencing their food, though, I had another name for them.

Somehow I survived the transatlantic trip. We docked in Bremerhaven, Germany, in October 1951. It was my first time on foreign soil. About three o'clock that morning, we were put on trains and sent to Munich. The trip was a long one, so the army provided Pullman sleepers. But I stayed awake for much of the trip, staring out at the countryside, fascinated.

I will never forget the faint sound of the train running on the tracks, almost silent, whispering, totally unlike the metallic racket of trains back in the States. It was as if the wheels never came in contact with the rails. I was later told that when bombing raids took place over Germany, blackouts might render targets invisible, but sounds from the ground below could sometimes be heard, and those sounds became targets. So the Germans learned to muffle their trains.

I had dark expectations of what I was going to see in Germany. World War II had ended only six years earlier, so what were the people like now? Without feeling? Still warmongering monsters whose leaders engineered the annihilation of millions of innocents? Such were my thoughts just prior to falling asleep riding through the heart of Germany.

We arrived at our destination the afternoon of the next day. The army loaded us onto two-and-a-half-ton trucks for the final leg of the exhausting trip. As we traveled through the countryside, I noticed that the towns we passed seemed to be untouched by the war. Bavaria, in particular, was beautiful in the summer and even more so in autumn. The towering Alps were already capped in snow.

My regiment was billeted at Warner Kaserne, outside of Munich. During the war, this place had been occupied by the SS, and only a few kilometers away was Dachau. One visit was enough to tell me everything I'd heard back home about the "Final Solution" was true. The revolting evidence of the Holocaust was enough to place the beauty of the countryside into sobering contrast.

When I finally met some of those German civilians I had been so curious about, I was left with a welter of confused feelings. Many times I encountered wounded German war veterans, some of them blind, missing a leg, or having some other visible wound. Poverty-stricken, they begged for handouts, offering a piece of paper documenting their military record.

The odd thing was, every single veteran could show evidence of having been wounded while fighting Russians on the eastern front. I could never figure out the truth of it. Were these disabled veterans claiming to have fought not Americans but Russians because they were afraid we would turn our backs on them? At first, I hesitated to help because of what I had seen at Dachau. Soon enough, though, the common humanity of their plight earned them my sympathy.

It was the winter of 1951–52, and most of my time was spent out in the field, specifically in the district of Hohenfels, living in a pup tent and digging foxholes. I threw live hand grenades with fifty-caliber machine guns firing two feet above my head. It was the coldest I had ever been in my life, with the temperature hitting fifteen degrees below zero.

The army didn't change its expectations just because our asses were frozen solid. We performed the same tasks as we did in good weather. When it was time to eat, it didn't matter if it was in the middle of a blizzard. We had to stand in the chow line, running in place to keep warm.

Our rations weren't going to win any taste awards. The exception was my first Thanksgiving away from home. The military did it up right, serving up turkey breast, sweet potatoes, mashed potatoes, and cranberry sauce. Of course, we had no teacups or pretty dishes, just our mess kits and our canteens.

One afternoon during that first raw winter in Germany, a host of dignitaries arrived at camp for a parade and inspection. I stood in front of my battalion, holding the Stars and Stripes in parade rest position. General Dwight Eisenhower walked by and stopped in front of me, and I snapped to attention.

"Where are you from, soldier?" Ike asked.

"Fort Benning, Georgia, sir," I said.

"What's a rebel doing in this Yankee outfit?"

"Oh, no, sir," I said quickly. "I only meant that I took my combat training at Fort Benning. I'm from New York, sir."

Ike looked me up and down and gave me a word of praise that I've remembered my whole life. "You're a fine-looking soldier, son," he said. Soon afterward he became the president of the United States.

I made some great friends while stationed in Germany. Most of them came from New York City. Some had enlisted, others were drafted. Among my best buddies were Red De Filippo, Sal Portillo, and Tony Antrilli, a ranked boxer from Philly, with whom I used to spar. Some of my army friends, like Joe Zappala, I still see even to this day. Later on in civilian life, President George H. W. Bush appointed Joe as ambassador to Spain.

Placed in among all these men from varying backgrounds, I began to feel my lack of a formal education more keenly. I resolved to improve my vocabulary, so I worked at educating myself. I got a dictionary and picked out four words a day to learn and use.

Slowly, with small, tortured steps, I discovered the glories of the English language. I came to like certain words, like "tantamount," "nomenclature," and "rodential."

Then, and not for the last time, baseball intervened in my life.

The regiment fielded a team that would play in a league made up from divisions that were stationed all over Europe. A certain Lieutenant Edwards from Texas became the reason I no longer had to go out on maneuvers. He was the manager of the 172nd Regimental Baseball Team.

At tryouts, I so sufficiently impressed Edwards that he named me as a starting first baseman and an occasional pitcher. The years of stickball in the streets and sandlot baseball in Crotona Park had paid off.

I learned the magical army acronym TDY—"temporary duty." It meant no more marches, no more mess details, no more drudgery. When springtime came, my one and only military obligation was to play baseball.

This was in the early 1950s, the period during which the Cold War was ramping up. There were almost as many U.S. soldiers in Germany as there were in Korea. To the quarter million American servicemen stationed in the country, we were their entertainment. I must have played a hundred games over the course of my two summers in Germany.

My teammates and I had it made in the shade thanks to temporary duty. We got weekend and evening passes and spent a lot of time at Munich supper clubs, including one in particular, Studio 15, where all the beautiful German actresses hung out. The food in Germany was amazing. The Wiener schnitzel! And the bread and butter was like nothing I had ever tasted before.

Lieutenant Edwards established one hard-and-fast rule. We held our baseball workouts across the street from the regimental barracks. If we were on the field when the regiment was headed out on a forced march, Edwards ordered us not to provoke our fellow soldiers in any way.

"As they pass us, you will not look in that direction," he said. "You will keep playing ball. You will make no eye contact whatsoever, and you will definitely not engage in heckling."

The enlisted men as well as the officers, he said, hated our baseball-playing guts. "They all want to do what you're doing. And they want you to share their misery. If they have to go out on marches and maneuvers, why not you?"

We did as we were told. It made me feel guilty, but not too guilty, and never for very long. I was enjoying the feel of a baseball bat in my hands too much to have any negative reaction to what was clearly a piece of good luck. I had joined the military and was seeing the world, just like the recruiting posters had promised.

But I could just imagine the conversations I would be having after my days in the service. "What did you do in the war?" "Well, I played a little ball." That answer didn't sound too good.

I spent twenty-eight months in Germany. I left the States a kid, but I came back a man. In January 1954, honorably discharged from the army, I was back in the Bronx and wondering what the hell I was going to do with myself. I was always wondering that. But I was determined that my life would be different. My nickname had always been "Junior." Now I insisted that everyone call me "Danny."

The reason you can't go home again is that home isn't the same as when you left it. The flight to the suburbs was beginning to hit my old neighborhood. I had an uncanny feeling that there were social forces afoot that I couldn't quite understand. Where did I fit in? Ike was in the White House, and America appeared to have settled into a peaceful period of prosperity. But in truth, the economy was already in a downturn and jobs were scarce.

I found myself back at square one. I felt restless. The streets were familiar but I had changed. There was more of me—I had filled out and come into my full height while I was in the service. I might have been tall, but I was still a bundle of uncertainty. I left the army as a corporal. That didn't mean a hell of a lot in civilian life.

I moved in with my mother in an apartment at 1419 Stebbins Avenue. Mom had more trouble with her eyesight, which she was losing to glaucoma. I think all those years sewing and doing piece-work had aggravated her condition. My sister Gloria told me that my mother needed an eye operation. It turned out Mom had saved every penny of the dependent payments that I had sent home.

"She wanted to use that money to buy you a car," Gloria said.

I almost cried. "Take the money!" I said. "Take it all! Give it to her for the operation!"

She had the operation, the first of several. This is the new role that I wanted for myself, to be a provider, a breadwinner, a dutiful son who took care of the ones he loved. Meanwhile I was living on my three-hundred-dollar mustering-out pay and a twenty-six-week stretch of unemployment benefits, at seventy-five dollars a week.

Even the warm cocoon of my family seemed to have changed while I had been gone. I rarely saw my siblings. My brother Joe worked with my uncle at his business, Aiello Junior Moving and Storage, at Ninety-Sixth Street on Manhattan's East Side. My sisters were married and living their own lives.

Mitchell Eddis, a baseball scout from the New York Giants, took a look at me on the ball fields of the South Bronx. He came up to our apartment a few times, having lunch or just coffee with me and my mother. I had last been scouted a half decade before, when I was still in high school.

Eddis was a genial man, a real old-fashioned aficionado of the game, the kind of shoe-leather scout you don't see much anymore. I reacted to his interest in a peculiar way. At that point in my life, in 1954, I had just been away from home and in a uniform for my stretch of time in the army. I simply did not want to don a baseball uniform and go out on tour with some minor-league franchise. It sounds like a whim, refusing a professional baseball scout for such a reason, but I just wanted to stay around my old neighborhood.

My time in the army might have made a different man out of me, but I slipped back into my old South Bronx ways with my former number-running buddies. I played a lot of pool and got to the point where I could knock down some coin hustling other players.

Then I had the greatest piece of luck I ever had in my life.

I found what I was missing. I discovered my heart's desire, right there in my old neighborhood.

Chapter Six

Sandy

I remember the first time I saw the most beautiful girl in the Bronx. It was April 1954 and I was standing on the corner of East 170th Street and Wilkins Avenue. Walking toward me was a knockout: blond hair, five foot two, maybe eighteen years old, with the most gorgeous blue eyes imaginable. She wore scotch-blue plaid slacks and walked like a little duck. She was alone and I wondered how the hell that could be.

I must say, I looked pretty good myself. I was twenty years old and had come out of the army at six foot three, weighing in at one hundred eighty pounds. The blond girl stopped a few yards down the sidewalk. Looking straight at me, she said, "Are we going to the movies?"

While I desperately wanted her to be talking to me, I knew that she really wasn't. I was like a pane of glass to her. She was looking right through me, focusing on another guy standing on the street right behind me.

He approached her and whispered something in her ear. They embraced and walked off, passing me by as if I were begging to be ignored.

At the time, I was with my friend Larry Leifbaur. I asked him if he knew the girl.

"She lives on Boston Road," Larry said. "Her name is Sandra, Sandy Cohen."

"Sandy," I said, already dreaming.

"You want to meet her?" Larry asked.

"Well, that's her boyfriend, right?" I said.

"So you don't want to meet her?"

"I didn't say that," I said. Right about that time, there was no one I would have rather met. "She's the girl I want to marry."

"You've only seen her once!" Larry said, scoffing.

After that, as fate would have it, I kept encountering pretty Sandy Cohen. A few days later I was in a candy store on Boston Road, drinking an egg cream (New York's favorite drink, which, despite its name, has no egg or cream in it—only seltzer, Fox's U-bet chocolate syrup, and milk). I had stepped into the store's old-fashioned phone booth to make a call.

Sandy entered soon after and fell into a conversation with the store owner. She never once looked over at me. I couldn't make out what they were saying. I stayed in the phone booth like Clark Kent afraid to change into Superman. My time in that damned booth seemed like forever. I kept asking myself, how many occasions could I possibly end up in the same place with this girl and not get up the nerve to speak to her?

Finally she left. I emerged from the booth and asked the store owner what the two of them had been talking about.

"She comes in here all the time with her boyfriend, Stanley," he said. "Now she tells me that they broke up."

There was a chance for me, I thought, but she didn't even know I was alive. But I kept bumping into Sandy: on the sidewalks of Wilkins Avenue, in a park, or at a café. I thought it was a series of coincidences, but all of those "accidental" meetings were actually carefully planned by my future wife.

The very next day, after our nonencounter at the candy store, I was playing baseball with a sandlot team in the Federation League at Crotona Park. I was playing first base and looked over into the stands. And there she was, sitting next to a friend of mine who also happened to be named Sandy—not an old girlfriend, but someone dear to me from the neighborhood who had thoughtfully sent me care packages while I was in Germany.

I hit a home run that day, three hundred and fifty feet over the left center-field fence, but Sandy Cohen didn't see me do it. She had left the game by that time, but had given her phone number to her friend Sandy with instructions for me to call her.

I was equal parts excited and flustered. When I finally called, her mother answered.

"Can I speak to Sandra?" I said, my voice trembling.

"She's out," her mother said. "Who's calling?"

"Danny."

"Danny who?"

"Just Danny," I said, panicking. I didn't want to give my last name, because I didn't know if an Italian suitor would be acceptable to her mother. Now thoroughly embarrassed, I thanked the woman and hung up.

I was shooting pool later that same evening at Charley's—a pool hall that was one of my main hangouts in that period, right across Boston Road from where I first saw Sandy—when my friend Larry came in.

"I gave you her number," he said. "You didn't call?"

"I did! Her mother answered."

"So?"

"I got all nervous when she asked me my name. I told her 'Danny,' thanked her, and hung up. Her family's Jewish, right?"

"What's that supposed to mean?" Larry asked.

When you live in a melting pot like the South Bronx, there are mix-ups like these all the time. Sandy's mother had told her that a boy named Danny had called and didn't leave his phone number. But little did I know that Sandy had *anothe*r boy after her: Danny Fisher. It was a case of two Dannys and two Sandys. What the hell else could happen?

Without telling me, Larry had contrived to have Sandy come into Charley's poolroom that very night. When Sandy showed up and the moment came for me finally to introduce myself, I froze once again. I could not force my feet to walk or my mouth to speak. I made no move to go up to her. I continued to play pool.

"Say hello, Danny," Larry said. I couldn't do it. I knew I was being foolish. I was so messed up that if Larry had laughed at me right then, I would have busted his head open.

Sandy had come into the place with a girlfriend. They went over to the pool hall's shuffleboard game and started to play. She knew that I wanted to meet her. She could also see that I couldn't work up the nerve to speak. It was a classic, romantic beauty-and-the-beast standoff. I was a full head taller than her, and I probably outweighed her by a couple of weight classes. Yet this sweet, tiny thing flattened me as sure as if she had knocked me out in the ring.

While I shot pool, Sandy and her friend continued to play shuffleboard. Out of the corner of my eye, I watched her plug nickel after nickel into her game. I couldn't even look directly at her. She gave up and prepared to leave. I had the desperate thought that I had totally blown it, and she was walking out of my life forever.

Instead, Sandy strolled over to me.

"Here," she said. "I think this is yours." She tossed a plastic wristwatch onto the green felt of the pool table. A high score on the shuffleboard game won a prize courtesy of Charley's, and Sandy had gotten it.

I remained totally tongue-tied. I had forgotten every word of the English language. I simply stood gaping and watched her walk out. Larry and everyone else in the place except me broke out in laughter.

From that stumbling beginning, I rose to the occasion, romancing the girl I thought was more beautiful than any other creature on earth. She was Jewish and I was Italian and this was the Bronx, where everyone fought each other tooth and nail. But it didn't matter to me. We were together.

Sandy's parents did not welcome their daughter's new beau and made their feelings known. "But he's Italian," her mother protested, stating the obvious, as if that fact was enough to derail the relationship right there.

"Ma, I'm just going out with him," Sandy would reply. "What's the big deal? I'm not going to marry him."

Sandy herself had second thoughts all the time. In her eyes, I was this rough, macho street guy who was a little too ready with his fists. I kept a cigarette pack rolled up in my sleeve. I wore a T-shirt in winter, and a suede jacket without a collar and a zipper up the front.

"You're a hoodlum," she declared more than once, whenever she was mad at me.

The pool halls of the South Bronx were my second home. Lefty's on Whitlock Avenue, over by the Bronx River, was a favorite. Pop Bennet's at Tremont Avenue and Southern Boulevard was almost like a holy place to me. But after I met Sandy, Charley's became my main base of operations. What I didn't know at first was that Sandy's family had a fourth-floor apartment right across the street. She had a view out her window directly down into the place.

I found this out in a particularly painful way.

Sandy called the pay phone at Charley's one evening. My brother Joe was there with me and happened to answer. She demanded to know why I was so late for a date we had scheduled.

"Danny's home sick," Joe said, scrambling to cover for me.

"Really," Sandy said.

"Poor guy," Joe said.

"What if I told you I'm looking at him right now playing pool?"

Rattled at being caught in a white lie, my brother abruptly hung up the phone. The episode spooked him, as though Sandy was all-knowing, all-seeing. She laughs about the incident now, but back then she wasn't so civil when I apologized for Joe's white lie.

In general, my family was a lot more impressed by Sandy than her family was by me. "She looks just like Lana Turner," Mom would say. She was right that there was a resemblance, but I thought Sandy was much prettier than Lana.

In those days of summer and fall 1954, Sandy worked in Manhattan as a secretary at a candy company. She would catch the downtown IRT at the Freeman Street el station. Her route from her home to the subway brought her directly past my apartment building. We lived on the ground floor. I had moved in at 1401 Stebbins Avenue with my sister Gloria and her husband, Johnny. I stayed there with Mom and my sister Annabelle.

Every morning Sandy would come by on her way to work and knock at my window. We would start talking and pretty soon I had made her late. That morning stopover became something of a ritual, so much so that she finally had to quit her job.

I was deeply in love. It was an unlikely pairing, a feisty Jewish girl and an explosive Italian boy. At first, she balked when I asked her to marry me.

"Why don't we just go steady?" she said.

"I'm a grown man!" I exclaimed. "I don't 'go steady.' That's kids' stuff. Let's get married."

I finally wore down her resistance. When Sandy told her parents that I had asked her to marry me and she had accepted, they did not exactly sit shiva, but almost. Her mother had a novel way of trying to talk me out of it, emphasizing how expensive it would be to support her daughter.

"You know she needs hay fever shots, right? Do you realize how much money those cost?" I just laughed it off.

We were married on January 8, 1955, in Mount Vernon, New

York, the nearest place we could find a justice of the peace. My sister Gloria bought me a dark blue suit for the occasion, the first one I ever owned. The reception was at the home of Sandy's family, 1461 Boston Road, with twenty friends and relatives in attendance. As was the tradition, the well-wishers lined up single file to congratulate me, kiss the bride, and present their gifts, mostly envelopes of cash.

My father, in a rare appearance, attended both the ceremony and the reception. My mother was ecstatic, and I remember feeling happy to see him there, too. For this one day, at least, the Aiellos gave the appearance of being a complete family. My father presented me with a five-dollar bill at the reception. As he left the party later that night, he asked to borrow it back.

On the surface, Sandy's parents liked me and treated me well. But I once overheard her mother say to her father, "It will never last."

As of this writing, Sandy and I are enjoying our sixth decade together.

Sixty years of marital bliss? Even those people who are happily married know how difficult that is. There are always hard times in every relationship. Sandy and I are no exception. We fight well, but more importantly we make up well. It took a long time for us to figure out how to do that. For a time, our marriage was a bumpy road.

The first hint came at the wedding breakfast. The morning after we became Mr. and Mrs., we went out to a restaurant, just the two of us and our parents. Sandy ordered a sardine sandwich, a perfectly normal request. She didn't count on my deep loathing of all forms of seafood.

"Sandy, please change your order," I said, speaking low so her parents wouldn't hear.

She refused. She absolutely would have a sardine sandwich, and that was that. I was upset and made my feelings known. She finished every morsel of that sandwich. To this day, Sandy still loves sardines, but after that wedding breakfast, she made sure to never eat them in front of me again.

Our first son was born in September 1955, almost nine months to the day from our wedding night. Sandy chose the name Rick. At that point, though, I was one step removed from the situation. Sandy and I were living apart.

She had come to learn what a bullheaded guy I was, and I began to understand how headstrong she could be. We were young. We didn't know how to disagree without allowing the situation to escalate all out of proportion. She moved out of our place and into her parents' apartment. It wasn't far—I still lived right across the hall.

The day my son Rick was born was probably the happiest day of my life, and also the scariest. *How will I do this?* I asked myself. *Is there a manual on how to be a good father? A better husband? What kind of work will I do? Will I be able to get a job?*

I tried to calm my anxieties with the thought that I had held a position in the U.S. Army for three years and had been honorably discharged. That was a job, wasn't it? Yes, but not one that would translate well into civilian life.

From that point on, I realized life as a married man would be a lot more difficult. I started asking myself hard questions. Were the same kind of worries I was having the reason my own father was never around? Did those worries contribute to why my parents' marriage had failed? Maybe there was truth in all of that.

I made a solemn promise to myself that my father's mistakes were never going to be mine.

The new baby brought Sandy and me back together. Another son, Daniel Aiello III, came along in January 1957. In 1960, we moved out of her parents' building to the Marble Hill projects on West 228th Street. Our third son, Jaime, was born there in March 1961. Later on, after we moved to West 238th Street in the Riverdale section of the Bronx, our darling daughter, Stacey, came into our lives in November 1969.

Our family was complete. After years of fumbling around, never knowing who I really was, always searching for the true me, I thought I had finally settled into my role in life as a father, a family man. I vowed that I would always be there for them. More than anything, I would be their guardian and protector.

Maybe it was the influence of my brother Ralphie, who had died before I was born. Maybe it was the uncertainty I felt about my father. How it developed, I'm not sure, but I have always had a strong protective streak in my life.

Here's an example. I had an odd habit as a young child. Whenever my family went to the beach while we were living that summer in Coney Island, I would watch out for them like a little lifeguard. Standing at the shoreline with my back to the ocean, I made sure they didn't get too close to the dangerous waves. I didn't know what I would do if one of my brothers or sisters got themselves into trouble, since I couldn't swim myself. It didn't matter. I was the self-appointed sentinel who would protect them from harm.

I was like this as the head of my own family, too. I remember a blizzard when my children were young, and New York City came to a total stop. Rick and Danny III were at baseball practice at an indoor gym, four miles across town. All forms of public transportation were halted. The streets were piled high with snow. But I was going to get them home, no matter what.

When we were out in the storm, I plowed ahead of my boys and made them walk behind. I held the flaps of my coat out wide to shield them from the wind. I looked like the Caped Crusader, but we got there. That was me, acting in my role of protector. To my sons, I must have appeared crazy.

My love for my children was mixed with dread that they would somehow be taken from me. I remember once having a jolt of fear go through me when my son Danny III passed out in church one Sunday from the smell of incense. I was sitting in the pew next to him. I looked at his white-as-a-sheet face and thought that my son had died. I picked Danny up in my arms and ran out of the church.

"My son, my son!" I screamed, tearing down Southern Boulevard. I didn't know where I was going. Lincoln Hospital was miles away. Danny woke and was fine, but from that day on, I knew I had to worry about my boy. I experienced many sleepless nights. He became stronger as he grew up but was still left with lingering problems.

I was a hands-on parent all the way. Maybe, because of my experience with an absent father, I was overcompensating with my own children. I signed my sons Rick and Danny up for Little League baseball. I attended their games religiously. I volunteered as a football coach when they started playing the game at school.

Somehow, I had turned into a sports version of what they call today a helicopter parent. "Mom, does he have to come to every single game?" Rick complained to Sandy. I was thunderstruck when my wife related his comment to me. I had been a real presence in the athletic lives of my sons, cheering loudly from the stands. I thought I was supporting them, but it turned out I was only embarrassing them. I immediately dialed back my participation.

They did all right without me. My son Rick was a big kid. I had known from the outset that he was going to be an athlete. He turned into a very good one. He was an All-City football player for DeWitt Clinton High School in the Bronx, playing both defense and offense.

Never once did I lift my hand to any of my children. But I did administer discipline. I was a yeller. There are several scenes in my movies when the audience can witness me in a state of anger. Seeing it from the outside, I can understand how frightening I could be to a kid when I'm fuming mad.

But underneath all that bluster, I nursed a secret fear. What if I failed as a father? I was a working-class man. What if the jobs disappeared? What if I was a protector who could not save those I loved? What if I was a guide who got himself lost?

What if, what if, what if? On the surface, I was happy. I loved my wife and children. I never confessed the insecurities that were plaguing me. What I didn't realize was that at the dawn of the 1960s, when I hit the labor market, the blue-collar way of life was changing. Manufacturing jobs were vanishing.

I first learned this lesson in 1955, when I landed a job on the assembly line at the Curtiss-Wright aircraft plants in Garfield and Wood-Ridge, New Jersey. I worked at Curtiss-Wright for three years, carpooling from the Bronx. It felt good to have steady employment. Then, suddenly, the rug got pulled out from under me and I was laid off. My anxieties came roaring back worse than ever.

Sandy saved me. Well, actually it was her uncle. Through his contacts, I landed a job as a baggage handler at the Greyhound station in Manhattan. I was starting out at the bottom there, but it was solid work and the company was unionized. The year was 1957. I experienced a newfound sense of security. This is what I was, and this is what I would be for the rest of my life: a working-man, a good provider with a steady job. I tried to tell myself that I was all set from now on.

For a while, it even seemed to be true.

Chapter Seven

The Big Grey Dog

Beginning in 1957, when someone asked me what I did, I said I worked at Greyhound as a baggage handler. That answer classified me as blue-collar as surely as if I had shown them my union card. From the start, I fit right in at my new job. The Greyhound station at 245 West Fiftieth Street in Manhattan had waves of humanity crashing through it on their way to elsewhere. This was in the days before air travel became commonplace. For the vast majority of Americans, the "Big Grey Dog" was the transport of choice. The passengers in the terminal were visiting relatives, traveling for work, or setting off to seek greener pastures.

The midtown Greyhound station was built in the 1930s, and by the time I started there, it had become worn out a bit from hard use. I liked it anyway. As I got used to the job, I looked upon the place as my own personal turf. The constant to-and-fro of travelers made it seem like something was always happening.

Other people's luggage seems random, but it is intensely personal. Handling baggage all day, humping hundreds of bags, suitcases, and boxes, I was getting an up-close view of America. There were hard-traveling bags and upper-crust monogrammed luggage. If there was a cord tied around a valise, it probably meant the owner was down on his luck. Mostly, I didn't have time to think about which bag was whose. I just slung.

With a solid job, I thought all the uncertainty, worry, and secret doubts that had troubled me would vanish. They didn't. Instead, my anxieties increased in severity until a strange affliction started to kick in. Several times a day, a tightness would seize the back of my neck. I was sure that I was about to pass out. I suppose these sudden fits were a kind of panic attack, but no one used that term back then.

I didn't know what was happening to me. I had a wonderful family, had a steady paycheck, and was living in the greatest city in the world. I should have been content. Instead I was laid low by a mysterious opponent. A street fight was one thing. A punch to the head that sent my brain reeling, that I could handle. But these attacks came out of nowhere. I tried to deny what was happening. I dodged talking about it to Sandy.

Finally, with the tempo of the episodes increasing, I checked myself into the Kingsbridge Veterans Hospital in the Bronx. I was examined and told by the military doctors that they could find nothing physically wrong with me. I didn't understand. Feeling the way I did, how could that be true?

The hunt for a cause moved from the physical to the mental.

This development made me uneasy. The disgrace attached to ill-nesses of the mind held sway. Me, a nutter? It couldn't be. I was the strong one, the reliable one, the guy who could always get the job done. Yet the shrinks kept poking and prodding at my stub-born anxieties, which turned out to be the root of the problem.

The diagnosis? Nervous exhaustion.

"That's one step below a nervous breakdown," my physician told me. "If you keep on like this, a breakdown is exactly where you'll find yourself."

I ended up in a locked psych ward for two weeks in the sum-mer of 1963. I was too ashamed to tell anyone at Greyhound the specifics of my illness. I was just "out sick." The doctors on staff prescribed sedatives to calm me down. I refused to take them. I had never put anything stronger than an aspirin into my system. I wasn't going to start now. I was the classic example of a guy who always declined to see a doctor no matter how ill he was.

In my confusion and anxiety, I held fast to the idea that there was a physical cause to my illness. There were times I thought that I'd rather have a brain tumor—something, anything, rather than be afflicted with a wimpy-sounding condition like nervous exhaustion.

A psychiatrist suggested physical therapy. A male nurse took me out to the huge lawn on the hospital grounds during the day. I carried a bat, and the nurse had a dozen softballs in a bucket. He would pitch to me for hours. Many of the balls I hit ended up fly-ing out onto Kingsbridge Avenue.

In my precarious mental state, my love of the game comforted me. The solid thwack of the bat hitting the ball centered my mind. It was something I knew. Playing ball had smoothed my time in the military. Now slamming away at those pitches helped me in a different way. It wasn't the first time that the sport wound up saving my ass, and it wouldn't be the last, either.

I felt good while I had a bat in my hands. But when I went back to the ward, I immediately fell sick again. I would sit on a couch and watch patients a lot younger than I was, who appeared to be a lot healthier than me. They paced up and down the corridor, staring directly at the floor, not making eye contact, with nothing alive in their expressions. Pharmacology wasn't as sophisticated back then as it is now. The pills my fellow patients swallowed had turned them into the walking dead.

Sandy and my mom came to the ward for visiting hours, but I let none of my neighborhood friends know what had happened. It was enough to see my wife and mother devastated by my illness. Sandy had witnessed my attacks. She saw me stare into the mirror and start to cry, moaning, "I feel like I'm going to die." Even though she knew that the hospital was the right place for me, my wife was still knocked for a loop seeing me committed to a mental ward.

There is no misery sharper than the dread that you might be losing your mind. I shared a double bunk bed with a city bus driver who seemed like the most normal guy in the world. I would lie there at night, and incredibly enough I could look out my window and see the Marble Hill projects, where I lived. Sandy kept a bright light shining in our fourth-floor window for me to see.

The night I decided to leave the hospital, I was staring longingly at that bright light of home when the bus driver in the bunk below me began to cry. He was a strapping guy who looked as if he could be playing football for the New York Giants, but he wept like a son of a bitch, huge racking sobs that continued on and off all night.

I do not belong here, I told myself, listening to him. *These guys are all nuts, not me!* Meanwhile all those other patients in the ward might have been looking at me and thinking the same thing.

The next day, I asked to be discharged.

"Well, Corporal Aiello," my veterans' hospital doctor said, "you admitted yourself voluntarily, so you are allowed to leave at any time. But I have to tell you, it will be AMA."

The military loves its acronyms. "What does 'AMA' mean?" I asked.

"'Against medical advice,'" he said.

"If that's the way it has to be, then that's the way it has to be," I said. "I just have to get out of here. If I don't, I think I'll go crazy."

I thought he might get the joke, but he didn't laugh. Instead, he gave me a good piece of medical advice. "If you have this feeling of yours again, whenever you believe you are going to pass out, I want you to lie down. I don't care where you are, at work or at home or on the street even; if you feel an attack coming on, lie down."

That suggestion helped, but it didn't cure me. Whenever an episode started, whenever that familiar tightness would start to grip my neck, I would immediately prostrate myself on the floor. Anyone around me would be convinced that I was indeed nuts. It happened once while riding the subway. Down I went, flopping over into some surprised stranger's lap.

I returned to work at Greyhound, humping baggage. Whatever doubts Sandy harbored about my mental state, she remained relentlessly positive and encouraging. For two years after I left the hospital, the attacks persisted. I experienced the same panicked feeling, but I willed myself into going to work every day. It was my self-prescribed therapy.

Looking back, I think my mind must have been trying to tell me something. I was in my late twenties at this point. A question hung in the air back then: *Is this all there is?* Perhaps my illness was my mind's way of insisting that baggage handling at Greyhound could not be my only option in life. Maybe I had a secret desire to be more than what I was. Maybe I didn't *know* who I was.

Two years after they began, the attacks gradually tapered off. I no longer had the conviction that I was in my death throes every other day. Looking back, the end of my affliction coincided with a change in my daily work.

One thing I especially enjoyed about the Greyhound job was the godlike tones of the public address announcer, reciting the far-flung destinations all across the country. For each departure, the names of the towns echoed through the terminal. It was like living inside an atlas. The words had a rhythm, speaking of the romance of the road.

Hearing the announcements so often, I had the reaction that I'd like to be the one calling out the distant bus stations. I wanted to be the voice over the loudspeaker. A lowly ambition, maybe, to go from baggage handler to station announcer, but what the hell, it was still an ambition.

When I saw a posting for a public address announcer job opening at Greyhound, I put in for it and got the gig. There was a small increase in pay. My new position had me interacting much more with the other personnel in the terminal, getting to know the drivers, the secretaries, the company bosses.

More than that, I heard my own voice every day echoing through the bus terminal. I won't deny that it fed my ego. I can still recite in order the bus route destinations all over the country:

"May I have your attention, please? Across from platform three, a departure to Philadelphia, Harrisburg, Pittsburgh, Wheeling, Columbus, Indianapolis, Terre Haute, Effingham, Saint Louis, Tulsa, Oklahoma City, Denison, and Dallas, Texas, with connections in Jersey City for Montclair, Denville, Dover, Budd Lake, Hackettstown, Strasburg, Mount Pocono, Tobyhanna, Scranton, Wilkes-Barre, Clarks Summit, Nicholson, Hallstead, O'Toolesville, Binghamton, Canandaigua, Pittston, Towanda, Waverly, Elmira, Corning, Batavia, Mount Morris, and Buffalo!"

Sure, it's easy enough to write it down, but try letting it roll off your tongue. Years later, during an appearance on David Letterman's show, he asked me to reprise my old public announcer "act." When I sang out the final word, "Buffalo," the audience went nuts; it ended up as one of the best times I ever had on a talk show.

I have to confess that one of those towns I called out is a ringer, an inside joke. I always inserted "O'Toolesville" into my spiel because one of the bosses was named O'Toole. But there was no such town, and no one ever came up to me demanding to know where the hell O'Toolesville was either.

I wasn't going to stop at being the terminal announcer. I now had ambitions beyond that. The Greyhound drivers, baggage handlers, and other workers were represented by the Amalgamated Transit Union, Local Division 1202. I attended shop meetings and became known as a loyal union man.

My experience as a kid on the streets of New York City gave me the world's best education in human psychology, so when issues arose at Greyhound, I came across as a dependable guy. I got along with most of my coworkers, and more importantly, I was able to stand my ground when it mattered.

In 1961, four years after I started working at Greyhound, the union membership voted me in as shop steward. By the end of 1965, I was elected president of the twelve-hundred-member Local Division 1202, the youngest person and the first nondriver ever to hold the post. I won the vote by a five-to-one margin.

As union president, I conducted meetings in front of scores of my fellow workers. I would speak off the top of my head. At first I had no idea how I would do it, but my communication skills turned out to be quite good. I got a copy of *Robert's Rules of Order* and studied up on parliamentary procedure.

The union rank and file favored me with their support as a result. The terminal personnel had always felt that they were second-class citizens compared to the drivers, and I lifted them up. The experience was tantalizing. I began to dream about a move into politics.

As part of my job, I used to travel to Montreal, the home base of some of the drivers represented by our local union. I'd go give a talk in front of a whole crowd in the city's Laurentian Hotel ballroom. Most of the union guys up there were proud French-Canadians who didn't speak much English, and I didn't know a word of French. Somehow, I got through to them. I was getting unanimous approvals on the measures I put up for a vote.

"What's going on?" I asked one of the English-speaking drivers. "I don't even speak the language. How come they trust me?"

"They trust your eyes," the driver said in a strong French accent.

I thought I was hot shit, and I was—for about a minute. Humble as my success was, it all came apart during the long hot summer of 1967.

Greyhound came down with a new directive that June. They wanted our drivers to submit to a different schedule. Instead of two days on, two days off, management ordained that henceforth, the schedule would be two days on and *one* day off. I thought this change would be unsafe for both drivers and passengers.

The "past practice" clause in our contract stipulated that any alteration in the work rules had to go through a vote by the union membership. The Greyhound executives informed us that the vote didn't need to happen. The new rules would go into effect without any input from the union.

The Greyhound bus drivers decided they weren't going to accept longer hours without a fight. As president of the local, I supported them. The national Amalgamated Transit Union, however, did not. They removed me from office pending an investigation. In protest, my coworkers went out on strike.

Wildcat strike! That's what it's called when workers go off the job without the backing of their union. They went out on June 21, 1967, the day after my thirty-fourth birthday. Greyhound had moved farther downtown into the Port Authority terminal by then, meaning we were smack-dab in the middle of Lincoln Tunnel traffic. The work stoppage completely disrupted the streets of midtown.

The Port Authority became a battleground. Company supervisors stood facing off with a vocal squad of wildcat strikers. Buses arriving at the terminal stopped short, refusing to cross the picket lines. Soon enough, traffic backed up across Ninth Avenue. Cops screamed and supervisors yelled, but nothing moved.

Some of those Montreal drivers I represented took it a step further and got violent about it. They waylaid Greyhound buses that were headed down the New York State Thruway to Manhattan, first carefully emptying the vehicles of passengers, then smashing windshields and attacking the buses with sledgehammers. It was sheer insanity.

I was a little stunned by the pandemonium we had wrought. Unfortunately, given my nature, I was such a strong representative that I refused to bend. Nor would the workers. I stood solid as a rock, failing to do what a savvy politician might, which was keep a back door of compromise open.

If I had handled the strike differently, if I had been amenable to concession and negotiation, perhaps I would be a politician today. Those who know how to play the game always leave themselves a way out. They're able to emerge from difficult situations and come back to fight another day.

I couldn't do it. In my own way, I was an idealist. My mind balked at the idea of what the company supervisors might think of me if I caved. I didn't want them to believe for one moment that my decisions were based on strategy and calculation. That to me was a lie. My position flowed from principle, not politics. So I stood my ground and locked that proverbial back door.

My world ended when the national union sided with the Greyhound corporation against the wildcat strikers. They took over our local. My coworkers felt as though they'd been stabbed in the back. Whoever heard of a union favoring the company over the rank and file?

As a parting gift when I was kicked out, Greyhound hit me with a $500,000 civil suit for the damages the striking drivers had done to the buses on the thruway. The company wanted me gone. Suing me was just a scare tactic. *Leave the office for good or we'll drag your sorry ass through court*—that was the message they were sending me.

If the national board had stood with me, I could have fought back. Instead, it asked every officer of our local union to take over my position as president. One after another, my executive board members refused. Four stand-up guys stuck by me when the going got tough. Vice President Joe Daly, Recording Secretary Charlie O'Keefe, Financial Secretary Art Mason, and Garage Representative Buddy Casano—all are enshrined on my personal honor roll, and I will never forget them.

The whole episode, of course, was devastating. The life that Sandy and I had built together depended on my bringing in a paycheck every week. Little League for the kids, the nice apartment at 238th and Broadway, the food on our table—all seemed about to disappear as if they had never been there to begin with. Ten years at Greyhound, all gone. My old fears about failure and homelessness now returned with a vengeance.

My experience at Greyhound was meaningless in the job market. Try looking for a job as a union president. The bottom dropped out of my life. I had nothing. I was nothing.

I resorted to desperate measures, doing many things I'm not proud of today. None of it worked to drag me out of the hole I was in, and none of it was pretty.

Chapter Eight

Breaking In

The 1960s were staggering to an end, and American society seemed to be coming apart at the seams. There were riots, war protests, assassinations. Half of the Bronx was in the process of getting burned out or abandoned. Success was the furthest thing from my mind at this point. Survival was more like it.

Where was I in my life? I can give it to you in one word: nowhere. I was flat broke with no job, never knowing where my next nickel was coming from. As far as I could tell, I was unemployable.

I hustled pool, playing in halls all over the South Bronx. Once in a while I was able to knock down a couple hundred bucks over the course of a few days, but I didn't make a ton of money doing it. Most of the money I made in that period came from a pool hall called Jimmy's. All the Puerto Rican players there liked the game of nine-ball.

Nine-ball is all about position. You have to sink the balls in numerical order, and when I scored the final nine, that was my sign to sweep up whatever money had been bet on the game. There was also pill pool, a game that had each player picking a number out of a leather cup. If I sank the ball with my number on it, everyone in the game paid me. If I sank the ball with your number, I got paid by you. It was the potential of getting paid twice that made pill pool exciting.

Whatever I did, and however hard I hustled, my fortunes kept spiraling down. The Aiello family was on the ropes. Twice, and for a few months each time, I had to go on welfare. My veteran status made me eligible for public assistance. The shame I felt about being on the dole made me push myself to do better. I took all sorts of jobs, having to accept whatever was offered. Frequently, that meant hiring on as a bouncer at after-hours clubs, working off the books and getting paid cash.

The official closing time for bars in New York City has always been four a.m. After-hours clubs illegally catered to those who didn't want to go home even then. Those after-hours joints were brutal places, with guys looking for fights just so they could tell their buddies that they kicked your ass.

Management always had a rule: no fights inside the club. If I ever got into a fight on the premises, I'd lose my job. So a customer could feel free to insult me as the bouncer, knowing the most I could do was order them out of the place. I got around the rule by telling the offender that I'd meet him outside. I'd slip out a side door and the two of us would then battle it out in the street.

For a while, I ran a Manhattan after-hours club on West Ninth Street called the Toy Top. There were fights every night, the police constantly busting the place for being open after-hours. The butch lesbians who hung out at the Toy Top used to take the rap for me, knowing I had kids and a straight home life. They'd step in and swear to the cops that they were the ones managing the club, not me. They had hearts of gold.

After the Toy Top, I got hired as a bouncer at the world-famous Roseland, but that didn't last long, either. I could never bring myself to crack heads. The patrons there were too sweet. They were all big-band aficionados, and it was as if they had been trapped in the year 1945. I bounced no one, so management bounced me after only three nights on the job.

Hustling pool was feast or famine, and so were the club jobs. Day by day, I could feel my life slipping away. As a result, self-respect went out the window. Out of sheer desperation, I made a series of bad moves that almost landed me in prison.

I began to steal. A longtime friend of mine, Barry, was my partner in crime. I met him when we were both pin boys at Metropolitan Lanes on Whitlock Avenue. He was a great bowler. I wasn't. When our fortunes hit the skids, Barry recruited me and we embarked on a petty burglary spree all over the South Bronx. I was doing it just to make ends meet. Barry liked the thrill.

The two of us would break into isolated businesses after hours. We'd find ways into local stores, bakeries, and warehouses by prying open windows or back doors. Barry was the second-story man. He'd do all the climbing and scaling of walls. He'd squirm inside somehow and then open up the place for me.

We took safes, when we could find them. We weren't these high-style cinematic safecrackers, either. If I had tried twirling the dials and listening to the tumblers, I would have been there for years. Instead, we broke them open by force right on the spot, or took the easy route and tossed the safe out a window to the pavement.

If a safe still didn't open after all that, I would heft it into the trunk of Barry's car and we'd drive it to a junkyard that he had access to, deserted in the off-hours. The two of us would attack it with sledgehammers. Hard as we went at it, more than once we couldn't break a safe before daylight came. So we would bury the stubborn fucker and come back to work on it some more the next night. After all that effort, the most we ever got from a safe was $80.

We had to really move it along whenever we hit bakeries. Bakers had a habit of coming in predawn to open up and light the ovens. We also liked to target bowling alleys, including ones where Barry and I had worked as pin boys. Sometimes we burgled the same places over and over. One bowling alley got hit maybe a dozen times.

They couldn't keep us out. Whenever I played pool at one of our neighborhood bowling alleys that had tables, I was doing two things at once: I was setting up my next shot and casing the joint, trying to find locks to jimmy or windows to force. These were local places I was in and out of all the time. But I never hit Pop Bennett's pool hall. That would've been like busting into a church.

Barry and I were a two-man crime wave. There was never cash in the tills in any of these places, so instead we rifled the candy and cigarette machines. That was our take, chump change, quarters, dimes, nickels!

Shooting pool one day in a bowling alley, I saw a skylight over the tables that I thought would be a perfect way in. We came back that night, broke open the skylight, and used ropes to lower ourselves down from the roof. Since the skylight was right over the billiards lounge, we didn't land on the floor but wound up on one of the tables. Then we hit the cigarette machines, took our loot, and beat it.

The next day, I went back to the same bowling alley. I remember clearly racking the balls for a game and seeing my own telltale footprint on the green felt of the pool table. That was me, the cat burglar from the night before.

"What's all this?" I remember Sandy saying one night after she found me at our kitchen table, stacking up rows of coins.

"This is rent money," I replied. For months at a stretch, I paid the rent with stolen cigarette machine coins. My wife was none the wiser. She thought I was bringing in the money from hustling pool.

Once in a while, my father had me come down to where he occasionally worked at the New York Coliseum, across from Central Park on Columbus Circle, nowadays replaced by the towering Time Warner headquarters. My uncle Sal Aiello was president of Local 814 of the International Brotherhood of Teamsters, and sometimes I'd get work through him. I'd have a day's paid labor, unloading trucks.

The Coliseum hosted a lot of trade shows and exhibitions, so there was constant action. The place was also a feeding trough for the Mafia. The FBI spent fifteen years investigating pilferage at the place. Merchandise was constantly falling off the back of a truck, as they say.

If a vehicle came in without a helper, union rules dictated that a Teamster had to be assigned to work the load. We didn't know what kind of shipments we would be working. A full "thirty-eight"—a semi with a thirty-eight-foot trailer—could take all day to unload. A "shorty" was a smaller truck that might have only a couple of boxes in the back. But I got paid the same—$100 per load—no matter how much work it took.

My dad had to explain the workplace facts of life to me. "Danny," he would say, "you gotta kick back."

At first, I thought he was telling me to relax, take it easy. But he jerked his thumb toward one of the wiseguys who hung around the place. Then I got it.

"What do you mean, Dad?" I said. "I'm not giving him money!"

Soon afterward, I found myself called to account, sitting in a diner across the street from the Coliseum with my father and his wiseguy boss.

Bobby C., I'll call him. My experience with made guys was that they were nice enough—until they weren't. You could sit and have coffee with them and never feel any fear. But the minute you crossed them, they turned vicious. I wondered what I was getting into. This was my dad's world, not mine.

Bobby C. wasn't a real high-ranking mob boss. He was just the captain of a crew. The first thing Bobby did was hand over his keys and tell me to move his car, at the moment double-parked outside the diner.

"You're asking me to *park your car*?" I said. "No way."

My dad grabbed me out of the booth and pulled me aside. "What are you doing?"

"I'm a married man with kids, for chrissakes," I replied. I wasn't going to act as anybody's gofer.

In fact, all the pushback I was giving Bobby C. worked like magic. The mobster actually liked the fact that I wasn't intimidated by him. The next thing I knew, he put me in business with his son. Bobby bought the two of us our very own legitimate union charter. He sent his son and me out to recruit workers. I was the president of a union again, but it was a paper union, with no members, just officers.

Our job was to decertify the current union and get the workers to transfer to ours. Despite the shady players in the background, this was a legitimate practice, sanctioned by the government's National Labor Relations Board. One of our first targets was the Star Factory, a machine parts plant in Poughkeepsie, New York. I was hired on, pretending to be nothing more than a common laborer. But my secret agenda was to bad-mouth the electricians' union that had a lock on the factory's labor force.

"Oh, man, that goddamned union is here?" I'd moan to the other workers. "I had a lot of trouble with them on my last job. They're no good. If they're here, then I'm leaving."

I kept working the pitch, talking to workers, insinuating myself into their confidence. I thought they bought it. I told Bobby C.'s son that I had them convinced. At the next election, the plant workers could check a box for our own union, one for no union, or one for the now-maligned electricians' union. Due to my efforts, I predicted our union would be certified. It wasn't.

I might have been a little naive. Two weeks after I started at the Star plant, I walked out to the parking lot to find the van I was driving had every single one of its windows smashed in. This was the electricians' union's retaliation for my bad-mouthing activities.

I drove home with the breeze blowing in my face, going about five miles an hour without a windshield to protect me.

My union job was only part of the game, though. Whenever I went around with Bobby's son, I noticed that he was constantly popping in and out of places along our route. "Hey, Danny, I have to make a stop," he'd say, directing me to an apartment building in the northern Bronx. He'd go inside and wouldn't come back for fifteen minutes. I didn't think anything of it. I just stayed in the car and waited.

But it happened again and again. Bobby's son had me make stops all over the Bronx. I suspected he was dealing drugs, and I was unwittingly serving as his driver. But I certainly couldn't complain to Bobby C. about what I thought his son was doing.

How the hell do I get out of this?

Eventually, I felt I had to make a move, and I went to see Bobby C. in the same coffee shop across the street from the Coliseum. "Bobby, I can't do this. It's not for me," I said. "Since my time with Greyhound, you know I'm all disillusioned about unions. I don't want to have anything to do with them."

Bobby C. was silent. I couldn't tell if I was digging my own grave.

"Your son," I continued. "He's really the one who should be taking the lead on this. He should be president of the local."

"My son," Bobby replied. There was an awkward pause. He stared at me for what seemed an awful long time.

"Okay," he finally said, and that was it.

I was out. I couldn't believe it. I felt a sick kind of relief. I think my father, too, felt relieved. In his heart of hearts, he didn't want his boy going down the same path that he himself had traveled.

A certain kind of future died when I said no to Bobby C. But there was only one problem. I didn't have another future to replace it with.

Ball fields are scattered all over Central Park, a couple dozen in all. But the ones I knew, my home diamonds, were the Heckscher Fields just to the north and east of Columbus Circle. They're used for the city softball leagues, and for the Broadway Show League in particular. Unemployed actors, writers, musicians, and students all congregated there in the summer.

I wasn't an unemployed actor or an unemployed writer. I was just unemployed. Whenever there was no work at the Coliseum, I'd drift over to Central Park and those ball fields, soon becoming a familiar face. Naturally, I got recruited into the Central Park softball games. Every team was clawing for any scrap of advantage it could get. The use of ringers wasn't technically allowed, but there were always ways to bend the rules. No one was checking Equity membership cards.

The New York Yankees sponsored the Broadway Show League. I played on the CBS team first, alongside people like retired Yankees star shortstop and announcer Phil Rizzuto. Also in the mix was football great Frank Gifford and local CBS anchor Jim Jensen. For a while, I was on the team fielded by Sparks Steak House, the midtown restaurant where years later the notorious John Gotti would have his boss Paul Castellano rubbed out in cold blood.

Mostly, though, my teammates were actors. Tony Lo Bianco, the *French Connection* star, was a pitcher so competitive you would have thought he was playing in the World Series at every game.

Back in those days, I was called "Tree City Danny," so nick-named because I always swung for the tree line in left field, 275 feet away. In softball, there's no crack of the bat. The sound made is more like a solid thud, like the punch of a fist into a gut. I still remember the satisfaction when I would connect with a ball and send it sailing into the trees. Nothing could have been sweeter.

I used to live for those games. They represented time off from the grind of always hustling for work. I was a man in a hurry, look-ing for a job where I could make solid money in a short amount of time. I needed a break.

My family didn't really grasp the level of desperation in my life back then. At home, I tried to present a calm, fatherly face. I loved watching Sandy spoil Stacey, our little girl. But outside the home, I was a madman. I made frantic dashes from one end of the city to another, hustling up games at pool halls, commit-ting those second-story jobs with Barry, trying to cadge work at the Coliseum—and hanging around the softball fields of Central Park.

There wasn't any money there. But there was a human connec-tion. One of the people I met was Budd Friedman, who ran a fa-mous comedy club called the Improvisation on West Forty-Fourth Street off Ninth Avenue. The Improv was a phenomenon, one of the pioneer clubs in what would become an explosion of stand-up venues. In contrast to the dozens of comedy clubs around the city today, back then there was only the Improv and one other fore-runner, Rick Newman's Catch a Rising Star.

Friedman fielded a team in the Broadway League made up of the staffers and performers at his club. When he and I spoke, de-tails of my situation inevitably came out. As an unemployed high school dropout who was expecting his fourth child at any moment, I was carrying a heavy load of trouble and anxiety.

Was it my sad-sack story or my power hitting that prompted Budd to offer me a job at the Improv?

"You had a kind face and good heart," was all Budd would admit to later when I asked him about it. "You also needed the work."

Budd recognized me for my talents, so he hired me as a bouncer at his club, and he put me in at first base on his softball team.

I didn't even know it at the time, but I had my foot in the door.

Chapter Nine

At the Improv

Budd Friedman's Improvisation was in the Hell's Kitchen neighborhood of Manhattan. The place is gone now, a Mexican restaurant and a brick-oven pizzeria in the space where the Improv used to be. But for me, that area will always be a sort of personal shrine.

Inside the Improv, a barroom at the entry led into the main performance space. A small stage was set against an exposed brick wall that would soon become the trademark of the place.

To me, Budd Friedman was the real attraction, one of the most honorable men I ever met in the business. He had opened the Improv in the early sixties after he had served during the Korean War. When I compared our experiences in the military, mine paled next to his. I drew a long straw twice, while Budd was one of the heroes who got wounded in the famous charge up Pork Chop Hill.

The night I started at the Improvisation, Budd took me under his wing. When I asked if he could give me a general job description, he said, "I'm not sure myself. I've never had a bouncer." He paused to think. "Do not hit anyone. Unless they're attacking me," he added with a smile.

I like this guy, I thought. *He's just making it up as he goes along.*

"Heckling's fine," Budd said. "It's part of the scene. But it can get out of hand, and you will have to be the judge of that." If customers walked out without paying the check, the waitresses were held accountable and would have to reimburse the club. "So help them out and keep your eyes open," Budd said.

The gig was six days a week with Sunday off, starting at eight p.m. and lasting until the stage went dark and the crowd left, usually at around three a.m.

"When I'm not around," Budd told me, "you may have to take on other responsibilities, like emceeing."

I didn't know how I felt about that. The idea made me anxious and excited at the same time. The closest I had gotten to a microphone was in the announcer's booth at the Greyhound bus terminal.

I realized that I hadn't asked Budd one of the most important questions of all. "How much do I get paid?"

"One ninety-five a week." Relief and gratitude flooded through me. It was enough to keep the wolf away from the Aiello family door.

Landing the bouncer gig at the Improv turned out to be one of the most important steps of my life. It was there that I got to know people who gave me the confidence to pursue a career that I would never have thought possible.

The list of performers I met at the club reads like a who's who of comedy and entertainment: David Brenner, David Frye, Richard Pryor, Andy Kaufman, Steve Landesberg, Robert Klein, Rodney Dangerfield, Jimmy Martinez, Mike Preminger, Marvin Braverman, Bobby Alto, Buddy Mantia, Marty Nadler, Buddy Hughes, Jimmy Walker, Doc Pomus, J. K. Kleinhaus, Larry Reed, Vaughn Meader, Bette Midler, Ray Serra, Anthony Conforti, Joe Peck, Freddie Prinze, Lenny Schultz, Elayne Boosler, Liz Torres, J. J. Barry, and Raymond Johnson. You may not be familiar with some of these people, but they were all talented and great to get to know.

During my time at the Improvisation, I met Jerry Stiller and his wife, Anne Meara. They appeared at the club frequently. From their comedy teamwork on TV variety shows, the two of them were already well-known to the public, but they came into the Improv to work new material. Audiences went wild for them. Of course, both Jerry and Anne would later go on to sitcom renown, with Jerry playing grumpy fathers on *Seinfeld* and *The King of Queens*.

I spent two and a half years employed at the Improv. Sandy was now a "comedy widow" six nights out of the week. I had a single line in my repertoire, which I memorized and delivered flawlessly: "How many are there in your party?"

The work wasn't complex. The situations I dealt with were mostly black-and-white. My job as bouncer was to post myself near the end of the bar, at the entrance to the main room. "Look big," is what Budd told me. That was easy enough. It came naturally. If anyone hassled the comics, or if anyone in the audience was loud or obnoxious, I'd stroll over and introduce myself.

Budd acted as the emcee for the evening's acts, breaking some of the biggest names in comedy. I watched Rodney Dangerfield perfect his "I don't get no respect" act at the Improv. While Budd didn't think the late David Brenner was a particularly funny guy and told me never to put him on in prime time, I loved him. Whenever I took over emceeing duties in Budd's absence, I'd give David a plum position in the lineup.

Before she took off into the heights of stardom, Bette Midler was the darling of the Improv. Budd acted as her informal manager and adviser. In those days, she was already on Broadway doing Tzeitel in *Fiddler on the Roof.*

The great songwriter Doc Pomus collaborated with Bette on material back then. He used to arrive in a cab outside the club. Because he was a paraplegic, I would pick him up and carry him inside. We'd park his wheelchair while Bette sang and did her routine. Bette would soon go on from the Improv to sing at the Continental Baths in the Ansonia Hotel. After that, there was no stopping her.

With all the comedians coming up, I never, ever had the feeling that I could do stand-up. I could never be a "monologist," one of my favorite words back then. To this day, I believe that stand-up is the most terrifying kind of performance. It's a high-wire dance— it's physical, mental, and spiritual hell. And you are all alone up there. If you don't kill, you bomb.

Working as a bouncer, I tapped into my personal hatred of rude behavior. Loud talking, heckling, drunken boorishness—if you indulged in any of that business while at the Improv, you were mine, baby. I was on your ass in a heartbeat. I felt simpatico with the performers. If they were willing to put themselves out there, risk everything just to try to make you laugh, I figured the least you could do as an audience member was to be polite.

Just to indicate my attitude, I'll tell you about one night when a guy named Doug Ireland started to sound off at the Improv. I found out later he was the press representative for Bella Abzug, the most outspoken female politician of the day. Ireland was also a huge man, maybe five-ten and four hundred fifty pounds. That night he was with a drunken crowd of staffers of Mayor John Lindsay, and this guy obviously thought his position gave him the liberty to be a loudmouth.

He was talking and interrupting the acts. I went over and told him that he needed to shut the fuck up and that I didn't want to have to come back. Then I took up my post again near the bar. But Ireland wouldn't quiet down.

"All right," I said to him, returning to his table. "Out you go!"

I still recall the bleary, arrogant look Ireland gave me. "Do you know who I am?"

"Yeah," I said. "You're the loudmouth prick who's leaving the club."

He then made a huge mistake: "Does your fucking mother know you talk like that?"

On the street, there's a time-honored code about how you react when someone insults you. You give him a second chance. You don't start in with the fists right away. You ask your opponent to repeat what he just said. If the asshole backs away, maybe he can avoid a beat-down.

In this case, I duly invoked the warning. "What'd you say to me?"

Doug Ireland didn't take the hint. "I said your mama—"

He didn't get all the words out. I punched him on the top of his fat head so hard that he fell forward and split apart the tabletop. The Lindsay minions all of a sudden became a lot less drunk. They somehow managed to carry the massive, unconscious Ireland from the club, which was no easy task.

Worried about possible retaliation from city authorities, who could have easily closed the Improv down with a bogus building or fire inspection, Budd put me on ice for a couple of weeks. He was nice enough to make it a paid vacation. No political blowback ever developed, and Doug Ireland never showed his face in the Improv again. After my two-week suspension, I was back in the mix.

A great mood of camaraderie held sway around the club in those days. Even after hours, the Improv comics, singers, bartenders, and regulars would hang out together. Almost every night after closing we'd board what we used to call the "bagel express" to go out as a group. Budd had a bagel delivery guy, Hy Lipstein, who pulled up outside the Improv at around four a.m.

Hy was a fan. He filled the walls in the back of his truck with eight-by-ten photos of comedy stars and actors. The whole gang would pile in among the racks and racks of fragrant bagels. With Hy Lipstein rolling through the deserted streets and us holding on for dear life in the back, we'd head east toward the Brasserie, a French bistro that was open round the clock.

One big happy Improv family, bagel-trucking it through the night.

These were great days for me as a workingman but not so much as a family man. I worked nights and slept during the day, which made it difficult to spend much time with my kids. I was preoccupied with making a living. My youngest son, Jaime, bore the brunt of my being away from home a lot.

Jaime was the third in line behind Rick and Danny, and I think he always felt that number three was not a very good position to be in. He was born in March 1961, four years after Danny and six years after Rick.

As he grew to school age, I was a nine-to-five man at Greyhound. While I still spent as much time as I could with my boys, it was my wife who kept tabs on my youngest son. I didn't realize it at the time, but Jaime needed his father's attention. My work circumstances made that impossible. Things became even more difficult when I became night supervisor at Greyhound. When Jaime went off to school in the morning, I was just getting home. I would be asleep when he got back from school.

Things began to turn around one summer when I was offered a position at a bungalow colony in Monticello, New York. In addition to my gig as an Improv bouncer, this would be a second job for me. My family and I would run the food concession. We couldn't afford to rent one of the bungalows, but if we operated the concession, lodgings would be thrown in for free.

I came up every weekend to help run everything with my wife and children. It was at the colony that I learned what an outstanding basketball player Jaime had become, largely without help from me. During those beautiful Catskill weekends, he and I played basketball with each other, as well as softball and paddleball. We made up for lost time.

Even though I couldn't be there much, those were some of the happiest days we had as a family. Sandy and the children remained at the colony for the entire summer season, two years in a row. I spent only Sundays and Mondays. The remainder of the week I was back in New York, working nights at the Improvisation.

A couple of times Jaime would drive home with me to see his friends. Keep in mind that I had to be at work by eight p.m. I would always lie down for a while before going in to the club, and my son would spend a couple of hours with his friends while I slept. But he would eventually get bored and ask to go back to the Catskills.

I never wanted to disappoint him. I felt guilty not seeing him all week, so I would drive back to our summer bungalow, drop him off, then immediately turn around for the return trip to New York City. Eight and a half hours on the road.

Besides running the food concession, once in a while I would perform for the colony guests. It was nothing too formal or spectacular. I would sing one song, the Beatles hit "Something." I followed Budd's lead and tried to emulate him as a master of ceremonies.

The colony couldn't afford to pay big money for entertainment, so I asked a few of the Improv comics, including Rodney Dangerfield and David Brenner, to come up and perform. Also pitching in was Steve Landesberg, soon to become popular on the ABC sitcom *Barney Miller*. All the Improv guys did the colony gigs largely as a favor to me. I was like a booking agent for them, but one who didn't get a fee.

If my time behind the microphone at the bungalow colony represented my out-of-town tryouts, then I guess emceeing at the Improv was my informal, unofficial New York debut. I'd get up, introduce the acts, and manage not to make a fool of myself. Doing it over and over, stepping in whenever Budd wasn't there, allowed me a tiny seed of confidence.

I was just getting my feet wet. No one heckled me. I took one small step, then another and another. Some nights, I would even act as a straight man for one of the comics.

Once in a while I got jobs through my contacts at the club. The comic and impressionist David Frye hired me on as his road manager at $500 a week. Budd gave me permission to leave my post at the Improv and go on Dave's West Coast tour with him. Even though Frye called me his road manager, I was basically a step up from a gofer. The guy was a huge, happy drinker, so one of my main jobs was to make sure his whiskey flask was filled.

But there were some chores I refused to take on.

"Look, kid," Dave said to me during his first club appearance on the tour, even though I was far from a kid at this point. "I'm up there, I got to pee all the fucking time, so you got to clear the ice bucket whenever it fills up."

I couldn't believe my ears. Dave's drinking and his weak bladder made him have to go urgently and often. He incorporated it as part of his routine onstage, ducking back behind a screen to tap a kidney every ten minutes or so.

"If you think I'm going to empty your pee-filled ice bucket, that's not happening," I told Frye. He backed off and got some poor busboy from the club to do it instead. Better him than me.

Dave did uncanny impersonations and was one of the best at what was even then a dying art. He impersonated everyone from Jimmy Cagney, Clark Gable, and a host of other Hollywood stars as well as political figures such as Richard Nixon.

One night in San Francisco, he was doing Cagney at the upscale Fairmont Hotel. Whenever he impersonated the actor, he'd wave his arms a lot and walk in an exaggerated manner. The Fairmont had a thrust stage that reached out into the audience. Dave-as-Jimmy strutted forward, saying Cagney's signature line, "You dirty rat!" Only he kept going until he walked right off the end of the stage.

I watched in disbelief as Frye's legs kept moving even though he was treading air, like the cartoon character Wile E. Coyote. I thought he was going to break his legs. But somehow he landed without falling, managed to stay upright, and continued walking, right out of the club. He never came back. The audience members roared, thinking it was all part of the act.

All this exposure to the ins and outs of show business was paying off for me in the form of increased confidence. At the Improv, my comfort level developed to where I would go onstage myself, not to do comedy, but to sing. I still didn't have the guts to perform for an audience, so I waited until everyone but the staff had left the place. Then I serenaded the empty tables and chairs.

I did the same tune every time I got up, "Some of These Days," a song that the red-hot mama Sophie Tucker made famous, a song that every singer in the world had done before me. I belted it out, giving some of my first onstage performances at four a.m. in a deserted comedy club.

An actor who hung around the Improv was always trying to encourage me to go into acting. Carmine Caridi was a legit guy with a lot of stage credits on his résumé, so support from him really meant something.

"You! You're a natural!" he would tell me. He was always like that, brimming with enthusiasm for people. "Yeah, Danny, you should do it!"

"I'm too old," I said.

"Knock it off," Carmine responded. "You're still a young guy."

"I'm too old to begin acting," I said insistently. "I live in a fucking project up in the Bronx. I have kids to support."

It's not like he'd bug me about it all the time, but Carmine didn't give up, either. He used to watch me on the stage at the Improv when Budd had gone home and I would step in as emcee. When I sang or did dramatic readings, I'd look out and see Carmine there. Gradually, the outlandish idea he was selling me—that I could work professionally as an actor—began to stick.

I ventured into doing late-at-night monologues from *The Godfather*. The movie hadn't been made yet, but I did a few of Sonny's speeches from Mario Puzo's bestselling book. I thought I *was* Sonny Corleone. The Puzo language was flowery and distant from what I heard on the street, but it sounded good up onstage.

As an actor doing a monologue, there was a psychological barrier between the audience and me. I could be anyone I wanted. For a short time, I wasn't me, I was the character. It felt like a revelation.

In the beginning, doing those lines from *The Godfather*, I was very shaky and shy, because I was ill equipped. I learned that the key to a successful monologue is to be prepared. I worked on phrasing, emphasis, pacing. In those early days, I had a simple approach to acting: pure, unadorned energy.

I was half-hoping nobody would see me. Deep down, though, I actually dreamed I would somehow magically be discovered. I didn't have a clue what I was doing, but I started to be more of a regular on the Improv stage. With Raymond Johnson on the piano, teamed up on vocals with Buddy Mantia and Buddy Hughes, I'd do backup singing for Bette Midler or Robert Klein.

When I finally told Sandy that I thought I might try acting for a living, she actually laughed. I didn't blame her. I thought the whole idea was pretty unlikely myself. But some stubborn, hidden dream within me wanted to come true. No matter what anyone said, no matter who laughed or who ridiculed my hopes, the dream would not die.

Sandy thought I might try acting for a year or two. After the inevitable disappointment, I would get it out of my system. Then I'd settle down with a "real" job.

The next step and sensible move for me would have been to sign up for some acting classes. That would have been the advice of show business professionals. But I felt I was too old and too much in a hurry to take the traditional path. In order to learn the craft of acting, I decided that I would have to study it on the run.

I remember when I first started carrying scripts around. The reaction of the guys at the Central Park ball fields was typical.

"Now you're an *actor*?" they'd say, shaking their heads in disbelief. They knew me as a ringer, as an athlete, as a long-ball hitter. They had me pretty well pegged. It didn't make sense to them that a big tough guy like me would try his hand at what they were doing. Acting was their game, not mine.

What happened next represented one of those curveballs that fate tosses at you every once in a while. Most of the time you whiff at them. If you're lucky, though, you can hit one out of the park.

A Hoboken guy came into the Improv every once in a while. He had narrow eyes and a big shock of black hair. Louis LaRusso II introduced himself to everybody as a writer and was very big on the language of the working class. That was his thing.

Lou LaRusso hadn't had anything produced, but that was okay. Everywhere you looked in those days, there were actors who had never been cast and producers who had never gotten a show on the boards. There were so many unproduced playwrights around Broadway that you could hardly throw a rock without hitting one.

Together, Lou LaRusso and I were about to change our lives.

Chapter Ten

Steps Forward and Steps Back

I had never seen a play before acting in one.

Louis LaRusso II didn't inspire a lot of confidence at first. He was one more of the numberless showbiz wannabes who passed through the Improv. No one called him by his full name; he was just Lou. He wasn't considered a professional writer. He'd been struggling to be one for a long time. His struggles plus thirty cents would have gotten him on the subway back then. But Lou had one attribute that is essential for success.

He didn't quit.

He wrote and wrote and wrote. Most of his stuff was rooted in his working-class upbringing in Hoboken, New Jersey.

Every so often in the early seventies, Lou would approach

me at the Improv. "So, Danny, I got a play I want you to be in," he'd say.

"Why are you asking me?" I said. "I'm not an actor."

"Yes, you are!" Lou said. "You just don't know it yet."

He was persuasive. "Try it," he kept urging me.

Eventually, I came around. "What the hell, Lou," I told him. "I'll give it a shot."

Lou LaRusso II's hometown of Hoboken sits right across the Hudson from downtown Manhattan. Looking across the river, you can almost touch the magic, but it's just out of your reach. Hoboken is the kid with his nose pressed up against the shop window, an outsider looking in.

Lou tapped into that outsider feeling within me. The play he gave me to read, which he called *Lamppost Reunion*, turned out to be a barroom drama. The plot centered around success and failure—stars who achieve fame and ordinary folks who don't.

The main character, Fred Santora, was a Hoboken singer who made it big and climbed to the heights of success. The model, of course, was Frank Sinatra. In Lou's play, "Fred" comes back to Hoboken, massively popular. Earlier in the evening, he headlined a fabulous Madison Square Garden concert across the river in Manhattan. Now he wants to see his hometown friends and bask in nostalgia for old times' sake. It doesn't work out that way, as resentments crop up and old beefs surface.

Lou put out a casting call for *Lamppost Reunion*, which meant he went around the Improv and begged people to be in his play. There were five characters: the famous singer, an alcoholic, a bookie, a bodyguard, and a bartender.

There were five of us. One was a longtime actor with a lot of credits, two others were part-time actors, another was an actor-comedian. As a final cherry on top of the sundae, Lou chose a partly deaf director who had little directing experience.

Then there was me, the fifth wheel. At that time, I wouldn't have known acting if it bit me in the ass.

What a lineup. We were a gang of misfits along the lines of the Dirty Dozen, but with fewer members, like the Filthy Five.

The whole arrangement looked pretty shaky. But as I read Lou's play for the first time, I began to get excited. He used language that I recognized. It wasn't refined. Usually it's called "earthy." Lou had nailed the reality of the American dream: great for some, a nightmare for others.

The course of true love never runs smooth, but if you ever really want to see rough, just get involved in mounting an off-off-Broadway play. Like a lot of situations in life, if I had known how crazy the production history of *Lamppost Reunion* would become, I probably would have had second thoughts going in.

We planned what was called a showcase production. The idea was that financial backers would see the show and might recognize the commercial possibilities. We were each given a script and would have to rehearse for two weeks. Budd Friedman at the Improv supported my career moves and made it easy for me to get time off. The run was limited to twelve performances, if we weren't thrown out on our asses before that.

I remember feeling a bit dismayed when we gathered two weeks before we opened in what was to be our performance space. We set up in a converted building on West Fifty-Third Street between Ninth and Tenth Avenues. The place served as a church during the day and a bingo hall on most nights. It sat about forty people on benches and metal chairs. Leaking radiators constantly hissed, and every once in a while the heat pipes erupted in mysterious bangs and rumbles.

Lou LaRusso paid a small amount of weekly rent. He dubbed our makeshift theater the Churchyard Playhouse, but I began to doubt that it was ever a church at all. There was no evidence of religious denomination anywhere. The gentleman who hung around the premises claimed to be a priest, but he didn't wear a collar. The Churchyard Playhouse became our theatrical home.

Chaos immediately descended during rehearsals. All of the people involved were strong-willed, and a few actively despised one another and didn't make a secret of it. I was too much of a rookie to realize that this is how the theater usually is. The company fought all the time. Shouting, name-calling, and even shoving were commonplace.

Observing all this from his post in the audience, Lou LaRusso never said a word. But he sure as hell looked as if the sand in his hourglass was running out. His play, his baby, was being tortured right before his eyes. Whenever Lou was nervous, he had a habit of constantly running his fingers through his hair as if he wanted to rip it all out.

J. J. Barry already had a well-established career and was a consummate character actor. You might possibly know him as Mr. Compton in the TV series *Three's Company* or Uncle Gonzo in *Happy Days*. In *Lamppost Reunion*, though, he played the lead of Fred Santora, the Frank Sinatra character.

I remember the rehearsal when we went "off book" for the first time, meaning we could no longer refer to the script and had to have our lines down solid. I had been working on it day and night since we started. I had Sandy run them with me. I recited them walking down the street. I must have mumbled them in my sleep. I was terrified of embarrassing myself onstage.

Miracle of miracles, on that initial run-through I somehow managed not to stumble too badly.

"Okay, let's block," our director called out.

I swear to you, my first thought was about a football lineman. That's what I knew about blocking. I didn't know it was the term for charting out the movement of actors around the stage.

The cast member who gave everyone the most difficulties was Ray Serra, a little guy given to boosting his height by wearing lifts in his shoes. As he crossed the creaky wooden floor of the Churchyard stage, his clunky footwear sounded like thunder. The director, who had enough trouble hearing as it was, laid down an ultimatum.

"Either come in wearing sneakers tomorrow or don't come in at all," he told Ray.

Serra blew up, cursing the director and quitting the company. I ran after him as he stalked out of the theater.

"You can't quit, Ray!" I said. "I've got a good feeling about this play." Ray looked at me like I was crazy.

"Fuck him," he snarled, about the director. "He's a loser."

For a last-minute replacement, we simply went back to our casting pool at the Improv and recruited an actor-artist regular at the club.

Unlikely as it was, the production slowly took shape. How it all came together, I'll never know. In the fall of 1970, I made my debut on the New York stage in an off-off-Broadway showcase production of *Lamppost Reunion*. I was on a stage, acting in a play. And I loved every minute of it.

The first week was slow. The rule in theater is that if the cast ever outnumbers the audience, the show doesn't have to go on. But word of mouth slowly began to build. We began to sell out every night, and the initial showcase got extended. I started to believe that the whole enterprise might actually work out.

Could it be that we had a hit on our hands? *Maybe the space really is a church*, I thought. *Maybe the priest really is ordained, collar or not.*

Lamppost Reunion somehow became a must-see. Now real movers and shakers from the theater world started to show up for the performances, agents, managers, actors, directors, and producers.

The actor who played the drunk had connections with money, and Lou met with them. The money men informed him that they had heard his play was very good, but naturally, they would want to see it a few times before committing to back the production. Lou agreed. They came, they saw, we conquered. The money guys loved the play and decided to provide backing.

My first real stage work represented only a small baby step into the world of show business. At first I didn't believe that anything would come of it. And for a long, agonizing stretch of time, nothing did. The funding didn't come through right away, and we were left hanging with a vague promise there would be money for a full-blown Broadway production sometime in the future.

When I consider how I broke into acting, I always think of three men, recalling each one of them with a sense of gratitude. Budd Friedman of the Improvisation is one. Lou LaRusso is another.

The third is Carmine Caridi, an actor with a true gentleman's soul. He saw something in me that I didn't even see in myself. Carmine and I gravitated to each other because we had things in common. We were both Italian-American, both born in New York City, both about the same height and age. We could have served as each other's stand-ins.

Among the ragtag Improv crowd, Carmine was respected because he was getting parts. He had an agent and went to casting calls. When I began working at the club, Carmine became a true friend. Back then, I didn't put a name to what he was doing for me. I didn't think of him as a mentor. I thought he was just a good guy, being generous to me as he was with everybody else.

In the spring of 1971, Budd Friedman threw a party for Carmine at the Improv. We were celebrating the news that Carmine had just won the role of Sonny Corleone in the big-screen adaptation of *The Godfather*.

This was huge news. None of us realized what a cinematic classic director Francis Ford Coppola would create with this movie, but there was definitely a buzz around town about it. Mario Puzo's novel had been immensely popular, and actors are always hungry for work. For a while, *The Godfather* was all anyone talked about.

And now my friend Carmine had knocked down a huge role. The character of Sonny was one of the most interesting in the book. Hotheaded, cocky, and mercurial, Sonny offered an actor great opportunities to display anger, brashness, and a young and sexy brand of confidence. Carmine was perfect for the part.

All the congratulations died in our mouths the night of the party, as Carmine had just been informed he was out and James Caan was in. At the time, none of us grasped the magnitude of the sudden switch, though we all knew that an actor could wait a lifetime for that kind of role.

The producers had officially given Carmine the part. The contracts were signed, i's dotted, t's crossed. The commitment was so firm that Carmine wound up getting paid for the part that he didn't get. For me, the whole experience turned out to be a lesson in the cruelties of show business, the way producers could dangle a plum role in front of somebody's face, only to whisk it away when it was within reach.

The Improv party turned into a wake. Carmine never complained. He met the bad news with a philosophical shrug. "That's the business," he said. "That's the business now and that will be the business forever. It's the world of broken dreams."

Since that time, I've realized that they make more broken hearts than movies in Hollywood. I always remember the example of Carmine Caridi and the role that almost was. I can never say I wasn't warned about the ups and downs of an acting career, but I went ahead with it anyway.

Of course, James Caan became a huge star as Sonny Corleone. In part to try to make up for what the producer had done to poor Carmine, Francis Coppola offered him a role in *The Godfather: Part II*. It was a nice gesture. If I had been in Carmine's place, I might have told Coppola to stick it up his ass. But not Carmine. He had too much class. He and I wound up being cast together in the film, playing the Rosato brothers.

What do you do when you get flattened? You get up and move on. That spring, while *The Godfather* was gearing up to film in New York City, Carmine landed work on Broadway. The ragingly popular production of *Man of La Mancha* was continuing its run, and Carmine got the part of Head Muleteer. He doubled as the back end of Rocinante, Don Quixote's horse.

We all laughed bitterly about that. Carmine had gone from Sonny Corleone to a horse's ass in a heartbeat.

While Carmine was doing *La Mancha*, he was offered another job. A road company was going out with Jason Miller's basketball play, *That Championship Season*. When Carmine couldn't take the gig, he forced me to go to an audition. When I say "forced," I mean that quite literally, as he walked me to the rehearsal hall.

It's no secret that every actor hates to audition, and I was apprehensive to the extreme. I have always held to the notion that if directors can't tell what kind of man I am just by sitting down and talking with me, then maybe they're in the wrong business.

At Carmine's urging, and with all my fears tripping me up and holding me back, I read for the part.

And got it.

Within a month, I found myself out on the road with one of my heroes, Broderick Crawford, who played the lead as the coach. He was one of my silver-screen father figures. I considered him a model of what a real man should be. But he was having trouble at that point in his life with making himself understood by the audience. His dental work got in the way. Halfway through the tour, the great character actor Harry Bellaver replaced Crawford.

The next year I again went out on the road with *Championship Season*, this time with William Conrad in the lead role. Conrad's career was taking off with the TV hit *Cannon*, and he was none too happy to be gigging on a touring stage play during his off-season. None of us in the company were aware of his dissatisfaction until the last stop of the tour, in Chicago.

Conrad took us all out for dinner and presented each cast member with a gold watch. Mine was inscribed: "To Danny, a champion of all seasons, Love, Bill." We were all stunned by Conrad's generosity, thanking him profusely.

"Now I want you all to go fuck yourselves," Conrad said calmly. "This has been one of the worst experiences of my life." He walked out. We were left speechless.

During this period when I was cobbling together a stage career, Sandy and my children never really took my involvement in acting that seriously. They didn't see me tour in *Championship*. Of course, Sandy, Mom, and my family came to see me for every single one of my New York openings. But I think that until I started to get press notices, until I was interviewed on talk shows and got my name mentioned in reviews, acting was a bit hypothetical for my near and dear ones.

I had doubts myself. I felt like a juggler with one too many balls in the air, thinking that at any moment it could all come crashing down. I was getting gigs—the work with Lou LaRusso, the job offers for minor parts—but it was as though I didn't really want to believe it was happening. My life at that time was a perpetual knock on wood.

Touring in *Championship* paid off in a big way. At the end of my initial run, I received my first formal recognition for my acting. Great as that was, it was made all the sweeter because of who presented it to me.

Every year the Faberge Straw Hat Awards honors promising newcomers in the worlds of film, theater, and dance. The ceremony was held at Jimmy's restaurant in the Theater District. I walked up to receive my award and was greeted by one of the most recognizable people on the planet—Cary Grant. There he was, the impossibly handsome movie star whom I had seen dozens of times on-screen.

I stood next to him, a smile frozen on my face. "I'm scared," I muttered.

"So am I, kid," Cary Grant said, a great gentleman from first to last.

I began to feel as though I was actually putting together a career as an actor. This was all happening during that time we were waiting to know for sure if we were going to Broadway with *Lamppost Reunion*. But before Lou's play made it there, I landed a part that showed me where my true destiny lay.

The silver screen.

Chapter Eleven

How Baseball Saved My Life (Again)

With *Lamppost Reunion* still in limbo seeking financing, I was feeling frustration about my stuttering start to acting onstage. My film career hadn't exactly taken off like a rocket, either. Early in 1973, I was involved in an ill-fated production of a movie called *The Godmother*, written and produced by Lou LaRusso. Made with a budget of about fifty cents, the misbegotten comedy concerned that most unlikely of characters, a gay Mafia boss.

The Godmother was a humble, homemade project all the way. There should have been a line in the credits: "Conceived, written, and cast during late-night sessions at the Improvisation Comedy Club." Budd Friedman had a part. Carmine Caridi and I both played bodyguards of the lead mafioso.

To this day I believe if *The Godmother* ever got released, it would have meant the end of my acting career before it even got started. Instead, it was never screened, never distributed, and never released on video.

Oddly enough, my involvement in Lou's movie did have one positive outcome. I can date my membership in the Screen Actors Guild from *The Godmother*. Getting my SAG card for work on an unreleased film sounds like a good-news, bad-news joke, but that's how it was.

So, my first venture into the movies crashed and burned. But I didn't give up. Mixing with the actors, playwrights, and drama professionals of the Broadway Show League in Central Park, I heard about a lot of opportunities. There are always tons of auditions going on in New York City on any given day.

"Hey, Danny, they're casting a baseball movie," Elliot Cuker told me in the summer of 1972. "You ought to go out for it." Elliot was a charismatic actor who would go on to become one of the world's foremost collectors of vintage automobiles.

The movie was *Bang the Drum Slowly*, released in 1973 and based on Mark Harris's acclaimed novel. I showed up to the area of Central Park where the casting was taking place. The director, John D. Hancock, put a bat in my hands and had me toss a ball around while I told stories of pro-ball scouts reaching out to me when I was a teenager and playing on the CBS softball team with Phil Rizzuto.

At the end of that first day of casting, Hancock uttered the magic words. "Okay, you're on."

What did that even mean? I really didn't understand what part exactly I had been auditioning for in the first place.

"You're playing Horse Byrd," Hancock said.

"Who's he in the movie?"

"He's a relief pitcher."

I was overjoyed. Here I was, with no acting class experience or anything like it ever, and at thirty-nine years old I had been cast in a major motion picture.

In the original novel and in the first drafts of the screenplay, my character Horse Byrd spent most of his time in the bullpen. "No, no, I want you on the field," Hancock said after he became more familiar with my ball-playing skills. He reworked the role, and Horse was transformed into a first baseman, primarily because I was one of the only real ballplayers in the cast.

The plot centers on a dying ballplayer, Bruce Pearson, played by Robert De Niro. Michael Moriarty, whose father played ball on one of the Boston Red Sox farm teams, had the lead as pitcher Henry "Author" Wiggen, Bruce Pearson's friend. Vincent Gardenia was a comic wonder in his Oscar-nominated role as Dutch Schnell, the cantankerous coach.

De Niro's career was just beginning to take off. He had already been involved in *The Gang That Couldn't Shoot Straight*, a Mafia comedy based on the book by the journalist Jimmy Breslin. But it would be 1973's *Bang the Drum Slowly* and that same year's *Mean Streets* that really put Bobby on the map.

A lot of the actors involved in *Bang the Drum* didn't know a bat from a hole in the wall. De Niro especially had no clue about baseball. I would end up coaching him on some catcher's moves: how to block a wild pitch, how to dig a ball out of the dirt, stuff like that. Vince Gardenia didn't know a lot about the game either, or at least he pretended that he didn't.

"I want you all to line up along the third-base line!" shouted assistant director Allan Wertheim before one particular scene.

"Danny," Vince whispered to me, "which one is third base?"

Playing the team's coach, Vince had another scene where he went out on the field to speak to the pitcher. I clued him in on one of the traditional superstitions of baseball. "When you walk back to the dugout from the pitcher's mound, don't step on the foul line," I said.

"I shouldn't step on the foul line?" Vince asked, mystified.

"That's right," I said. "The chalk line that runs along the base path? Hop over it instead of stepping on it."

I don't have a clue about where this superstition came from, but I knew it well. Sure enough, in the film, Vince is careful to step over the foul line on his way back to the dugout. It's a small detail, and one that only a baseball aficionado would pick up on. But it made the role that much more authentic.

Confident as I was about my knowledge of baseball, I was less sure about my acting. Throughout the shoot, I was always second-guessing myself. I remember being in a corner rehearsing my lines, when Vince asked me what I was so worried about.

"What if I'm lousy?" I moaned. "If I'm lousy in a movie, it's bad for all time. If I see the movie fifty times, I'll see myself suck fifty times."

"That's okay, kid," he said. "You'll probably never work again anyway."

Vince was most likely kidding, but his words had a sharp edge. It was a reminder that nothing in the world of acting is certain. Out of all the people I worked with on *Bang the Drum Slowly*, Vincent Gardenia became a lifelong friend.

Actors always remember their first speaking scene in their debut film. My first one was with Bobby De Niro, who was not bad company for busting my cinematic cherry. The four-word line that is enshrined in my memory? "He always did wonder."

Baseball was a thread that ran through my whole life. My involvement in our national pastime gave me the Improv, Lou LaRusso, and *Bang the Drum Slowly*.

As I started out in acting, I would have been hard put to list any resources that might help me in my career. I thought I had nothing, but I had baseball. And that made all the difference.

Soon after *Bang the Drum* hit the movie theaters, *Lamppost Reunion* came back into my life. The money men had finally come through, and we were headed to Broadway.

There was laughter and tears over the news. I was elated. *Lamppost* had turned into a real acting job, and even more important, I was going to get paid. We had done the showcase run at the Churchyard for lunch money. By contrast, a Broadway production paid standard salaries. Wages were set by Actors' Equity, and every performer had to be compensated. Those of us who weren't in the union—that was four out of five—would join.

It didn't matter that I had no idea what I was doing. I would get an Equity salary for acting! I was on my way.

After one month of rehearsal, we were scheduled to open at the Little Theatre on West Forty-Fourth Street, only a block away from the Improv. Today the venue has been renamed the Helen Hayes Theatre. Then as now, it sat on hallowed ground—right next door was Sardi's, the most celebrated Theater District restaurant of them all.

When we had been rehearsing for two weeks, we were asked to report to the office for a meeting, where it was announced to the cast that the director and J. J. Barry, the lead, had been fired. The two most important people responsible for our reaching Broadway, gone! None of us in the cast knew what the hell to say.

There was an actor who hung out at the Improv, someone who had been in the profession for a long time. I had shared the screen with him on *Bang the Drum Slowly*. He had been coming to watch us rehearse. We'd nicknamed him "the Shadow," because he was always there. No one thought anything of it. If there was something wrong with his being there, I would have been the last to know. I didn't understand anything about show business rules and traditions.

Lo and behold, with the original director and J. J. now out of the building, one of the producers introduced our new director—the Shadow. He came onto the stage with a smile on his face, as if he believed we would greet him with open arms. What we all should've done then was leave the production immediately.

The feeling of betrayal was complete. We had gone through hell to get to Broadway, and I have never forgiven myself for not walking out of the fucking theater in solidarity with J. J. and the director.

The Shadow made a little speech, telling us that J. J.'s replacement was a good friend of his from California, Gabriel Dell, formerly one of the Dead End Kids. Gabe greeted the cast as if nothing out of the ordinary had happened. He simply thought he was an actor coming in from the West Coast to do a part on Broadway.

I found out later that the cast member who had the connection to the Rhode Island backers was responsible for the conspiracy. He was able to engineer the firings and planted his friend the Shadow at the rehearsals. All along, the Shadow had been watching the original director with the intention of replacing him.

But what goes around comes around. We were in previews when it happened, before the show formally opened.

Walking up the backstage stairs on my way to begin the second act, I passed two guys I had never seen before. My street sense told me immediately what they were.

Sure enough, they started to beat the shit out of one of actors, working him over with blackjacks. I assumed this guy was somehow disrupting the show, and now that the money boys had invested in it, they were getting serious about not letting him fuck things up. Of course, this was New York, so it could have been something else entirely.

At the opening of the second act, the actor was supposed to emerge from the barroom's toilet, behind a door, stage right. At the cue, I turned to react to his entrance. The door opened, and out came his replacement instead—the Shadow. Talk about changing horses in midstream: this was changing actors mid-play!

This kind of double-dealing was familiar to me from the streets of the Bronx. Somehow, I thought Broadway would be more civilized, but I was wrong. From the start, I guess I should have felt right at home in the theater.

Lamppost finally opened on Broadway on October 16, 1975. In an irony of ironies, the Shadow, who had the advantage of all of the original director's insights into the direction of the play, received a Tony nomination for it.

I was building on my collaboration with Lou LaRusso. The next year, I did Lou's *Wheelbarrow Closers*, another showcase that wound up going to the Great White Way, opening at the Bijou on October 11, 1976. All the cast members in Lou's plays were now being talked about in the theater community. It was as though we were part of a new, different breed of actor.

Broadway wasn't through with me yet. The next play I was cast in went on to become the biggest hit of the season.

Chapter Twelve

Gemini

My birthday is June 20, meaning my astrological sign is Gemini. Though I don't even follow my daily horoscope, it does strike me as remarkable that a play of the same title boosted my stage career to a whole new level.

Gemini was the product of a young Yale-educated playwright named Albert Innaurato. His producers had seen me in *Lamppost*. They cast me as the blue-collar Italian father Fran Geminiani, which was very close to the character I had played in *Lamppost Reunion*. I almost didn't accept the part, as I didn't want to play a forty-year-old father. My delayed start to an acting career already made me feel older than the other actors around me.

"Sure, Fran is forty," Albert said, trying to convince me to take the role. "But, Danny, he still thinks of himself as a nineteen-year-old." That made sense to me, because I felt the same way. I reconsidered and took the role.

Gemini was a crazy kind of comic opera, featuring a woman who climbs telephone poles in an overstuffed costume, a four-hundred-pound boy who flies around on his scooter in pajamas, and my character's son, Francis, whose sexual orientation is ambiguous. The Geminiani family is not quite sure what he is, but they're hoping for the best.

The entire play takes place in the backyard of the family's South Philadelphia home, around a table where the family members and their guests eat, with gusto and enthusiasm. My character's wife, Lucille, was played by Anne De Salvo, and she picks food from the plates of others. This impolite habit prompts my character to throw an entire pot of spaghetti at Lucille. Night after night. I had fun. I'm sure Anne didn't.

The Geminiani family backyard was like hellzapoppin', with characters ducking and weaving through the food-fight crossfire. The kids in the play were terrific: Robert Picardo (who would go on to a supporting role in *Star Trek: Voyager*), Reed Birney, Jonathan Hadary, and Carol Potter.

Gemini had me serving up spaghetti and meatballs eight times a week, matinees and nightly performances included. I didn't cook the food myself; the producers had it brought in from Mamma Leone's, the famous Theater District red-sauce restaurant. I wouldn't have been able to eat it so often if it wasn't from a quality kitchen.

After an out-of-town trial in Huntington, New York, we opened *Gemini* off-Broadway in March 1977, downtown in Greenwich Village at Circle Rep. Audiences loved it. I discovered there's nothing quite like being onstage in a comedy when laughter threatens to bring down the house. But it wasn't only that *Gemini* was funny. It also perfectly matched the mood of the times. The gay pride movement was really ramping up during that period.

As she always did, my wife, Sandy, came to see the show at Circle Rep on opening night in March 1977. She wanted to meet the wonderful Jessica James, who was terrific as Bunny Weinberger, the telephone-pole-climbing nutcase. After the performance, I told Sandy to go ahead and visit Jessica in her dressing room.

Sandy is always very unassuming, and she didn't know a lot about show business, despite hearing some of the ins and outs through me. When she knocked on Jessica's door, it swung open to reveal the actress without a stitch of clothing on, and Jessica remained that way for what felt like an eternity to Sandy. My embarrassed wife stood there talking up at the ceiling for about five minutes, never once looking directly at Jessica.

Carol Potter's understudy was a twenty-three-year-old beauty named Kathleen Turner. She was doing a soap in New York at the time. Kathleen was in every way a very alluring young woman, full of laughter and smarts. In the play's concluding scene, two boys and a girl run to catch the train back to school. My character is there to send them off. During one performance, when Kathleen the understudy had stepped in to play the role, I kissed her good-bye.

It was the most normal thing in the world, a stage kiss, a father bidding farewell to one of his son's friends. It was supposed to be a peck on the cheek. That night, Albert Innaurato thought I had made it into something a little bit more with Kathleen. He came running backstage, screaming but not really angry. He always spoke in exclamation points.

"This is a different play!" he said, raising his forefinger in the air like offended royalty. "This is not the one I wrote! In my play, the son runs away with the girl, not the father!"

The whole cast broke up. Incidents like that happened every night. Unpredictability, in my opinion, makes for beautiful theater. *Gemini* played to waves of laughter.

Two months after we opened at Circle Rep, in May 1977, the play headed uptown to the Little Theatre, the same venue where we had opened *Lamppost Reunion*. For the third play in a row, a small, limited-run production I appeared in was moving to Broadway. Theater people are superstitious. It didn't hurt that they began to believe my presence in the cast worked like a good-luck charm.

Broadway is like a gauntlet for egos. The critics line up and take their whacks as you pass by. But the reviews for *Gemini* were ecstatic. Albert's play became a huge hit, eventually running for four years.

I won an Obie for my performance. To appear in a hit on Broadway, to receive a prestigious acting award for my part in it—what could be better?

Naturally, I decided to leave the play.

No one guided my moves in the early part of my acting career. I was like a blind man feeling my way around. I didn't know how things were done, so I operated on a gut level. I ditched a Broadway hit simply because I didn't want people to believe that I couldn't get another job. I also didn't want to be associated with a single character, Fran Geminiani. I didn't want to be typecast. I wanted producers to understand that I could play something other than an Italian father.

Looking back, my logic didn't make that much sense. But I was new to the theater game and had no grasp of how rare it was to land a part in a smash play. Up until then, almost everything I touched had turned to Broadway gold. Actors would kill to enjoy the success I had. I turned my back on it because, basically, I didn't know what the hell I was doing.

The odd thing was, my presence in the cast of *Gemini* continued long after I left. We had filmed a TV ad for the play that aired continually on local television. I was prominently featured, delivering my trademark line: *"This is gonna be suummm party!"* Fans would stop me on the street and ask me to say it. There came a point where I didn't want to disappoint them by noting I was no longer in the play. The TV spot turned into a zombie ad, giving my performance as Fran a life after death.

By the late 1970s, another appearance of mine had taken on a life of its own as well. Francis Ford Coppola's *Godfather* saga was a huge critical and commercial success, with both the original and the sequel winning Academy Awards for Best Picture. I had a brief but memorable role in *The Godfather: Part II*. I had only a few lines, but one stood out that would be identified with me long afterward.

I never knew how I came to Coppola's attention. Perhaps Carmine Caridi recommended me for the role of the thug hit man Tony Rosato. Another possibility is that one of the producers of the film, Gray Frederickson, used to frequent the Improv and could have noticed me there. Whatever the reason, I didn't audition for the part. I never even met Coppola until I was on the set.

The original script had me in two scenes. One got edited out of the final cut, but the other appearance made it in. I was to come up behind actor Michael Gazzo, who was playing Corleone underboss Frankie "Five Angels" Pentangeli. My character would perform a classic Mafia hit, garroting Pentangeli, making him another casualty of a large-scale mob war.

"Okay, let's rehearse it," Coppola called out.

Technically, it was a difficult scene. I had to appear as if I were violently lifting Gazzo from his chair with the cord I had wrapped around his neck. I wanted to make very sure I wasn't hurting him. The prop crew had rigged a harness for Gazzo, so I lifted him up not by the garrote, as it appeared on film, but with the hidden harness. I had to hold it and look as if I was tightening the cord at the same time.

We rehearsed the scene, and it went off without a hitch. But I ended up ad-libbing a line during the strangulation.

"What was that you said?" Coppola asked after the run-through.

I hesitated. I didn't know if I was in trouble with Coppola for improvising.

"What was it?" he asked again.

"I think I said, 'Michael Corleone says hello.'"

Coppola considered this for a brief moment. "That's good," he said. "Keep it in."

With cameras rolling, we did the scene again, and I hissed out the same line. As the movie gained in reputation, that improvised four-word phrase came back to haunt me. Fans started to quote it to me on the street. "Hey, Danny," they'd call out, "Michael Corleone says hello." The line has stayed with me all the way through to today. On the Internet, aficionados still debate its meaning.

Although the *Godfather* films are cinematic classics, it doesn't take anything away from Coppola to say that both movies present a highly romanticized view of the Mafia. The language and the truth of the characters are nothing that I recognize from my life on the streets. Real mobsters never talked the way Marlon Brando, Al Pacino, and Robert De Niro spoke in the films. Coppola portrayed the mob as viewed through rose-colored camera lenses.

My work on *Lamppost Reunion* had benefited me in a lot of different ways. A theatrical agent named Richard Astor came to the showcase during its off-Broadway run at the Churchyard Playhouse. When theatrical professionals and moneymen see the play and actors in showcases, good things are supposed to happen.

That's not often the way it turns out, but with *Lamppost Reunion*, I wound up getting proper representation. Richard Astor saw something in me long before I had an established body of work. After all, my New York theater experience consisted of a single play, and a limited-run showcase, at that. It took guts for Richard to follow his instincts and take a chance on me.

Richard's company, the Astor Agency, had a small office on Fifty-Seventh Street and Broadway. He represented a lot of actors, including Robert Duvall and Martin Sheen before they broke big. They became A-list after they left him, but he was the one who helped them on their way.

In 1975, Richard set me up with a part that would change my life. He let me know that Woody Allen was involved in a movie, a rare project that Woody would act in but not write or direct. It was called *The Front*, and it dealt with the dark days of the

Hollywood blacklist. Walter Bernstein, who had been blacklisted in 1950, wrote the Oscar-nominated screenplay. The director was Martin Ritt, who made the film version of *The Great White Hope*, as well as *Hombre*, starring Paul Newman.

I met Woody for the first time with Martin Ritt at the film's production office. In *The Front*, Woody plays a lowly theater cashier deep in debt with gamblers, who to make extra cash serves as a front man for blacklisted writers. Ritt told me that I would play Danny LaGattuta, a bookie for Woody's character. The part was not a large one.

No rehearsal, no audition. Many times, an initial meeting with a show business professional would simply be a test as to whether you might be a pain in the ass, might have bad personal hygiene, or were in some other way unsuitable for the job. At this stage of my career, my parts came in a limited variety of flavors. I was a bartender, a bookie, or a father. In *The Front*, I appeared in only a few scenes, but my involvement in the film turned out to be vital for me later on.

Woody Allen would remember me. Down the line, I would encounter the mystery of his hot-and-cold personality. I would also have to endure major heartbreak in our professional relationship before it bore fruit. I could never say that *The Front* was the beginning of a beautiful friendship. But it was certainly the beginning of what would be some of the highest achievements of my acting career.

Around this time, Richard Astor got me my first television gigs. I had a strange animosity toward the whole idea of TV. I was a child of the movies, born into a world where the silver screen was the most popular form of entertainment. We plunked down good money to see movies—although, truth be told, I didn't always pay.

When TV came around, I remember everyone saying that this new medium would replace film. I hated hearing that, because so much of my life was wrapped up in the movies. I never felt the same emotional connection watching TV in my living room as I did in the darkness of a movie theater.

My master plan, such as it was, was never to go into television. I didn't consider it real acting. I was biased against TV right from the start. I took the roles that were offered to me not to further my career but to keep my family's head above water.

Producers offered me roles on cop shows such as *Kojak* and *The Andros Targets*. I did a TV movie called *Lady Blue* that spun off into a full series. Jamie Rose played the lead, and we shot a season's worth of episodes in Chicago.

Throughout the late seventies and early eighties, TV was the Aiello family's bread and butter. It kept me a busy boy. *Gemini* came back into my life as a TV movie, where I acted alongside Sheree North and Scott Baio. I had a turn as a master of ceremonies in a skit on *Saturday Night Live*. I did a TV pilot based on the hit movie *Car Wash*.

I would eventually appear on every TV talk show there was, with Tom Snyder and Charlie Rose being my personal favorites. In contrast to shows that focused on always getting the laugh, their programs were more like warm conversations among good friends.

My family only slowly came around to understanding that my acting career was more than just a passing whim. Sandy and I rarely discussed it with the children. Her support was simply part of her character, being a strong, loyal wife, always in my corner. Truth be told, however, she would have probably rather had a more conventional lifestyle, with a man whose work did not require travel all the time, one who remained home where she could keep an eye on him.

I tried to be as understanding as I could. After a two-month stretch shooting in Chicago on *Lady Blue*, living in an efficiency apartment and keeping in touch with Sandy mainly via the telephone, I decided to award my wife with a token of my affection. I purchased a brand-new black Pontiac Grand Am and drove it home. I parked the gorgeous vehicle out in front of our house and put a big red ribbon on it. She loved the surprise. A new car represented a concrete sign that my career as an actor was solid and reliable.

Sandy would occasionally join me when I was doing shows out of town. During this period she first earned her nickname "Sandy Sheets," since my wife always traveled with her own linens. She refused to lay her head on a hotel pillow or use the linens provided. Many times I would find myself on one side of the bed with her cocooned in her own sheets on the other. Needless to say, this arrangement made intimacy a little problematic.

At first, my boys were pretty reserved about my newfound celebrity as a TV actor. As time went on, though, they began to take advantage of it, as kids will. My daughter, Stacey, was different. She was genuinely embarrassed by it all, being extremely shy and not looking for any kind of notoriety.

"Class," Stacey's teacher said one day in the fall of 1980, "there's a film on television that is required viewing." It was an ABC After-school Special called *A Family of Strangers*, about a widower who remarries and must raise his own two daughters along with the daughter of his new wife. The subject of blended families was causing a lot of public discussion back then. I would go on to win a daytime Emmy for my work on the movie.

Stacey didn't let out a peep at school about my participation in *A Family of Strangers*. Her classmates had to watch the drama to find out that her father was the star of the movie that their teacher had assigned as homework. My daughter endured all the attention only after the fact.

"Why didn't you just tell them?" I asked her.

"Daddy, I didn't want them to think that I was something special," she said.

Because I started acting so late in my life—thirty-six years old for my first play, forty for my first film release—I used to lie a lot about my age, knocking a few years off from the truth.

In show business, producers always seem to think you might be too old for whatever part you're up for. It's as if they're trying to get rid of you as quickly as they can and shuffle you off into the retirement home. It was a never-ending battle, with producers adding on the years and actors subtracting them. I kept lying about my age. It got to be ridiculous when various media outlets cited different numbers.

Finally, my oldest son, Rick, called me to account: "Dad, you keep this up, in a couple years I'm going to be older than you are."

The job of acting is rarely a steady one. You work, you're unemployed, you work, you're unemployed again. The obligation of having to support a family had once forced me to do terrible things like stealing. So I could live with telling a few white lies about how old I was in order to land an acting job.

In the meantime, my work in TV represented a strictly practical endeavor. I may not have been a fan of television, but it sure beat robbing cigarette machines in the middle of the night.

A lot of fans believe that celebrity actors chum around with each other all the time. If you've acted in a movie together, the idea is that you're friends for life. With most actors I've worked with, our relationship was close only while the specific project lasted. I would see someone every day for a ten-week shoot, then rarely stay in touch, with each of us retreating into his private, personal world.

I would never claim that I'm a close friend of Robert De Niro. But during the period when he and I worked together on *Bang the Drum Slowly*, he came over a few times to my apartment in the Riverdale section of the Bronx. An actor like De Niro is a sponge, always observing people around him, soaking up local accents and personal quirks.

I recognized myself in one of Bobby's most famous movie lines. When I was younger, if I was facing off with some bullshit guy in the neighborhood, I would put a sneer in my voice and ask, "You talking to me?" Then my wife and I saw *Taxi Driver*, with De Niro uttering the same phrase. We looked at each other and Sandy whispered, "Danny, he's doing you!" De Niro could have just as well picked it up from the street himself, but it does make me wonder.

In 1973, after Bobby and I appeared together in *Bang the Drum Slowly*, I got a call from the offices of movie mogul Dino De Laurentiis. A writer there, Pete Savage, invited me up to the Gulf and Western building on Columbus Circle. Back then, Gulf and Western owned Paramount Pictures.

Dino De Laurentiis and Paramount were big-time. I couldn't figure out why they would bother with me. I had hardly any credits to my name.

I met with Pete Savage and a producer named Ralph Serpe. They had a great project, Savage said. "You know who Jake LaMotta is?" he asked.

I was a boxing fan. Of course I knew who Jake LaMotta was.

"Along with another writer, Joe Carter, I did a book with LaMotta," Savage said. "It's his life story. He calls it *Raging Bull*."

De Laurentiis was developing a script based on the LaMotta autobiography. My heart leaped. I conjured up visions of playing Jake LaMotta, the legendary "Bronx Bull" of boxing, who was a madman in the ring and out of it.

Savage quickly disabused me of the notion. Sure, there was a part for me, but not the lead. Eventually I realized that Savage, Serpe, and De Laurentiis were trying to get to Robert De Niro through me. Bobby was hotter than hot due to his work in *Bang the Drum* and *Mean Streets*. If I could get the *Raging Bull* book to De Niro, Savage said, Bobby could do a great job as Jake LaMotta.

De Niro knew as much about boxing as he did about baseball, but the movie would be less a fight film than a character study. If Hollywood ever remade *Somebody Up There Likes Me*, one of my all-time favorites, starring Paul Newman, Bobby would be the natural choice to play Rocky Graziano.

Savage gave me the *Raging Bull* book, which I read. LaMotta's life made for great drama, and Savage presented the story in a straightforward, easily understandable way. On one of the evenings that Bobby came over to our apartment, I told him I had something for him.

"I don't know how to do this," I said, uncertain how to proceed. "Some guys gave me a book for you. You know who Jake LaMotta is?"

Bobby didn't. I told him that LaMotta won the world middle-weight crown in 1949. Then I recounted details of my meetings with Serpe and Savage.

"I don't want to play a boxer," De Niro said. But after encouragement from me, he agreed to read the book.

From that point on, Pete Savage repeatedly invited me back to the Gulf and Western offices. "How's it going with Bobby?" he kept asking. Ralph Serpe lavished attention on me also. It was the first time I had been romanced by a studio. Paramount certainly had all the techniques to turn an actor's head. The courting went on for months.

Then, suddenly, nothing. The connection went dead, and all the phone calls and invites stopped. I could never reach Savage or Serpe or anyone else at Paramount. It became apparent that I couldn't have gotten into that office if I had a key.

Bobby was pretty much out of my life by that time. We would work together again, but not for a while. He was in Italy preparing himself for *The Godfather: Part II*, playing a young Vito Corleone in what would be an Oscar-winning role for him. He wanted to meet Italians from the turn of the century to pick up their speech patterns.

As I said, relationships between actors are a temporary sort of thing. Outside of a movie set, I have seen Bobby De Niro maybe twenty times over the course of my life. Show business friendships are formed quickly but often are not sustainable. De Niro might have gotten me my first answering service and recommended a financial adviser, but we weren't exactly buddies.

I slowly pieced together what had happened via the rumor mill. As far as the LaMotta project went, Dino De Laurentiis was out and the producer partnership of Robert Chartoff and Irwin Winkler was in. On top of that, director Martin Scorsese had come along with the new producers.

At the end of the seventies, when Scorsese finally got his production financing together and started to cast *Raging Bull*, I did indeed get a call to come by his office.

Bobby was there. Marty offered me what was essentially the part of an extra, a bodyguard role with no lines. I didn't expect Bobby to intercede on my behalf, because he always had a strict professional rule never to interfere with a director's vision. As far as he was concerned, it was all up to Marty.

At the time I was doing *Knockout* on Broadway and I was feeling pretty good about myself. I thought that my career had advanced beyond a role with no lines.

Scorsese had made me his offer. I thanked him and left.

Chapter Thirteen

Knockout

Boxing wasn't through with me yet. At the end of the seventies, playwright Lou LaRusso wanted to work with me again. At first, Lou and I kicked around the prospect of doing an Elvis Presley character, but the more we spoke about it, the more the idea began to feel a little stale.

I knew LaRusso's gritty, working-class style of drama. "How about an over-the-hill boxer?" I suggested.

I had a friend at the time, Anthony Conforti, who entertained me with stories of a cousin of his who kept fighting long after he should have quit the ring. Sly Stallone's *Rocky* had been a huge hit, so I felt as though Broadway audiences would be open to a down-and-dirty play about a boxer. I put Lou and Tony Conforti together, Lou filled out the story of Tony's cousin, and we were on our way.

Lou called his new play *Knockout*. I played the lead, an aging, gentle-minded fighter named Damie Ruffino. The set included a regulation boxing ring erected onstage. Just as my experience with baseball got me a part in *Bang the Drum Slowly*, my boxing chops set me up well for *Knockout*. With Lou as playwright and Tony Conforti as associate producer, we had the great good luck to connect with Hollywood showman H. William Sargent.

Bill Sargent was a Texan wild man who had made a fortune in electronics. He would go on to pioneer pay-per-view and closed-circuit events for television. To give you an idea of Bill's style, he once proposed a closed-circuit battle in a swimming pool that pitted a human diver against a great white shark.

Broadway productions are difficult and audiences are fickle, but our producer Bill simply never said die. He loved the play and backed it to the hilt, paying his actors a living wage. I made $3,000 a week, which I'm sure at times sent the production into the red. Eventually, Bill sank almost a million dollars into the play.

Knockout became one of the most difficult projects I was ever involved with. In six weeks, I lost thirty-five pounds to get in shape to fight eight shows a week, with ninety-eight punches thrown in each show. Believe me, I counted. We landed real blows, not fake pulled punches as had been the rule in other boxing stage plays. I wanted to make sure the audience heard the sound of fist to flesh.

Eddie O'Neill, soon to become well-known as the lead of the hit TV show *Married with Children*, played my bullying opponent, Paddy Klonski. The boxing was choreographed, of course, but that didn't stop Eddie and me from kicking each other's ass every performance.

Putting the play together was not easy. Director Frank Corsaro was more accustomed to staging operas. I don't think he had ever attended a boxing event in his life. He felt *Knockout* was a great challenge for him. In the mid-fifties, Corsaro had made his name directing *A Hatful of Rain* on Broadway with a cast that included Anthony Franciosa, Ben Gazzara, Harry Guardino, Henry Silva, Shelley Winters, and an understudy named Steve McQueen.

Corsaro concentrated on helping the cast to talk, while I helped them to box. The fight blocking, in and out of the ring, was done by my son Danny III. The light heavyweight champion of the world, Jose Torres, was responsible for my training.

Because my character was an over-the-hill boxer, I had to get in shape and at the same time look as though I wasn't in shape. I never worked so hard in my life. *Knockout* ran for an entire year. Throughout that time, I did not miss a single performance. Training meant hitting the gym, sparring, running through the streets of New York City. My friends barely recognized me. "Is that you, Danny?" fans would yell. "No!" I'd respond. "I'm just a reasonable facsimile."

On opening night, my entire family attended, all dressed to the nines: Sandy; my three sons, Rick, Danny, and Jaime; my daughter, Stacey; and my mother, Frances.

By then, my mom was legally blind from glaucoma, so she was given a seat in the front row. Mom had been to three Broadway shows before this and I was in each one of them. It didn't surprise me when, in the middle of my performance, I could clearly hear Mom talking to another member of the audience.

"That's my son," she said in a conversational tone. "He never curses like that at home."

The opening was a smash, with a standing ovation and curtain calls. After I took my bows, I staggered back to my dressing room, totally drained. I fell into the shower. The next thing I knew, my three sons had burst in on me, crying. They were still wearing their tuxedos and were getting all wet from the shower, but they didn't give a damn.

This was my family moment. I had managed to prove myself to my sons in a way that I never could to my own father. Rick, Danny, and Jaime immediately recognized that their old man was good at what he did. They just wanted to tell me how proud they were. In my mind's eye, I can still see us in the shower, crying and hugging, like a snapshot that will never disappear.

The play might have been well received by audiences, but the reviews were, at best, mediocre. "If we want to see a fight, we'll go to Madison Square Garden," or so said the critics. Everyone in the theater community expected us to close in a week.

Bill Sargent fought back as hard as I did in the play. The *New York Times* panned us with a lethal review. Bill paid for an ad that ran on the opposite page, testifying to how great he thought the play was and how much the audiences loved it. He asked me to do back-to-back performances to keep the box office up. We'd do a show, close for an hour, then do another show. I was taking a total of a hundred and ninety-six punches in a day.

Everyone attached to *Knockout* tried everything humanly possible to keep the play running, not for ourselves as much as for Bill. I remember an interview I had with the influential Broadway columnist Earl Wilson. He had seen the show and observed that my performance must have taken a lot out of me every night. Not thinking about what I was doing, I opened my shirt and peeled down my pants to prove that I was black and blue from my ankles to my rear end. The next day, Wilson wrote about it in his column. Anything for the play.

A few nights, the crowds in the theater would be pretty light. I always tried to whip up the enthusiasm of the cast members, reminding them that even though the theater was only half-full, the people in the seats had come to see us give it our all.

The play ended on an upbeat note. In character as the battered but triumphant Damie, I would raise my arms over my head and scream out as loud as I could, *"Knockout!"* It never failed. No matter how many empty seats there were, audiences always reacted by erupting into applause.

From his closed-circuit event productions, Bill Sargent knew the wild-haired boxing promoter Don King. Willing to resort to desperate measures to keep *Knockout* from closing, Bill arranged to have Don bring in one of the fighters he managed, Larry Holmes, who then reigned as the heavyweight champion of the world. As a promotion for *Knockout*, Holmes and I would fight an exhibition match onstage in the theater.

Larry and I got into the ring. While we were putting on the gloves, I approached him. "Throw the right hand at me as hard as you can," I whispered to him.

"Are you crazy?" he responded.

The theater was jammed with people. I wanted to give them something more than a silly exhibition. After all, they had come to see me in character as Damie Ruffino. Well, a few of them had, anyway. Most of them were there to see Larry Holmes.

The bell rang, we danced the dance for a few turns, and then Larry threw that right hand just as hard as I had asked him to. If that blow had hit me square, I would have been laid out for a week.

I slipped the punch, taking it on my glove, and went down like I was shot. There wasn't a person in the theater who didn't think I was hit, including Don King, by now thinking that his favor was about to turn into a major lawsuit.

But I suddenly jumped up from the canvas, raised both arms over my head, and yelled, "Knockout!" at the top of my lungs. The audience bought the whole gag and went wild. Anything for the play.

Stacey, the youngest of my four children, is probably the most truthful person I have ever met in my entire life. She would not tell a lie if someone offered her a million dollars to do it. I admired her for this personality trait, but her devotion to honesty resulted in an uncomfortable situation in the aftermath of an incident that almost derailed my career.

Sandy and I had three children before Stacey, all boys. My wife desperately wanted to have a girl, and the fourth try was the charm. Stacey was born in November 1969. I was totally clueless when it came to raising a girl. I felt that it was hard enough raising three boys. How in the heck do you raise a little girl? Very carefully, I found out.

I was still trying to understand how my wife was able to bring up a trio of rambunctious sons. Remember, Sandy's life as a mother began when she was eighteen. All those years, she hardly had a life of her own. How she accomplished it all was beyond me.

With Stacey it was different. This was our little girl, something Sandy had dreamed of having all her life. She pampered that child as if she were pampering herself, which in a sense she probably was. The two of them grew very close. Me and the boys were the odd men out in that equation.

As a small child, Stacey was extremely sensitive. I raised my voice to her exactly once. She launched a hysterical crying jag that I decided I didn't ever want to experience again. I never repeated that mistake. Stacey inherited the shyness I had as a child. She didn't want her friends to know her father was an actor. Her habit of honesty continued as she grew older. If the phone rang in our house and I didn't feel like talking to anyone, I would ask Stacey to pick it up.

"If it's for me, just say I'm not here," I would say.

Uh-uh. Not Stacey. She would pick the phone up and say, "Hold on, please, he's right here."

I might have been a bit overly protective of my daughter, as I was with all my children. With Stacey, I was like a father from the last century. If I saw her hanging out with friends, I would go over and question the boys among them, to find out their intentions. Believe me, it wasn't pleasant for her. When she saw me coming, she wanted to run.

Stacey was never lazy. From the age of eleven she was working. She was a newsie like her father and delivered newspapers on weekends. She did it all on her own. Only when the weather was bad would she accept my help. As we drove her route together, she had a teenager's horror of being seen with her father. She sat in the car and made me deliver the newspapers.

"Hey, Danny!" her customers would say. "Did you give up acting?"

"Just helping out my kid," I'd say, and jerk my thumb over my shoulder to our car. But Stacey could not be seen. She had slunk down in the seat. God forbid anyone would conclude she was hanging out with me.

Today, Stacey is happily married to a loving husband, William. They have three children: Sydney, Gabrielle, and William Daniel.

On one of my days off on *Knockout*, Sandy, Stacey, and I headed from New York into New Jersey to go house hunting. We were finally contemplating moving out of the city. I was driving a Cadillac. On our way home, the three of us were in the front seat, ten-year-old Stacey between me and my wife. When we reached the George Washington Bridge, traffic was bumper-to-bumper all the way to the toll, with four lanes of cars maneuvering at a crawl.

We finally nosed up close to the tollbooth, where two lanes merged into one. In the car to my right, the driver began to harass us. He had three women passengers in the car with him. We were slightly ahead of them heading into the toll, but the driver refused to let us through. I got steamed.

Sandy realized what was about to happen. "Danny, please don't get out."

The occupants of the other car looked over at us, laughing and gesturing. Stacey started crying, thinking any minute I was going to get out of the car. She knew her father well.

The other car passed through the toll and went on. I thought the incident was over. Traffic remained slow. We took the upper roadway of the bridge. Once we were on the span, we somehow wound up abreast of the same car once again.

The driver rolled down his window and flipped a cigarette at Sandy. The butt hit the glass right next to her face. I couldn't stand for it. I released my seat belt to jump out of the car.

"Don't get out, Daddy!" Stacey begged, grabbing my coat, trying not to let me go.

She cooled me off just enough. "Okay, okay, don't worry, honey, I won't," I said.

Life with Father. At times the whole world is my Bronx. I get challenged and suddenly I'm right back in the neighborhood, going toe-to-toe with some asshole. This time, I held myself back. Barely.

Then traffic opened up. Just before the other car pulled away, the driver pitched a container of coffee onto the hood of my car, after which he took off. At this point I lost complete control of myself. I was out of my mind. I chased after him. We were speeding across the George Washington Bridge, with me twenty feet behind him and Stacey and Sandy screaming.

Suddenly the cigarette flipper slammed on his brakes. I hit mine. I ended up a few feet from his back bumper. I jumped out of my car and he got out of his. Facing off in the middle of the bridge, we began to fight.

I knocked him down. With my left hand I grabbed his hair and lifted his head, punching him with straight right after straight right. A stranger jumped out of a nearby truck and grabbed me from behind.

"Don't hit him anymore!" the guy yelled. "You're going to kill him!"

I shrugged the stranger off and walked back to console my wife and daughter. The female passengers of the other car helped the beaten driver into the vehicle.

"You rich bastards are all the same!" one screamed. The other called my wife a whore. They drove off, one of the women at the wheel, the guy bloody and unconscious in the backseat.

Stacey, Sandy, and I remained in the Caddie in the middle of the bridge, not moving, horns honking all around us as we sat there parked, trying to make sense of what had just happened.

"This is not going to end here," I said. "Somebody is going to report this. When we get home, I'll call the police. If they haul us into court, so be it." I turned to Stacey. "When that happens," I said, "you just tell them the truth."

"Daddy, I saw you pulling his hair and punching him on top of his head."

I shook my head at my daughter's innocent honesty. I said to Sandy, "Stacey *will not* be a witness."

When we returned home, I called the Port Authority Police at their George Washington Bridge office. I was passed through a few layers of bureaucracy before a desk sergeant came on the phone.

"We have a criminal complaint against you," he said.

"Who filed?" I asked.

"Three women who witnessed the assault."

"I defended myself!"

"That's not what they're saying," the cop said.

"Can I make a counter-complaint?"

"Not on the phone," he said. "You have to come down here in person. Is this Danny Aiello?"

There was no way the police could have known my name. The Cadillac I drove was not registered to me. Producer Bill Sargent leased it for me during the production of *Knockout*. But the police sergeant told me my name had been spelled out on the criminal complaint. I went in to the Port Authority station and filed a counter-complaint.

In court I was represented by my financial adviser, Jay Julien, who happened to be an attorney. I sat in the court listening to the women who were in the other car at the time of the fight. The complainant himself testified. He gave his age as twenty-eight. He was my same height, six foot three, and said he worked on the docks in New York.

Sitting there in court, he looked pretty capable of kicking my ass. At the time, I was forty-six years old. The guy had been taken to the hospital and kept overnight with a concussion. That gave his complaint a little more weight.

Jay Julien began questioning him. "You look to be in great shape," he said. "Do you work out?"

"Yes," said the cig flipper.

"What do you weigh?"

"Around one eighty."

"You work on the docks, don't you?"

"Yes."

"A lot of tough guys down there, aren't there?"

"I guess."

"You want this court to believe that Danny Aiello, a forty-six-year-old man, sitting in the car with his wife and ten-year-old daughter, jumped out unprovoked and kicked the shit out of you?"

The judge intervened, cautioning Jay Julien on language.

It came time to give our side of the story. Sandy was called as a witness and told the court what happened. Then it was my turn on the stand. I explained to the court exactly what I remembered happening.

I emphasized what to me was the strangest aspect of the case. Somehow the complainant knew my name, even though I was driving a leased car. "Starring Danny Aiello" was up in lights on a

Broadway marquee. My face was in TV advertisements for *Knock-out*. I thought that at the time of the incident the driver knew exactly who I was, and had set me up, looking for the possibility of a lawsuit.

"Danny, let me ask you a question," the judge said. "I know you're an actor. Are you a tough guy?"

"I am presently playing a boxer on Broadway," I said. "I am not a professional boxer. I'm not a tough guy."

"But you are in good shape?"

"Yes, Your Honor," I admitted. "I have to be, in order to do the show."

Under oath on the witness stand, I went through the entire incident blow by blow, the face-off at the tollbooth, the cigarette tossed at my wife, the cup of coffee thrown at my car, the meeting on the bridge, he got out and I got out.

I finished my testimony with a final statement.

"In the middle of the George Washington Bridge, Your Honor, and with these two hands, I beat the shit out of him."

"Again with that word!" the judge exclaimed. And with that he threw the case out of court.

Woolworth's five-and-dime store photo booth, Wilkins Avenue in the Bronx, 1945.

My army enlistment photo, taken at Fort Dix, New Jersey, in 1951.

Warner Kaserne Service Club, Munich, Germany, in 1953: (left to right) Red De Filippo, Sal Portillo, Joe Zappala (who became ambassador to Spain under President George H. W. Bush), and me.

Sandy and me in our marriage photo, taken January 8, 1954.

Me in my booth at the Greyhound bus terminal on West Fiftieth Street in New York City, where I announced the bus schedules.

At the bungalow colony swimming pool in South Fallsburg, New York, with my son Danny III in 1959.

Our apartment on West 238th Street in the Bronx: (left to right) Stacey, Rick, me, Danny III, and Jaime in 1972.

My three sons: (left to right) Danny III, Jaime, and Rick in 1965 at the Marble Hill projects on West 228th Street in the Bronx.

My son Danny III and me at the Marble Hill projects. At that time, in 1961, money was scarce, so I cut my children's hair. I had a photo taken so he could see the result. A beautiful little boy, he could have been a child model. And to think this little boy became a top stunt coordinator in film.

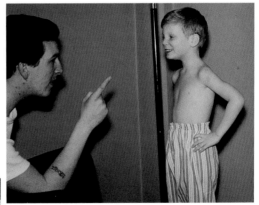

Easter Sunday, 1965: (left to right) my sister Rose (New York Yankees announcer Michael Kay's mother), me, Mom, my sisters Gloria and Helen, and my brother Joe, outside my sister Helen's apartment on Stadium Avenue, the Bronx.

Family get-together in 1979 at our apartment at West 238th Street in the Bronx, before moving to our first home in Ramsey, New Jersey: (left to right) Mom, my sister Rosebud, me, and my sister Annabelle.

"Swinging for the Trees," Broadway Show League in Central Park, 1971.

The replica of the Oscar presented to me in recognition of my Academy Award nomination by the cast of *Once Around* in 1990.

My son Danny III and me courtside at a New Jersey Nets basketball game in 1998.

Louis LaRusso II, author, the person most responsible for my life in show business. When I told him I couldn't act, he said, "Yes, you can! You just don't know it yet."

Fort Apache, the Bronx riot scene: John Aquino and me in action during filming in 1980.

Fort Apache, the Bronx: Paul Newman and me talk on set during a break in filming.

In Cannes to promote the 1984 film *Once Upon a Time in America*: me, Bobby De Niro, and the great Italian film director Sergio Leone.

Training at a New York City gym with my son Danny III for the Broadway show *Knockout* in 1979.

Killing time with Woody Allen during the *Purple Rose of Cairo* shoot in 1985, with first camera operator Dick Mingalone acting as referee.

My wife, Sandy, and I at the Mirage Hotel and Casino in Las Vegas, Nevada, where I performed with Ben E. King at a testimonial dinner for Augie Renna, vice president of MGM Entertainment Corporation, in October 2010.

My beloved mother at my son Danny's wedding reception at our home in Ramsey, New Jersey, on June 28, 1980.

Celebrating the second birthday of my eleventh grandchild, Willie D. Poppe, at my Saddle River, New Jersey, home, with my daughter, Stacey, his mom, on February 12, 2014.

Sofi Belle and me at Willie D.'s birthday party, 2014.

Tuning up the pipes during
a sound check at Monmouth
University, West Long Branch,
New Jersey, before performing
with my band in 2005.

"Besame Mucho" music
video shoot on Gansevoort
Street in New York City's
Meatpacking District, 2007.

Chapter Fourteen

Fort Apache

In the late seventies, I finally shot a scene in a movie that Woody Allen was directing, what was then an unnamed comedy. I had a small role playing opposite Harvey Fierstein. Afterward, Charles Joffe, Woody's producer, told Harvey and me that it was one of the best scenes in the film.

During this shoot, I watched Woody interact in scenes with his costar Tony Roberts. Afterward I joked with him: "Enough with the two Jewish guys! When I was growing up in the Bronx, I lived in a Jewish neighborhood. It was never two Jewish guys going around together. It was always the Jewish guy hanging out with the Italian guy."

In response to my transparent plea for a bigger role, Woody only smiled vaguely.

I never learned the name of that movie until I was invited to the premiere. It was *Annie Hall*. The production office generously provided me with enough tickets to bring along my family. Everyone was excited. The buzz around the film was tremendous. But there was only one problem: the scene with me and Harvey had been cut from the movie.

My disappointment over *Annie Hall* faded when I landed a role in 1981's *Fort Apache, the Bronx*. This was a major studio release featuring superstar actor Paul Newman, which represented a real kick upstairs for me in terms of Hollywood and the movies.

I had loved Newman for his great performances in classics like *Hud* and *Cool Hand Luke*. This guy had it all, with a great marriage to actress Joanne Woodward and charity work that raised millions of dollars.

Sitting in my trailer on the first day on the *Fort Apache* set, a feeling of unreality came over me. Naturally, I called my mother.

"Mama, I'm here making a movie with Hud!"

"Who's Hud?" she asked.

She might not have known the names of all his characters, but she knew very well who Paul Newman was. She was duly impressed that her little Junior, the boy who had given her so much worry when he was young, had wound up in a movie with one of the greatest stars of all time.

Something else was contributing to this strange sense of unreality. My life had looped around once more. *Fort Apache, the Bronx* was set in my old neighborhood, a place I knew all too well, having grown up there. The film's title referred to the same Forty-First Precinct house where cops had taught me a lesson for the high crime of stealing a candy bar, handcuffing me to a pee-stained radiator. Almost four decades later, I was coming back to the Four-One, not as a petty thief but as a movie actor.

The police precinct house was still there, but my old stomping grounds surrounding it were gone. The Four-One had earned its nickname of "Fort Apache" because it resembled a lonely cavalry outpost in the Wild West. By 1980, two-thirds of the people who had lived in the precinct had fled. Waves of arson and neglect had totally flattened much of the South Bronx.

I had returned to the old neighborhood once in a while before this, but as we settled into the shoot, the full impact of the urban decay hit me. We used the Four-One precinct house as our set, but everywhere in the area was the same desolation, with blocks and blocks of nothing but burned-out rubble. Here were the streets where I played stickball, where I worked hauling wet laundry and lighting stoves for observant Jewish households, where I first romanced Sandy.

All gone. Nothing was left. The tenement buildings on Stebbins Avenue and Boston Road, where I had spent so much of my teenage years, had been transformed into vacant lots. Of the ten South Bronx addresses I could recall from my youth, not one was left.

There were economic reasons for this devastation. At the time, conditions had gotten so bad that residents burned themselves out rather than live there, as they received new housing courtesy of the city when their homes went up in smoke.

My life looped around in another way during the *Fort Apache* shoot. I had my son Danny III with me. By this time, he was in his early twenties and had matured into a handsome man. He had become keenly interested in my movie work and accompanied me to the *Fort Apache* set. It was strange to have him with me on my old home turf, in the old neighborhood that wasn't there anymore. Here

I was, practically drowning in memories of my childhood, and there was my boy, just emerging from a difficult childhood of his own.

Up to that point, Danny III had not had an easy time in life. In his youth, he had been fragile and often hospitalized. Like his dad, he never enjoyed school, asking his teachers if he could sit in the back of the classroom.

A guidance counselor called my wife into school to speak about Danny's problems. He refused to participate in any class activities, the counselor told Sandy. Danny balked when asked to read or spell a word. He would shut down, put his hands over his ears as if he didn't want to hear anything.

Sandy and I didn't seem to be able to help the situation. We punished him at home. That made things worse. He went into a shell. It was hard to talk to him.

I began to search in my own past for answers. I hadn't enjoyed school that much, either. But I loved to get up and read or become involved in a spelling bee in front of the whole class. These activities were distractions from the childhood illnesses that were bothering me.

It turned out that my son had similar issues. A different illness, but the same result. Danny III was afflicted with a hidden syndrome that made it difficult for him in school. A therapist finally diagnosed my son with dyslexia. The syndrome was not well-known at the time. The therapist described how Danny would visualize words differently than other children. He would see the letters backward or in jumbles.

Psychologically, dyslexia could be devastating. Now I understood why he wouldn't read out loud. It broke my heart to realize that he considered himself stupid or backward. He wasn't. His problems had a medical basis. Danny was diagnosed with dyslexia in fifth grade. He was held back a year as a result, just as I had been when I missed school due to illness. It was as though my son's childhood was paralleling my own.

Danny was a shy, introverted young boy. His brother Rick once told me that if the two of them got in trouble and were running away, he would have to go back and help him over whatever fences they had to climb. I thought sports would bring Danny out of his shell, as it did for me when I was a kid. I got him into playing Little League ball. To succeed in athletics, you've got to be at least a little bit aggressive. At that age, even though he played, Danny tended to be more passive than not.

But as he grew into a teenager, the toughness came out in him. He was a standout football player at Kennedy High School in the Bronx. Danny learned how to battle his way out of difficulties with his fists. He soon came to be considered one of the hardest-hitting kids on the street. Later on, I was told of an incident where a neighborhood boy put a rifle to Danny's head.

"I'm going to shoot you," the kid said.

"Go ahead and shoot," Danny said calmly. "Shoot if you got the balls." The kid took off running. At that point in time, my own head must have been in the sand, or I was too busy trying to make money, because I had no idea that any of this was going on. My youngest son, Jaime, told me that no one would mess with him as a child because all the kids lived in fear of his older brother Danny.

Like his father, Danny dropped out of high school. Like his father, he enlisted in the U.S. Army. Unlike his father, he received not an honorable but a general discharge, being deemed "not adaptable" by the military authorities. Washing a soldier out was the way the army dealt with conditions it didn't understand, like dyslexia.

Just as I did, Danny discovered his true self on a film set. His visits to the *Fort Apache* set in the spring of 1980 changed Danny III's life.

I played a very bad cop in the movie. My character, Morgan, is a psychopath in blue. The entire plot and my role in it bothered me, as I'm very pro-police. I thought this kind of film might set the reputation of the NYPD back fifty years. But I was finally able to rationalize Morgan in my own mind as a cop who should never have been on the force.

In the film, tension boils up between Morgan and his lieutenant, Murphy, played by Paul Newman. The two of us get into a full-on sidewalk brawl outside a local bar. My son was on set the nights that we filmed the fight.

The director, Dan Petrie, called me over. "Would it be okay if we use your son as your double?"

"Sure," I said. "If he doesn't mind, I don't mind."

I didn't realize right away what Petrie had planned. My son was around the same height as me and had the same broad-shouldered build. Doubles and stand-ins are of course used all the time in movies. The lengthy lighting and prop setups require a warm body to take the place of the actors involved.

But the director wasn't talking about using Danny merely as a stand-in. He proposed that my son would stunt-double for me, which is a whole different thing. Stand-ins are inactive, but stunt doubles perform actions that at times involve a degree of risk. I didn't know whether or not I wanted my son to engage in film work at all, much less as a stuntman.

Danny was all for it, and one look at his eager face made me agree to the whole proposition. Vic Magnotta, the stunt coordinator on the film, would make sure that my son wouldn't be exposed to any physical harm. Vic told him what he had to do. Danny III would show-punch, grab, and wrestle with Paul Newman in all the long shots.

"Your father is with him in all the close shots," Vic said. "The audience will always know that Paul is fighting your father."

The scene turned out to be one of the best staged movie fights I have ever been involved in. On-screen, it looks as if real blows are being exchanged. When you're watching it, depending on the camera angle, you're seeing a member of the Aiello family, either father or son, battling it out with Hud.

From that day forward, Danny Aiello III was a stuntman. Vic Magnotta (who eventually died during a stunt on the set of the 1987 comedy *The Squeeze*, starring Michael Keaton) served as his mentor and friend. Danny doubled me in *Fort Apache, the Bronx*, as well as *Hudson Hawk, Do the Right Thing, 29th Street, Ruby*, and others. But he didn't limit himself to working on my movies; he went on to become a top stunt coordinator with more than three hundred films to his name. He also acted in movies such as *The Wanderers, Miller's Crossing*, and *Good Morning, Vietnam*.

Appearing in Robert Redford's baseball movie, *The Natural*, Danny III wore number twelve and played a first baseman, my same uniform number and position in *Bang the Drum Slowly*, over ten years before. It was just a wonderful coincidence, but I took it as a good omen.

Paul Newman had a wicked sense of humor. He used to mess around with me constantly during the shoot. Whenever I was on camera and he wasn't, he'd make faces, stick his finger up his nose, cross his eyes, anything to make me crack up. Of course, when he was on camera, I returned the favor.

The film turned out to be not all fun and games. Controversy arose over the project. The people who lived in the neighborhood were upset over the very concept of the movie, certain that it would portray their home turf in a negative way. In a sense, they were right. *Fort Apache* was certainly a warts-and-all portrayal of the South Bronx. Keeping it real were a couple of real police officers from the Four-One, Tommy Mulhearn and Pete Tessitore, who were on the set all the time as consultants.

Activists and rabble-rousers got involved, fanning the flames with legal threats. Reality began to imitate art. There were actors and extras portraying the antipolice rioters who figured in the plot. At the same time, *Fort Apache* protestors were agitating against the film, and the hostility spiraled out of control.

I was thinking about asking for hazard pay. The troublemakers would get up onto the roofs, just as we did in my days back with the Kingsmen, and toss shit down at the film crew. One afternoon, a porcelain toilet came flying from several stories up to smash into a thousand pieces on the sidewalk, right next to the set. Dan Petrie took it all in stride. He immediately incorporated a flying toilet tossed off a roof into the action of the movie.

The situation came to a head when it was time for Petrie to shoot the movie's riot scene. The chaos we attempted to reproduce on the set was mirrored by the chaos on the real streets. It got to be difficult to tell who was an extra and who was a protestor.

I pulled my son aside. "All the people rioting here are *not* actors," I warned him. "Some of them have guns. I've lived in this neighborhood. Maybe one of these fuckers will start shooting."

He took my advice and watched his back at all times. I was just worried that we wouldn't be able to tell a prop pistol from a real one. After the craziness on the set, I judged myself lucky to get out of my old neighborhood alive.

But disappointment lay in wait for me once the shooting wrapped, in the guise of another lesson about the film business. When I saw the finished cut of the movie, I couldn't believe my eyes.

I immediately composed a fiery letter to Alan Ladd Jr., the studio head at 20th Century Fox. Writing it wasn't so bad, but what was stupid was that I actually sent it. *I constructed the character of Morgan carefully*, I wrote. *Only a sick man would do what he did. The scenes that were cut were like the lower rungs of a ladder. When they were removed, there was no way to climb to the top. All my hard work collapsed. The character no longer made sense.*

I cited a removed bit where Morgan reacted with spite to an offer for help from Newman's character, as well as another edited-out scene where the audience glimpsed the lonely man's cluttered, filthy apartment. In my mind, these scenes established Morgan as a mentally ill individual.

Needless to say, I didn't receive a response from Alan Ladd. My well-rounded portrait of Morgan the insane cop went by the wayside. I felt I had done an oil painting, and what was in the final cut of the movie was merely a pencil sketch.

I thought that between the editing job and the ill-advised letter, I had destroyed any impact I would make with *Fort Apache*, but I was wrong. The film was a solid hit that boosted my visibility in Hollywood considerably.

Sandy and I had already moved out of the Bronx altogether the year before the *Fort Apache* shoot. For the first time in my life, I was living outside of New York City. I was finally earning enough money to purchase a small home in a middle-class area of Ramsey, New Jersey. The corner property at number four Thornhill Drive came complete with a beautiful white picket fence.

We had lived in apartments all our lives, so to some degree the new place represented a dream come true. But my anxieties moved right in with me. Having a mortgage payment every month is never easy for anyone, but it's doubly hard for someone in a catch-as-catch-can industry like show business.

For most actors, the wait between gigs can be an awful long one. There are a lot of people in the business and not enough work to go around. That's why 70 percent of Screen Actors Guild members make $3,000 a year or less. You have to be consistently very lucky to be among the 30 percent. The situation is even worse for Equity union members, who work in theater.

So of course, I was always hustling for another acting gig, leaving no stone unturned. A few years after my *Annie Hall* disappointment, and hard on the heels of *Fort Apache*, Woody Allen reached out to me again.

This time, he cast me not in one of his movies but in a play: *The Floating Light Bulb*. He wrote this comedy of childhood reminiscence himself but called upon Belgian-born Ulu Grosbard to direct. Ulu had numerous awards and nominations under his belt and worked in theater and movies both. Since it would be a live performance, there was no danger of my work being once again left on the cutting room floor, as it had been with Morgan on *Fort Apache*. The only danger would be getting fired from the play.

Woody had a hands-off approach to the production, which was to open at Lincoln Center's Vivian Beaumont Theater in the spring of 1981. He didn't interfere with Ulu's direction. He just sat in the back of the hall during rehearsals, reading a copy of the *New York Times*, holding the paper in a way that shielded his face.

Occasionally, the actors on the stage, myself included, would see him lower the newspaper slightly, peer briefly at us over the top of it, then duck down and go back to his reading. Most of the time, the cast members didn't even know someone was sitting out there in the darkness of the rehearsal hall.

I had little interaction with him during the production. But when I gave a performance that Woody thought was special, he slipped an encouraging note under the door of my dressing room. Some were brief jottings on scraps of paper: "Danny, you were great tonight, Woody."

Others were written on his odd brown-paper-bag stationery. He delivered one on opening night, after a week of previews: "Danny—Good luck. I think you're a great actor—now if we can only get you to believe it. Woody."

The Floating Light Bulb had a successful run and was a blast to act in. But to me, acting in the play was personally important because I got to know Bea Arthur, who remained a dear friend to me forever afterward and had one of the warmest hearts of anyone I ever met.

Throughout the seventies, Bea had starred in one of the top

sitcoms of the day, *Maude*, a spin-off of the popular show *All in the Family*. Audiences loved her, and she was a major factor in what made *The Floating Light Bulb* such a hit. I already knew Bea as a wonderful comedic actress, but I soon found out she was no one to mess around with. She was the consummate professional and took her acting very seriously.

As I sat in my dressing room during one of my offstage moments, I could hear the action onstage via the intercom. One evening during previews, a scene between Jack Weston and Bea was in progress. The two of them were taking no prisoners that night. They were killing, and the audience was going nuts.

Under the laughter, Jack muttered to Bea: "I can't wait to get the fuck out of here and get something to eat."

As the curtain went down, ending the act, I heard two things over the intercom: the explosion of applause, and Bea Arthur cursing out Jack Weston. "You fat fuck! You ever do that again, I'll punch you right in the fucking mouth!"

Bea loved Jack, and vice versa, but she wasn't going to put up with any shit. Onstage, she demanded that her cast mates be 100 percent professional.

All those good residuals from TV allowed Bea a lifestyle of tasteful luxury. She lived in Mandeville Canyon in L.A., where her private and gated compound consisted of two ranch-style houses. The main residence was very large, the guesthouse smaller but beautiful. Her great kids, Matt and Danny, lived with her, and Bea also had six huge German shepherds and Dobermans that had the run of the gated area near the estate's entrance.

When I visited Los Angeles one time to meet with studio heads, Bea put me up in her guesthouse. My son Rick and his wife,

Arlene, lived in nearby Studio City and were coming over to visit. Sandy and my sister Anna were flying together and were expected from NYC that afternoon. A healthy segment of the Aiello clan converged on Mandeville Canyon that day.

"Good," Bea said about all the visitors. "We'll have lunch."

My host wasn't working and that meant she was drinking a little, even though it was before noon.

"Do you think you have enough food?" I asked politely.

"The fridge is loaded," Bea said.

So is she! I thought. I opened the refrigerator to find a couple hard-boiled eggs and some overcooked roast beef.

"Let's reheat it," Bea said, not fully grasping the situation. There was not enough food to feed the Aiello hordes about to descend. I phoned my buddy Joe Peck, who lived in Los Angeles and was originally from New York City. A longtime friend, Joe was always trying to get people work, which he did on a regular basis.

"We're in trouble," I told Joe. "Bring over seven pizzas to Bea Arthur's house right away."

The Aiello clan arrived, maneuvered through the pack of dogs to enter the house, and sat down around the lunch table.

Bea was feeling no pain. She shouted out, "Let's eat!" But the cupboard was still bare.

At that moment Joe Peck entered with the pies.

Bea responded with surprise. "What are you doing here, you dago bastard?" She was in her cups, and it was a jocular question, not an insult.

Joe timidly offered his explanation. "I brought the pizzas," he said.

Bea grabbed her privates. "I got your pizza swinging right here," she said.

The table erupted in nervous laughter. Don't misunderstand when I mention the language Bea sometimes used. She never employed words to hurt. She said outrageous things to make people laugh, and making people laugh is what Bea Arthur lived for.

Two of Bea's friends were also stopping over to eat lunch with us that day. The gate bell to the compound rang. The actress Zoe Caldwell had arrived with her producer husband, Robert Whitehead.

After a moment, all of us sitting around the lunch table heard horrible yells coming from the gate area. Bea's dogs barked insanely. There was a small picture window to the outside yard. I saw one of the top theater producers in New York, Robert Whitehead, running past that window, screaming, with a dog attached to his ass.

Bea Arthur became the single person I trusted most in our shared profession of show business. When I was just starting out, she gave me advice that only a sister or mother would give, warm, truthful advice, not only about acting but about life in general. Sandy and the children loved her. She left us too soon.

My professional relationship with Woody Allen, the man who unwittingly brought me and Bea together, continued to have its ups and downs.

Chapter Fifteen

Sergio, Woody, and Madonna

Robert De Niro suggested me for a part in a film he was starring in, director Sergio Leone's gangster epic, *Once Upon a Time in America*. I had a small, barely-there role as a police official, but it was worth it just to work with Sergio.

While on set in Italy, and later on when I joined him to publicize the film in Cannes, I soon learned the director was treated like a national treasure. It was unbelievable—everywhere he went, he had a convoy of police cars and motorcycles leading him to his destination. Bystanders shouted out his name as he passed, sirens blasting. I called him "the Italian Santa Claus."

Sergio was crazy like a fox. He understood English well enough, but he allowed everyone to believe that he didn't comprehend a word of it. So he knew everything that was going on around him.

When I worked with him on *Once Upon a Time in America*, he asked me to suggest a name for my character.

"Let's call him Chief Aiello," I said. I thought, *What the fuck, no one knows me from Adam, I might as well use my own name.*

While I was in Italy filming scenes with Sergio, I noticed a young actor in the cast who looked familiar to me. His name was James Hayden. I recalled that while I was doing *Knockout* on Broadway, Jimmy would stop by and watch me working out with the heavy bag onstage at the Helen Hayes Theatre. Back then, he had been pretty green, just a great-looking kid studying to become an actor.

That had been three years earlier, and now he was cast as Patsy Goldberg, one of the young lead roles in Sergio's film. I didn't see him much while on set. We didn't have any scenes together but connected briefly over the days when he visited me during my run in *Knockout*. I liked what I saw of his work, and it appeared he had a great future ahead of him.

But Jimmy's story turned tragic. Frankie Gio, a friend of mine from New York, played a heavy in the movie and told me he had to slap the shit out of some kid in the film because the guy was constantly stoned and causing problems on the set. As I listened to Frankie, I realized he was talking about none other than the boy wonder, James Hayden.

Frankie was the wrong guy to get tough with. He was a professional boxer who could hit like a sonofabitch. Frankie also told me that while he was in the process of "correcting" Jimmy's degenerate behavior, the star of the film yelled out some advice.

"Don't hit him in the face," Robert De Niro said. "We've got a scene to do, so don't hit him in the face." Frankie hit him everywhere else.

I never saw Jimmy Hayden again after Italy, not alive, anyway. Sitting home watching television one night in 1983, I saw him being carried out of a New York apartment building in a body bag. Heroin overdose.

I heard later that he had gotten a standing ovation on Broadway that same evening, playing opposite his good friend and mentor Al Pacino in David Mamet's play *American Buffalo*. He died only a couple weeks shy of his thirtieth birthday. When I met Jimmy on the set of *Knockout*, he was so full of enthusiasm, so eager and brimming with the need for knowledge. What a fucking waste.

After *Once Upon a Time in America* wrapped, Sergio invited me to go to the Cannes film festival with the stars of the film. I felt somewhat embarrassed, because I didn't think my limited role warranted an appearance.

"It's such a small part," I kept saying.

"Danny," he'd reply, "you are going to be one of the stars in my next film!"

Just hearing him say that gave me a great feeling. His next movie was to be one he'd work on for the last ten years of his life: *The 900 Days: The Siege of Leningrad*, about the World War II battle in Russia. Unfortunately, he never lived to finish the project. I'm a little sad that Sergio Leone is known today in the U.S. primarily for his spaghetti westerns with Clint Eastwood. Not because those films aren't great, but because as a filmmaker he was so much more than that.

The trip to Cannes with Robert De Niro and Sergio worked out better than I could have expected. I'll never forget my experience at the Hotel du Cap in Antibes. The joint cost $25,000 a night, cash. The management didn't take credit cards. It's a good thing I wasn't paying. The film company was.

I checked in, exhausted from the trip. I came over on the Concorde, which was the only way I could handle cross-Atlantic travel. Jet lag had me still asleep in late morning of the following day.

I woke to a blast of horns in the hotel driveway down below. The room was like a palace, with big French windows opening onto the sea. I stumbled out of bed, still feeling the rush from the plane going so fast. Wearing a ripped T-shirt like Marlon Brando as Stanley Kowalski, I opened the shutters.

There below me stretched the Mediterranean, there were the Riviera beaches, there were the long tree-lined roads going down to the water. And there also were Bobby De Niro and Sergio Leone, honking the car horn to wake me up.

I started yelling out the window like I was in the fucking Bronx. "Bobby! Hey, Bobby," I shouted out. "You got the spaghetti ready?" I was in a fog and didn't know what the fuck I was saying.

"What're you doin'?" Sergio yelled up, shaking his head and laughing.

Bobby said later, "You looked like Brando yelling out the window."

That trip to Cannes was when Bobby first told me, "Nobody says 'fuck' like you. From your lips, the word sounds like a song."

Now there's a compliment I will take to the grave.

In the mid-1980s, the buzz around Woody Allen focused on a film project of his, about performers clinging to the lower rungs of the

New York show business ladder. The kinds of actors and comics featured in *Broadway Danny Rose* were not superstars and not particularly successful. Their most obvious characteristic was that they kept at it, year after year, show after show.

The title character was a talent manager, and Woody cast himself in the part. The action revolved around a performer whom Danny Rose represented, Lou Canova, a saloon singer who'd once had fifteen minutes of fame but was now just another lounge act.

I had been singing all my life. Not professionally, but whenever I felt the spirit move me. In *Broadway Danny Rose*, the role of Lou Canova called for a singer, someone who was professional but not too professional.

"Danny, you're my ace in the hole," Woody Allen said to me when we entered into casting discussions for the film. I took that comment as a positive.

What followed afterward had me feeling even more optimistic. Bobby Greenhut, the producer, and Gordon Willis, the cinematographer, kept talking me up for the role. I don't necessarily believe it was because they thought I was great, but they had both worked with me before on my aborted scene in *Annie Hall*.

I never saw the script for *Broadway Danny Rose*. Woody didn't give out script pages, only roles. He never once came close to promising me the part. Nevertheless, I cannot tell you how excited I was over the prospect of playing Lou Canova. While he didn't normally audition actors, for the singing role Woody had to hear what I could do. I sang my old Improv standby for him, "Some of These Days."

Broadway Danny Rose was to begin shooting in two weeks, and I waited for the call. And waited. And waited.

As things turned out, Woody gave the Lou Canova role to a singer named Nick Apollo Forte. The news was delivered via Brian Hamill, the brother of journalist Pete Hamill and a celebrated still photographer on numerous films, including Woody's.

I was devastated, heartbroken. I would have died for that part. I felt so close that I could taste it, and then suddenly it was gone. A few weeks passed by and Woody asked Brian Hamill how I was doing.

"Well, he's very disappointed," Brian said.

"Why?" Woody asked.

"Because he didn't get the part," Brian said, stating the obvious.

"Are you kidding? Danny works all the time!" Woody replied.

He then told Brian that he had given the role to Nick Apollo Forte because the guy wrote his own music. Forte would go on to compose the song "Agita" for the film. Woody felt that Nick *was* Lou Canova.

Even to this day, the website IMDb lists *Broadway Danny Rose* as among my movies, citing me as an "uncredited" member of the cast. I have no idea how this confusion arose, and I don't much care. The part of Lou Canova goes into the catalog of my performances that never were.

The whole episode became more troubling because, contrary to what Woody Allen thought, I *didn't* work all the time. My financial affairs got so difficult that we almost sold the dream home we had purchased only a few years before. I owed $60,000 on it, but the potential profits from a sale would total $40,000—I would still be in the hole and no longer have a place to live.

And right then, like a blessing, I got an offer for an action movie that ended up turning our financial prospects completely around. It was called *The Protector*, and I'd be costarring with Jackie Chan.

The call that saved me from losing my home came from producer Tom Gray, who was putting the Jackie Chan project together. I agreed to do the movie for a fee that would pay off my bills and have a little something left over. That was the upside. The downside was that *The Protector* would be filming in Hong Kong. I hate flying so much that I would have rather dog-paddled to China, but I had no choice.

Sandy accompanied me on the trip. I was wide awake the entire plane ride, as I never take pills of any kind. After a grueling nineteen-hour flight, the approach into the tight confines of Hong Kong resembled landing upon a postage stamp. The pilot must have been trained in aircraft carrier landings, but it was white-knuckle time for me.

When I met Jackie, I liked him right away. Even though I didn't know a word of Chinese, and he didn't speak or understand much English, somehow we were able to communicate. He knew of my work and he was the one who had chosen me for the part.

I had gotten to know much more about movie stunts since my son Danny III had become a professional. Danny III had hard-and-fast principles about risk on the job and always made a little speech to his crew at the beginning of every project: *We are not daredevils. We are not kamikazes. We are stuntmen and -women. Safe is what we always plan to be.*

But during the Hong Kong shoot, I soon realized that things

were different in China. If what Jackie Chan and his stuntmen do in movies looks real, it's often because it *is* real. If a telephone is to be smashed into an actor's face, sometimes it will be a real telephone, not a stunt prop designed to break apart on impact.

A stuntman might be injured as a result of all this hard-knock realism, but Jackie and his crew seemed to shrug it off. There were dozens of other stunt people lined up and on call, all of whom were ready, willing, and waiting to break bones. First in line was the star himself, Jackie Chan, who was well-known for doing his own stunts.

We were doing a scene one afternoon on the Hong Kong waterfront. Jackie was poised two hundred feet above me, fighting with a stuntman. They were kickboxing and pelting the hell out of each other with any object at hand, all while balancing themselves on a twenty-foot-square wooden platform. From down below, the action looked crazily fast and realistic.

Afterward, as they descended back down to earth, I realized that Jackie had not been hooked up to a safety harness. Such a rig would have rendered the stunt much safer, even though it would still have been frightening enough to watch. I spoke to Jackie in his trailer, communicating through his interpreter.

"You can kill yourself like that," I said.

Jackie answered me in broken English. "I can't do it, Danny. My fans expect more from me."

"Fuck your fans," I replied. I was speaking to Jackie, but I was thinking about the dangers that my own son faced every day on the job.

*   *   *

I've always tried to connect my acting to my street upbringing. I employed the same instincts on the stages of Broadway and in film that I used growing up in the Bronx.

But instinct could carry me only so far. When I became familiar with the feel of the stage and the movie set, that's when professionalism and experience started to kick in. By doing it over and over, I came to feel almost as if I were truly a classically trained actor. Macbeth lay within my grasp, Stanley Kowalski, certainly Willy Loman.

"Without doing anything, Danny, you're almost there at one hundred percent," Woody Allen once said to me. He also told the *New York Times* that I was "simply a natural."

But I nursed a secret grudge against comments like this. Even though it was looking a gift horse in the mouth, I resented being praised as a natural actor, which seemed to be code for "untrained." It implied that I didn't have to put in the hard work I knew acting required. It's like a sports commentator praising someone's "natural" athleticism. Meanwhile, the athlete is out there busting his balls every day trying to perfect his game.

Right after I completed my time on *The Protector*, Woody Allen called, offering me a role in his new movie, *The Purple Rose of Cairo*.

Michael Keaton had signed on to play the double role of actor Gil Shepherd and his movie-within-the-movie character, Tom Baxter, who's Mia Farrow's love interest in the film. One evening, while I was in Café Central on Amsterdam Avenue, my favorite hangout at the time, a visibly upset Keaton walked in.

"What's wrong, Mike?" I asked.

"He fired me!"

"Who?" The kid was a mess.

"Woody. He fired me."

"Why?"

"I guess he thought I wasn't funny enough."

Keaton was absolutely torn apart. I looked at him and saw my own experience in *Broadway Danny Rose*. The next day, Woody hired Jeff Daniels for the part. Because of the way Woody doles out only limited pages of his scripts, Jeff thought he was coming in to read for a small part. He only learned later, after being hired, that he had been given the lead.

On the set of *Purple Rose*, Woody and I would put on the gloves and box for fun. During downtime, we often tossed a softball back and forth. He was a very good athlete, a good actor, and a wonderful writer-director.

"Do it the way you feel comfortable," was one of Woody Allen's favorite phrases on the set. I interpreted that piece of direction as something of a test, as if he were telling me that I wasn't a good enough actor to do the words as written. Therefore, I should feel free to change his words to suit myself.

Fuck that, I thought. I would give Woody every line, every word, every letter precisely the way he wrote it. I have the capability to improvise my ass off. But Woody challenged me and I did the lines as is. Ironically, critics would respond to my performance in this film by saying it sounded as though I were improvising.

Around that time, I had developed the habit of warning people off from living inside their heads too much. "Don't be too analytical," I would tell my son Ricky about his own acting career. "You'll never be able to make a decision. And when you finally do, you're never going to be able to be happy with it."

Acting can be very, very easy if you allow it to be. You don't have to suffer for your art. You can just let it happen, whether you're classically trained or not. For me, I always had to make an emotional connection in a role, or else there was nothing.

Woody was always the ultimate minimalist as a director. He'd give you simple notes. "Be a little less angry." "Be just a little happier." That kind of stuff. With Woody, I felt myself falling into the same overanalytical trap I had been warning other people about.

Beyond the lines he wrote, I believed in my heart that I could give him something more, and I was never satisfied with my scenes. He'd praise me and I would say to myself, *He loves that? Really? What the fuck is he talking about? I just came on the set and did it. How the fuck could it be right?*

So I embarked upon a search for the "something more" that I felt I could give. We'd do the scene over again and again. Eventually, I'd wind up back with what I had done in the beginning.

This phenomenon was evident in the scene where my character Monk pitches pennies with his pals as his wife walks by. We did multiple takes, but the first one was the best. I embody the classic boorish husband, too busy with his meaningless pastimes to show his woman respect.

My character in *Purple Rose* is a bully. But like all bullies, he's also a pussy. I wanted to find the vulnerability lurking underneath the nastiness. There is a specific passage in *The Purple Rose of Cairo* that demonstrated this personality trait.

We called it the "Get me my meatloaf!" scene, after one of my lines. My character, the abusive husband, Monk, is with his wife, Cecilia, in their apartment. Cecilia is played in a cowering, mousey style by Mia Farrow. The scene is written in a spectacular manner. There is almost unbearable tension. The audience waits for this big, hulking bully—that would be me—to unload on his vulnerable missus.

Mia and I did a first take. It felt good. The action moves through the shabby rooms of Monk and Cecilia's Depression-era apartment, and the camera follows along. The energy was fantastic.

Woody watched the dailies and came back to Mia and me. "We're going to reshoot the scene," he said.

The consensus of Woody's inner circle, the half dozen people who watched dailies with him, was that the action had a grittiness and realism that reminded everyone of *A Streetcar Named Desire*. Normally, that would be a high compliment, but not this time. Woody finally decided the scene as shot didn't have the lightness of *Purple Rose*. It was too real, and therefore not funny.

The reshoot of the "Get me my meatloaf!" scene, the one that made it into the final film, did turn out to be lighter in mood. Mia and I still move through the apartment, talking back and forth. It works. It cooks. But I still believe we were much better the first time around.

In 1985, my friend Sean Penn married Madonna, the biggest pop star of the day. I had met Sean in New York in the early 1980s, during my hangout days at the Columbus Café. His new bride was of course world famous, but somehow her notoriety hadn't caught up to me.

"Hey, my wife is shooting a video and I think you'd be perfect to play a role in it," Sean said to me in early 1986, reaching out by phone.

My agent had already fielded a request for the project and had turned it down. Madonna's videos were elaborate dance numbers or mini-dramas that played out against the soundtrack of her songs. I had never seen a single one. I put Sean off, saying that I would think about it, which in Hollywood circles is a polite way of rejecting something.

I mentioned Sean's offer to Sandy.

"Sean Penn called me and said I should do a music video with the singer he just married," I said. "You know, the one who calls herself Madonna?"

My daughter Stacey happened to be in the room at the time. She immediately got excited. "Daddy, don't you know her? You've got to do it!"

"I don't know, honey," I replied.

"Oh, please, please—just for me!"

At Stacey's urging, I got back to Sean, saying I would be happy to be in the video. A short time later I found myself playing Madonna's father in "Papa Don't Preach." It was the first time a recognized movie actor would appear in a music video, something that became more common later. The scenes were shot in Staten Island, including on the ferry.

I found Madonna to be tremendously driven and professional almost to a fault. She had done herself up to look like the actress Jean Seberg and wore a T-shirt that read "Italians Do It Better."

As I had promised my daughter, I brought Stacey along to the set. She was sixteen years old, still a little shy and wholly naive about the ways of show business. I arranged to have an assistant assigned to take care of her while I was busy doing my job. This assistant approached Madonna and requested a photo be taken with her and Stacey.

The star was deeply preoccupied with the production of her video, and the assistant was told she would have to ask again later. But when that time came, my daughter politely begged off, saying she didn't want a photo after all. This represented Stacey's first on-set lesson in the whims of show business.

Throughout the daylong shoot, I had a bad attitude about doing a video. I didn't want to be there to begin with. The star and I exchanged only a few words over the single day we were on set together. I spoke more with James Foley, the director, who had worked with Madonna on the cult hit film *Who's That Girl*.

During our time together on set, I didn't see Madonna as a music star or a tabloid gossip queen. We were shooting a drama, so I viewed both of us through our characters. She was my daughter. I was her father.

At that point in her career, Madonna was not the Wonder Woman hard-body that she later became. She still had baby fat, with a softer, more rounded physique than she has now. The scene required me to take her in my arms in a fatherly embrace, her face to my chest. When it came time, I was deep into my character, so I really wasn't hugging Madonna. I was a father hugging my daughter. The shot of the two of us together represented the emotional payoff for the whole video.

When "Papa Don't Preach" came out, it landed right in the middle of the abortion debate. It was a controversial song to begin with, and in the music video, my character turns his back on his own daughter, ashamed because she's conceived a baby out of wedlock. I hadn't signed on for any sort of political statement. I accepted the role only as a favor to Sean and because my daughter was a Madonna fan.

"Papa Don't Preach" won Best Female Video honors at the MTV Video Music Awards, which played it in heavy rotation. You could hardly turn on the television without seeing me and the most popular singer in the world acting out our father-and-daughter drama.

For a quick job I didn't really think twice about though, "Papa Don't Preach" had enormous consequences for my career. Before I appeared in it, not many people under thirty years of age knew who the hell I was. Afterward, I suddenly had legions of young fans. I saw the effects of my newfound popularity every time I went out in public. My demographic began to skew much younger, as the Hollywood bean counters might say.

But the story told in the video began to bother me. I thought Madonna had presented only one side of the equation. I was the father of a teenage daughter myself. I tried to imagine what would happen in my own family if Stacey informed me that she was pregnant and unmarried.

Drama needs tension. James Foley, the director of "Papa Don't Preach," emphasized the conflict between father and daughter. I didn't think the brief reconciliation at the end of the video was enough. It felt tacked on. What you truly remember is the father and daughter being at odds.

So I conceived the idea of doing an answer song to "Papa Don't Preach," feeling that there was more to be said on the subject. Something was missing in the picture that Madonna had painted in her song and in the video: communication. The father-daughter relationship had to be a two-way street.

The result was a song and music video, a personal project that was never intended for wide distribution, called "Papa Wants the Best for You." The lyrics were written by my buddy Arthur Schroeck, who also had a daughter in her early teens, as did the producer, Ivan Bloch. In the video, I sing the lyrics and play a father searching for his wayward daughter. Sandy made a brief appearance as my character's late wife. The action ended on a conciliatory note, with my daughter's arm reaching out for me.

The whole impulse behind "Papa Wants the Best for You" was heartfelt in the extreme. In life, I couldn't stand the idea of alienation growing between me and my daughter, Stacey.

Chapter Sixteen

Moonstruck

In the late fall of 1986, I was called to the New York City office of Norman Jewison, the Canadian director famous for such classics as *In the Heat of the Night* and *Fiddler on the Roof*. Norman had indicated he might have a role for me in his new movie. He was also a well-regarded director for the stage, so I knew I'd be at ease working with him.

Our meeting turned into a two-man mutual admiration society, except I had a lot more to admire in his work. Norman told me he had a great screenplay written by the dramatist John Patrick Shanley. "He's calling it *Moonstruck*. When I first read the script, I knew that you were Johnny Cammareri."

I was over the moon, so to speak. Norman Jewison made the kind of quality movies that I respected, and a lot of other actors felt the same way. Cher topped the *Moonstruck* cast, which was filled out with Nicolas Cage, Olympia Dukakis, and my old pal Vincent Gardenia.

"I was thinking we could all get together and read the script," Norman said.

That stopped me cold. I took this as meaning that he wanted me to audition. At that stage in my career, I swore that I was through with reading for parts. The simple truth is that I didn't audition because I couldn't stand rejection. But I also believed that auditions weren't really necessary for the casting process.

Let's say I'm the director and you're coming in as an actor. An informal conversation tells me more than any audition. We casually sit together, talking about our lives. On that basis alone, I should be able to make a decision about whether I want you in my movie.

Woody Allen, for example, never has you read, though he will call you in to sing if the part requires it. When Woody comes to the initial interview, he already knows what you've done and is prepared to give you the role. So it always baffles me why directors and producers would have you read for a part.

I sometimes think that some directors are secretly looking for interpretations. They don't yet know how they're going to approach a character. They use auditions as a kind of fishing expedition, even videotaping the result. Auditioning actors are putting their own creative spin on a character, and some directors merely lift those character interpretations from the audition videos they've made.

"Mr. Jewison, are you asking me to read?" I said. If he had responded with a yes, I would have thanked him politely and walked out on one of the cornerstone parts of my acting career.

"Oh, no, no," Norman said hurriedly, much to my relief. "You've got the job. I just want us all to read the film."

A week or so later, he and I walked down Broadway together. I get recognized fairly often, but for some reason on this day, fans were coming out of the woodwork. I must have been stopped a dozen times within the space of a few blocks. It was as if I had planned it. After the fan interactions kept happening, Norman began looking at me with an amused expression on his face.

"Danny," he said, "I'm glad I negotiated your salary before walking down these streets with you."

Norman approached *Moonstruck* as if it were a stage play, which was well within my comfort zone. Since this was my first full-blown film comedy (as opposed to something like *The Purple Rose of Cairo*, which I saw more as a tragicomedy), I worried about whether I could furnish the laughs. But I knew I was in good hands with Norman.

We rehearsed quite a bit, running through a number of scenes in the script, and ended up becoming more like a theater group than a movie cast. Even Cher and Nicky Cage, who weren't known for their stage experience, joined in on the feeling of being one big happy theatrical family.

It was good to reunite with Vincent Gardenia. He and I behaved like the longtime friends we were, constantly ribbing each other. He always cracked me up. For example, I noticed that whenever Vinny cooked macaroni on the set, he refused to salt it.

"Vinny, how can you make pasta without salt?" I demanded. I thought it tasted like cardboard. He gave me his trademark deadpan look. When you've been deadpanned by Vinny Gardenia, you've been deadpanned by the best. I couldn't help it—I broke out laughing. Not salting his pasta was just one more of this lovely man's peculiarities. He avoided elevators and hated to fly even more than I did. Trains were his preferred method of travel.

On the opposite end of the age spectrum, Nicky Cage and I got along well, too. He was still in his early twenties when he was cast in *Moonstruck*. Cher lobbied Norman hard for Nicky to get the part of Ronny, my character's brother. In the end, it was her insistence that tipped the balance.

I remember well an act of kindness that Nicolas Cage extended to me and my family while we were in New York shooting the film. My oldest son, Rick, worked at a Varick Street club called Heartbreak, one of the most popular dance venues of the day. On one of his nights off, he was at the club and enjoying himself perhaps a little too much. I got a call that my son had collapsed and passed out.

Nicky heard of my troubles and vaulted into action. He didn't question and didn't hesitate but helped me mount a rescue mission. The two of us drove to Heartbreak. Wanting to shield Rick from the public eye, the club personnel offered a back way out.

"I don't want to hide him," I said.

"Let's bring him out the front," Nicky said.

With me and Nicky on either side of him, one arm each, holding Rick upright, we managed to exit Heartbreak gracefully. My costar was charmingly good-natured about the whole incident and brushed off my effusive thanks for his help.

The exteriors for *Moonstruck* were shot around the snowy streets of New York, but for the interiors, we transferred up to Norman's hometown of Toronto. There we were treated very well. Norman often invited the cast to his home for elaborate, festive dinners. He was like the Maple Syrup King of Canada, with every cast member going home with jars of syrup cooked from sap drawn from his own sugar maple trees.

Norman's directing was influenced not only by his stage work but by the opera. Before shooting a scene in Canada, he took the entire cast to see *La Bohème*, the Puccini classic that figures in the plot of *Moonstruck*. The operatic flavor is what gives the movie its air of heightened reality. This wasn't realism. We were in the land of fable and myth.

As I often did, I summoned up aspects of my own life to fill out my character, the aging mama's boy Johnny Cammareri. I used my childhood experience with eczema for Johnny's obsessive scalp scratching. I made him into a wimpy kind of guy who sure as hell would have gotten slapped around in my old neighborhood.

That spring, I was doing *The House of Blue Leaves* at Lincoln Center at night and rehearsing *Moonstruck* at a rehearsal space during the day. One afternoon, we did a series of scenes, all with cast members Louis Guss, Olympia Dukakis, Feodor Chaliapin Jr., Vincent Gardenia, Nicky Cage, and Julie Bovasso. In the close quarters, it soon became obvious that one of us was experiencing gastric distress that day.

Nobody wanted to say anything, but it got so bad that we began to mutter about it among ourselves. We didn't have any idea who was cutting the cheese, but someone was. The prime candidate had to be Louis Guss, who played the uncle. He had a practice of staying behind in the rehearsal room after everyone left.

Before going on in *The House of Blue Leaves* that evening, I was in the greenroom talking to three of the actresses who were playing nuns in the show. I didn't want to tell tales out of school, but I wound up mentioning what had happened that afternoon during the *Moonstruck* rehearsals.

All three of them immediately broke up laughing. "We know who it is," they all said practically at once. The person in question was a vegetarian who farted constantly—and it was *not* Louis Guss. The nuns had done shows with this performer in the past and had experienced the same kind of on-set explosions.

Before *Moonstruck* came out, people in my old neighborhood were accustomed to my doing versions of myself: a streetwise bookie, a quick-fisted cop, a boxer. My old friends had always dismissed my performances. "That ain't acting," they'd say. "You was just doing you." I always resented it.

Now, with Johnny Cammareri, it was different. "Hey, that's not you this time," they said, sounding surprised.

I half-hated my performance anyway. I'm a street guy. I told people that I hadn't wanted my mother to see the film because I didn't want her to see me as a weakling. I was embarrassed.

"Are you kidding?" Norman Jewison said when I told him this. "You're great in that role."

Norman always allowed actors to make suggestions and wound up incorporating a couple of my ideas into the action. There's a riff where I forget my suitcases on the curb when I'm taking a taxi. The cab pulls out of frame and then slowly reverses back into view. It helped to point out what a discombobulated mess Johnny Cammareri was.

Directing the scene, Norman must have liked my idea, since he developed it as a running gag. The same thing happens again later in the movie at the Castorini family home, where Johnny forgets his suitcases twice more and has to return for them. We did both scenes over and over. I felt as though I were back slinging baggage at Greyhound.

Another bit of mine is more subtle. My character is talking to Cher, telling her that he hasn't spoken to his brother in five years. I hold up my hand. "Five years!" I repeat, then do a dismayed double take at my outstretched fingers. At that point in the plot, the audience hasn't yet seen Nicky Cage's dismembered hand. But perhaps on repeat viewings someone would get the joke. His character had lost his hand because my character distracted him.

Moonstruck was a great critical and commercial hit. Audiences loved the spell that the movie cast. It earned Oscars for Cher, Olympia Dukakis, and screenwriter John Patrick Shanley. *Moonstruck* probably did more for my career than any movie I had done up to that point. People in Hollywood began to see me in a different light.

But *Moonstruck* also left a melancholy aftertaste in my mouth. There I was on the silver screen, playing a character who's flying to Palermo to see his dying mother. At the same time, during the film's theater run, my own mother had fallen mortally ill.

Fans on the street had no way of knowing this. People who had seen *Moonstruck* came up to me, saying jokingly, "Hey, how's your mother doing? Is she still dying?" None of it was anyone's fault. But it still gave me a terrible feeling, because my mother really *was* dying.

Mom passed away on June 5, 1988. I miss her terribly but stand in awe of her energy, her love of life, and her devotion to her family. I always say that if my mother had been born a man, she could have been the Pope.

Pope Frances and Pope Francis, one with an "e," one with an "i."

Throughout the eighties, I lost a lot of jobs in show business because of drugs. The cocaine culture ran wild in the film industry. So, yeah, I lost plenty of opportunities because of drugs. Because I didn't do them.

I don't know if it was a leftover influence from my childhood or what. As I said, Mom never had wine on our table when I was growing up. I never developed a taste for alcohol or anything else.

I grew to have a reputation in the movie business. It wasn't just that I wouldn't do cocaine but that I didn't hide my disgust for it. If someone was ever so ignorant as to push drugs in my direction, I went berserk. It wasn't a question of a polite "no, thank you." I blew up. It wasn't pretty.

"You offer me that shit? I'll rip your face off!"

In 1985, I was asked to step into Harvey Keitel's role in David Rabe's play *Hurlyburly* on Broadway. Harvey had another project. The character in question was a suicidal dope fiend.

Even from my experience as a nonuser, I felt as though I knew the contemporary drug scene. I could play a motormouthed addict because I had watched people like that, friends of mine who had habits. I studied the behavior. I listened to the jittery speech patterns.

David Rabe had nailed down those patterns brilliantly. My character Phil had lines such as this one: "Perverse is what she wrote the book on it."

The character of Phil freely expressed his despairing vision of the world. Words spilled out of his mouth in furious bursts. He was in every way different from me. A lot of actors coming up today think they must be dark, depressed people in order to get a good performance. That's bullshit. You don't have to be a sick fuck to play a sick fuck.

The show was up at the Ethel Barrymore Theatre. The great Mike Nichols directed. The cast was packed with terrific actors:

Christine Baranski, Ron Silver, Frank Langella, Alison Bartlett, Jerry Stiller, and Susan Anton. The action centers on a group of Hollywood degenerates in the movie business. The stage of the Barrymore was like a small piece of Los Angeles transported to Manhattan.

The company was one of the finest I've ever acted with. All the people involved were professionals who knew what they were doing. That didn't prevent us from having some riotous times, onstage and off. I loved all of them, but my old pal from the Improv Jerry Stiller stood out.

Jerry had been there at the beginning of my show business career. He boosted my confidence by always being so positive that I would be a success. Now we were appearing together on Broadway, and life couldn't get any better. He and I kept breaking each other up onstage. When we lost it too badly, we would hide ourselves by crawling behind a couch in the middle of the set. I would sometimes wrestle him to the floor and tickle him. The audience loved it, thinking it was all part of the show. It wasn't.

If a Q & A is attached to any theatrical piece I have ever done in New York City throughout my career, I can always depend on Jerry Stiller to come unannounced and be part of the audience. He will get up to say the most wonderful things that a friend could say about a friend. He is an angel on earth put there to make people feel good.

I wanted the original director, Mike Nichols, to direct me in *Hurlyburly*, but he had opened the show and had already moved on. I was directed by the stage manager and was unhappy about it. Nichols came to watch one of my performances and found me backstage.

"Hey, Danny, you were great," he said, gracious as always.

"Could you imagine how much better I would've been if you had directed me?" I said.

In the play, my character Phil walks around with a baby in his arms, a prop doll. It made for a terrifying contrast, this coked-up crazy carrying an infant. Just before the show was to begin one night, I was in the wings preparing to go on. Christine Baranski was there with her newborn, Lily, about three months old. Her husband was backstage holding the child in his arms.

I jokingly asked Christine and her husband if they wanted their baby to make her Broadway debut. They smiled but didn't really answer one way or another. For some reason, I took that as a yes.

With Lily now in my arms, I walked out onstage to begin the scene. I had a lengthy monologue to perform the moment I hit the stage. The footlights snapped on. I think it shocked the little girl, because she instantly began screaming at the top of her lungs.

With a squirming, squalling bundle of joy in my arms, I tried to deliver my lines. I didn't know what to do, so I handed Lily to Jerry Stiller. He took off running back and forth around the stage, rocking the infant in his arms. I swear he began singing a lullaby to her in desperation. It didn't work. Nothing worked. Lily cried on.

Jerry passed the baby on to Ron Silver, Ron to Frank Langella, as though Lily were a human hot potato. Meanwhile I attempted to complete my monologue. The whole cast dashed around the stage like the Three Stooges on speed.

In the end, Christine Baranski's daughter was probably the youngest child ever to make her Broadway debut. Why I did it, I'm not sure. Maybe I wanted to share the wonderful experience of being on the stage in a Broadway show with someone who might never have that chance. Lily should be about thirty years old right now. If her parents told her about her improvised debut in the theater, it might at least serve as a conversation piece for the rest of her life. It certainly has been for me.

In 1988, a few years after the Broadway run of *Hurlyburly*, the play looped back around into my life once again. I made a major push to mount a production in Los Angeles. I contacted producers and tried to line up talent. I reached out to two producers whom I respected very much, Barbara Ligeti and Fred Zollo. Fred had married into the Broccoli family, which controlled the James Bond franchise.

I wanted to appear onstage in Hollywood. It was a conscious move on my part. People in the film business had to see what I did for a living. Studio heads and movie producers rarely got to Broadway. What they saw of my acting was usually limited to segments in films. I wanted producers to witness the full intensity of my performances. I was more than a fifteen-or-twenty-minute player. I could sustain emotion over the course of a three-hour drama.

There was another reason why I wanted to revisit *Hurlyburly*. I felt that a crucial scene had been left out. When I first read the script, my character of Phil had a long exchange with Donna. We called it the "football" scene because both the action and the dialogue centered around the game. I loved the writing and the insight that the passage gave into Phil's poisonous personality.

I saw Harvey Keitel's great performance in the play on Broadway, and I immediately noticed that something was missing in the play.

"What happened to the football scene?" I asked Harvey.

"The prick wanted it out," he said—referring to Nichols, the original director. There was no love lost between him and Harvey.

"What are you talking about?" I said. "For your character it's the most important scene!"

Harvey didn't disagree. I almost refused to step into the role of Phil in the Broadway production because I felt there was a huge, noticeable hole in the play.

When I went to California with *Hurlyburly*, I planned on putting the missing passage back in. The football scene was explosive. I didn't think the show clicked as well without it. I wanted to do the play with the vital piece intact.

I would have to give up a number of other jobs in order to do *Hurlyburly*, forgoing offers for two major motion pictures to make $1,000 a week with no expenses. In making the push to do *Hurlyburly* in L.A., I thought that Sean Penn might serve as my ace in the hole. His talent and prestige could help put the production on the boards.

Paul Herman, the manager at the Columbus Café and a good friend, had first introduced me to Sean Penn. Even though we were at the opposite ends of the spectrum in terms of politics, we became friendly with each other immediately.

I liked Sean and his whole family: his father, Leo; his mother, Eileen; his brothers, Chris and Michael. Leo was an actor and a director who had been blacklisted during the fifties. I think that's where Sean inherited his own political activism. Michael was a wonderful musician. I was closest to Sean and Chris, a big bear of a guy with whom Sean had a tight, loving relationship. Chris would play my son in the Paul Mazursky movie *The Pickle*. I loved that kid.

I'll never forget a day at the Columbus Café when Sean walked in and encountered actor Mickey Rourke, who Sean felt had been bad-mouthing his brother Chris. I got to witness the spectacle of Sean Penn's rage.

"You ever open your mouth about my brother again, I'll fucking kill you." What could Mickey say? He had been wrong and he knew it. He remained mute and merely blinked his eyes in response. Sean stalked off. I've rarely seen a human being so broken up as Sean was later on when Chris passed away.

Having Sean's talent and prestige attached helped put the L.A. production of *Hurlyburly* on the boards. In fall 1988 we opened at the Westwood Playhouse for a two-month run, with Sean in the lead role of Eddie, a Hollywood casting director.

The notices were great. Like I said, I've never done a line of coke in my life. But every single audience member during our run left the theater convinced that I was a degenerate drug addict. Sean was superb, and the rest of the cast was terrific, too: Scott Plank, Michael Lerner, Jill Schoelen, Belinda Bauer, and Mare Winningham.

After *Hurlyburly*, the Hollywood establishment tended to look at me a little differently. But the play was just the first step in getting my name out there. Another would come not on the stage but on the screen.

Chapter Seventeen

Do the Right Thing

For a brief period in the wake of *Hurlyburly* and "Papa Don't Preach," I found myself hanging out with the most popular and controversial pop superstar of the day. Being with Madonna was one more indication of the strange turn my life had taken. I can't say we were best friends, but we had a few common interests. We were both raised Catholic and we both enjoyed Sean Penn's company.

Madonna taught me a few things, and one of the most important lessons was how to listen to music. I was invited to her home in Malibu for lunch. This was soon after Madonna and I had collaborated on the "Papa Don't Preach" music video.

Madonna knew I had a deep interest in music. She wanted my opinion on her soon-to-be-released album, *Like a Prayer*. I was anxious to hear it. Of course, she had a wonderful sound system in her home, and I thought we'd sit around and listen to her new album in the comfort of the living room.

"Not in here," Madonna said, and took me by the hand into the garage. "Here!"

She sat me in the passenger seat in her Mercedes convertible. "This is the way music was meant to be listened to," she said.

At full volume, the music soared. I thought the record was destined to be a hit. I told her so. The critics and fans alike have pretty much agreed that *Like a Prayer* is one of Madonna's best albums. It was certainly among the bestselling records of her amazing career.

From that time on, anything that I've ever done, anything to do with preparation—singing, acting, arranging, character development, learning my lines—I've done most of that while sitting in my car, sometimes in the garage, sometimes while driving.

My connection with Sean and Madonna paid off in other ways, too. In the late fall of 1987 I attended a party for Madonna in New York City. The music was pumping in the main room. After a while I got a headache and had to leave. As I was heading out, a stranger stopped me, somebody I had never met and didn't recognize. He sat all alone in a smaller room near the exit. It was as if he had been waiting there for me.

"I have a script I'd like you to read," he said.

I asked him who he was.

"Spike Lee," he said. The name didn't ring any bells. At this point in his career, Spike was still a relative unknown. He had done some student film work at NYU and released a small feature called *She's Gotta Have It*. That night we chatted for about five minutes. I told him I was on my way to Toronto on a film shoot (this was for *Moonstruck*) and that he should send his screenplay to my agent, Jimmy Cota at Artists Agency in L.A.

I left for Canada, pretty much forgetting about the whole encounter. While I was working on *Moonstruck*, Spike's screenplay showed up. I opened it, took one look at my character's first scene, and tossed the script aside. My reaction to what I had read was immediate and negative. Spike kept phoning and I kept avoiding him. I didn't want to be the bearer of bad news. Finally I took his call.

"Look, all I'm seeing in the character you want me to play is a guy tossing pizzas into the air," I said. "For an Italian-American, that's tantamount to showing a black man eating watermelon."

We talked some more. But I signed off with what I thought was my final word on the matter.

Spike didn't quit. He kept reaching out. He invited me to join him at a Knicks game. He repitched me his project. I was still not interested.

We could not have been more different if we tried. As was the case with me and Sean Penn, Spike and I were the opposite of each other politically. He was a knee-jerk liberal and I was a die-hard conservative. He was a Knicks fan and at the time I was a Boston Celtics fan. He loved Michael Jordan. I loved Larry Bird.

The Knicks lost that night, and Spike and I parted company without any sort of agreement between us. He still didn't concede defeat. In the spring he invited me to a Yankees game. Spike and I sat in the stands and talked about the character he had created, the owner and operator of Sal's Famous Pizzeria in the Bedford-Stuyvesant neighborhood of Brooklyn.

By that time, Spike had made some changes in the script for the better. Sal was still a cartoon, but he had been fleshed out somewhat. There were glimmers of a fully realized human being. My idea was to make the character of Sal more complex. I wanted the audience to think maybe he's a racist and maybe he's not. I hesitated to ask Spike if he would allow my input, since I was familiar with writers who feel very protective about their words.

"How about if I come up with ways to further develop the character?" I asked. "I could make suggestions, and if you like them, they stay in the script. If you don't like them, we could discuss it. If you still don't like them, they're out and we don't use them."

Spike was all for it. I didn't realize it then, but he always allows every actor in his movies to bring a lot of themselves to their part. His enthusiasm for the project was contagious. He won me over. Sitting there in the stands at the old Yankee Stadium, I agreed to be in Spike's movie.

It took a while for him to get his financing in place. *Do the Right Thing* came together and fell apart a couple times. Paramount had it and dropped it. Universal took it on. Finally, at the end of June 1988, I showed up on the Brooklyn set of *Do the Right Thing*.

Bedford-Stuyvesant. "Bed-Stuy." I recognized the turf. Bedford-Stuyvesant back then embodied all the aspects of urban decay. The neighborhood was not quite as burned-out and blasted as my old neighborhood in the South Bronx, but the crack epidemic had hit it hard.

I felt very much at home on the set because of the presence of producer Jon Kilik. I first met Jon in the winter of 1980, when I worked on a made-for-TV cop movie called *A Question of Honor*, with Ben Gazzara, Robert Vaughn, and Paul Sorvino.

Jon was a production assistant back then—in his words, "number one ninety-eight on the totem pole out of a crew of two hundred." But we connected on the set and became friends. I had no way of knowing he would turn into one of the visionary producers of the modern day, eventually guiding the *Hunger Games* franchise to box office glory.

Spike Lee had a perfect ally in Jon, who was a wizard with film finances. He would be able to squeeze every cent out of *Do the Right Thing*'s bare-bones six-million-dollar budget and put it all up on the screen.

The production headquarters for *Do the Right Thing* was located in the basement of a neighborhood school near the film set, which was on the block of Stuyvesant Avenue between Quincy Street and Lexington Avenue. There were no trailers or even campers for the cast. Instead of dressing rooms, we had areas in the school basement separated by shower curtains. Our actors' lounge was a TV set and a collection of a half-dozen folding chairs.

I still recall the sound of crack vials crunching underfoot as we walked back and forth from the school to where we were filming. The grittiness of all that got swept away in Spike's vision of the movie. There were no drugs in evidence in the plot. *Do the Right Thing* was like a fable of race relations. Spike's story had a political reality, not a street reality.

One small attempt to round out Sal's character came from my own past. I gave him his last name. "Frangione" was actually a stage name I was going to give myself when I started out in acting. I originally felt that "Aiello" was too difficult to pronounce. (For the record, it's "I-L-O.") So I experimented with calling myself "Danny Frangione."

My mother would have none of it. "When I see you up on-stage," she said, "I want everyone to know it's my son Danny Aiello Jr. up there."

Do the Right Thing is famously set on "the hottest day of the year." Tensions in the neighborhood boil over. But behind the camera our set ran without much conflict.

It was a forty-day shoot. The only troublesome incident I remember involved my son Danny III. The scene centered on an out-of-control mob attacking my character Sal. During the action, Danny III doubled for me. He went down, buried underneath the attacking mob.

While the scene was being shot, one of the actors spit in my son's face. All hell broke loose. Danny III wanted to kill the guy. He denied doing it, hiding behind the other members of the mob. But there it is in the finished scene, bigger than life, the jerk-off spitting on my son.

Things went a little more smoothly than that between me and Spike. We collaborated well. He accepted the adjustments to my character, incorporating lines I suggested into the script. Don't get me wrong. It was still Spike's script. Everything that went in was approved by him. Every word is his because it's his movie.

I don't want it to seem like I was responsible for wholesale rewrites, because I wasn't. But in a few scenes, the words that come out of Sal's mouth are mine. One scene is where Sal spouts a flowery speech in praise of Jade, played by Spike's sister, Joie Lee. (It was a nepotistic set. I had my two sons with me. In addition to Joie, Spike's father, Bill, scored the music for the film and his brother Dave did the still photography.)

The other scenes I had a hand in included what would become

the most cited lines in the movie. In one, Sal talks to his son Pino, who is advocating moving the pizzeria out of Bed-Stuy.

> I never had no trouble with these people. I look around and I
> see these kids—all these kids grew up on my food, on my food,
> and I'm very proud of that . . .

In another scene, Sal talks about the pride he has in his business.

> I built this fucking place with my bare fucking hands. Every
> light socket, every piece of tile—me, with these fucking hands.

The sentiments were straight from a workingman's heart, something that I knew well from all the blue-collar jobs I had worked in my life.

I came up with the "grew up on my food" lines about ten minutes before we were to shoot the scene. I said to myself, *Gee, that's corny.*

"No, that's not corny," Spike said. "Keep it in."

Do the Right Thing was so timely that film industry people were afraid moviegoers would riot. When Spike and Jon Kilik showed the movie to Universal for the first time, the studio heads were stunned. Spike hadn't allowed anyone to see dailies. Nobody from the studio could get on set. So the finished film hit Universal like a bomb.

I was shocked when people in the media stated that Spike's film would somehow incite violence. That's not how I saw *Do the Right Thing* at all. The movie doesn't leave you up on a roof crying for justice. Spike takes the audience to a whole different place. To me, he managed to lessen the impulse to riot, not heighten it. *Do the Right Thing* makes you think and makes you talk. And that can never be a bad outcome.

Most critics loved the movie. Gene Siskel and Roger Ebert were enthusiastic supporters of both the film and my performance, calling out my line "these kids grew up on my food" as the true heart of the story. I got plenty of accolades for my portrayal of Sal Frangione. *Moonstruck* was in the theaters. *Do the Right Thing* was in the can. I had trouble believing it all.

Chapter Eighteen

The Oscars

I met Eddie Murphy during my work on *Do the Right Thing*. He was one of the many celebrities who came by to visit the set of Spike's movie. By coincidence, I ran into Eddie later on the same day at a restaurant. We had lunch together and exchanged phone numbers.

Eddie didn't speak much about it then, but he was preparing for his first foray as a director. His acting career had been spectacular. Eddie reigned as one of the top-paid stars of the day. It was hard to believe he was still in his twenties. He had a lot of pull in Hollywood, which is why he was able to get multimillion-dollar financing for his movie *Harlem Nights*, which he wrote and planned to direct himself.

Eddie eventually offered me the part of a corrupt police sergeant. Although *Harlem Nights* was a crime caper, it had comedic elements, so every character had a larger-than-life feel. Oddly enough, *Do the Right Thing* and *Harlem Nights* both used a stuttering character for easy laughs.

I thoroughly enjoyed my time playing Sergeant Phil Cantone, whom I portrayed as a laughing cop with an evil smile. I made a good friend on that set, Mark Lipsky, who was Eddie's accountant and producer at the time.

There were some sly inside jokes. My character confronts Richard Pryor's character, Sugar Ray. "What are you?" Eddie's script has me saying. "You used to be a nightclub comic or something?" In real life, of course, Pryor was the most popular comedian around. He had already been diagnosed with the multiple sclerosis that would eventually lay him low, and his face showed evidence of scarring from a freebasing incident when he set himself on fire. But he handled his role with professional expertise.

Pryor heard that I had a daughter taking her first communion and requested that he act as godfather to my child. I would never have had the nerve to ask him, but I was surprised and gratified when he brought up the idea. Given the hectic quality of his life, it never worked out. I always liked Richie.

Throughout the *Harlem Nights* shoot, I watched Eddie shepherd the project with a sure hand. Here was this young kid, given a budget of thirty million to spend, the equivalent of double that amount in today's dollars. Yet Eddie was cool, calm, and collected. He controlled that set like the show business veteran he was. *Harlem Nights* went on to make more than $95 million worldwide, so the studio heads were right to trust him.

But Eddie was still Eddie. We had a scene to shoot at a location twenty miles outside Los Angeles, in the middle of nowhere, with hundreds of people in the crew. In one of the last shots of the day, my character was supposed to be seated in a bathroom stall. The whole scene was MOS, meaning without sound, with music to be filled in later.

"We're going to close the door of the stall," Eddie said. "All we want to see are your feet."

"All right," I said, and found my mark.

Eddie called in his direction to me. "When I ask you, just dance your feet," he said. "I'll be shooting it from outside, you won't see the camera, but we'll have a walkie-talkie. I can talk to you from here."

He rolled camera, I danced my feet, and Eddie yelled, "Cut!"

"Okay, Dan, stay where you are," Eddie said via the walkie-talkie. "Let's just assume that the music is a little slower, like a waltz-type thing, not a Lindy."

One more time. Roll camera. Action. Cut.

"All right, Danny, hold it, one more," Eddie said over the walkie-talkie. "Do it as if it was a rhumba, like interrupted steps."

Same thing. Roll camera. Action. Cut.

"Danny, Danny, just hold it a second," Eddie said. "I have to talk something over with the sound guy."

So I remained seated in the bathroom stall, humming to myself, waiting for things to come together. Everyone always does a lot of waiting on film sets, so it wasn't that rare of a situation. But after about ten minutes with nothing happening, I began to get impatient. I emerged from the stall, hoping I wasn't going to ruin the shot by doing so.

I walked out and everyone was gone. I mean everybody. All

two hundred or so people in the crew had packed up and left. The trucks weren't there, the craft people had folded their tent, makeup and hair were gone. There was nobody there but me.

Then, over the crackle of the walkie-talkie, I heard Eddie Murphy laughing. A practical joke. That was Eddie all the way.

Early in 1989, when I saw the finished cut of *Do the Right Thing*, my immediate impression wasn't positive. It was only later that I understood what Spike was doing with it, that the film was never intended to be cinematic realism, but rather represented a sort of urban parable. The comparison I always make is with the *Godfather* films, which didn't have much of a true street reality to them but rather had a more heightened, mythic truth.

If I stepped back and saw that *Do the Right Thing* was intended primarily as a political statement, I felt its power. When the movie hit the Cannes film festival that spring, I heard the boom all the way across the Atlantic. The movie got nominated for the top award at Cannes, the Palme d'Or. Spike was there at the festival representing his film. The French press lionized him.

Do the Right Thing opened in the States in June 1989. It became a huge phenomenon, a must-see movie. If a film has such a wide impact, the awards committees sit up and take notice. The Hollywood Foreign Press Association announced its Golden Globe nominations, and *Do the Right Thing* knocked down four, for Best Motion Picture, Best Director, Best Screenplay, and one for me as Best Actor in a Supporting Role.

That was just the first wave of the flood. For my performance as Sal, I won Best Supporting Actor awards from the Boston Society of Film Critics, the Chicago Film Critics Association, and the Los Angeles Film Critics Association.

I tried not to think about the possibility of getting an Academy Award nomination. I still felt as though I were somehow not as legitimate as the other actors who had gone to drama schools and went about developing their careers in a conventional way.

Luckily, I had enough work to distract my mind from the whole awards-season madness. With *Do the Right Thing* still burning up the box office, the Swedish director Lasse Hallström reached out to me with a part in his new movie. I loved Lasse's films, especially his 1985 Oscar-nominated sleeper hit *My Life as a Dog*.

The role Lasse wanted me for was in a movie called *Once Around*. The cast featured some great actors, headed up by Richard Dreyfuss, Gena Rowlands, and Holly Hunter. I signed on and toward the end of 1989 readied myself to head to the movie's North Carolina shooting location.

It was the night before the Academy Award nominations were to be announced. My wife and I found it difficult to sleep that night. We both rose early, at around six a.m. Sandy couldn't wait to watch the broadcast announcement of the nominations. All morning she sat glued to the television.

I didn't want to watch. I went out to my car and began packing my things for the trip to North Carolina. Even in the garage, I could hear the squawk of the television. It made me nervous.

"Why don't you turn it off?" I yelled in to Sandy. "Wait 'til I leave. Whatever happens, we'll find out soon enough."

Of course, the last thing I would have expected was that my wife would listen to me. As usual, she didn't. Sandy screamed when she saw the Best Actor in a Supporting Role category come up. I made a mad dash into the house. I was in time to see my image on TV and to hear the official academy announcement of that year's nominees for best supporting actor: ". . . Danny Aiello in *Do the Right Thing . . .*"

Sandy and I jumped around like two kids in a sandbox. We both began to cry hysterically, holding on to each other as tightly as we could, as if someone were going to steal this moment from us. One of my first thoughts was of Mom.

"If only our mothers were here to see this," I said to Sandy. Sadly, they had both passed before this ultimate recognition of my success.

The glow of the nomination had spread through my whole being. After telling my wife how much I loved her and how much I would miss her, I was on my way to my next job. On that car trip to North Carolina, I drove alone, talking to myself.

"You've been nominated for an Academy Award," I muttered. "Are you kidding me? How could this happen? How is this possible?"

I should have been having the time of my life. I should've been singing all the way to North Carolina. Instead I was overwhelmed. A thousand contradictory thoughts flew around in my head. My mother. My father. All my friends from the old neighborhood.

Traveling down the interstate at sixty-five miles an hour, I opened the window and started screaming to no one in particular, the same phrase over and over.

"I was just nominated for an Academy Award! I was just nominated for an Academy Award!"

Again, I had thoughts of my mother, and because I was alone, I could give those thoughts full voice. "What do you think, Mama?"

I shouted into the wind. "Your son Danny was just nominated for an Academy Award!"

Exhausted after an eight-hour drive, with no voice left to speak of, I arrived in North Carolina. Pulling into the driveway of the house where I would be staying, I saw something unbelievable on the porch: a six-foot replica of the golden Oscar statuette. It was a touching tribute from Lasse and my fellow cast members on *Once Around*. A huge inscription was emblazoned across the statue.

"Danny! You are a winner!"

Standing there to welcome me were Lasse and members of the cast, Richard Dreyfuss, Holly Hunter, and Gena Rowlands. My head was in the stars and at the same time I knew I had to buckle down and help Lasse make his movie.

Looming ahead of me, a few months down the road, would be the Oscar ceremony itself.

The distance from Stebbins Avenue in the Bronx to the Dorothy Chandler Pavilion in downtown Los Angeles ought to be measured in light-years. That's where the sixty-second Academy Awards were to be held on March 26, 1990. In the weeks before the ceremony, I had found myself at odd moments shaking my head in disbelief. But it was during the flight to the West Coast on the day before the Oscars that a sense of unreality really set in.

Sandy and I flew out to Los Angeles on MGM Grand Air, an all-first-class service that was briefly famous back then for pampering guests with every sort of luxury. We entered the refurbished Boeing 727 to discover a fantasy land.

In place of cramped airline seats, the plane had plush loungers that swiveled and reclined. A chef served from an elaborately equipped kitchen, and the drinkers among us had access to a full bar. The bathrooms boasted gold-plated fixtures, and all the flight attendants wore tuxedos.

From a palace in the air to a palace in Hollywood: once we arrived in Los Angeles, Sandy and I checked into the Beverly Hills Hotel. We had a wonderful suite on the first floor, with a huge terrace overlooking the bungalows below. I have always loved this hotel because there is so much Hollywood nostalgia attached to it. For its flamingo-colored walls, the place was nicknamed "the Pink Palace."

The day we arrived, Sandy and I proceeded straight to the hotel's Polo Lounge. It was like going through the Pearly Gates and gaining entry into movie star heaven. I recalled stories of Marilyn Monroe showing up in the bar wearing a mink coat with nothing on underneath and of Howard Hughes suffering a mental breakdown in one of the bungalows.

We had been invited to lunch by the film critics Roger Ebert and Gene Siskel. The two of them were at the height of their popularity. Being with them at the Polo Lounge was a pinch-me-I'm-dreaming moment for me, and I think for Sandy as well. As they had on their syndicated movie review program, Siskel and Ebert both praised *Do the Right Thing* and my characterization of Sal Frangione.

"Danny, you're a shoo-in for the Oscar," Roger Ebert told me. To top it all off, the two picked up the bill for the lunch. I was getting my first real taste of movie star life.

Sandy and I were riding high. Universal Studios took care of our expenses, including the first-class cross-country flight and the hotel. My publicist Jay Schwartz was on hand to make sure everything went smoothly. That night Sandy, my makeup artist Debbie Zoeller, and my buddy Joe Peck went out for dinner at Dan Tana's, the famous celebrity hangout on Santa Monica Boulevard.

The evening was filled with compliments and congratulations for my Academy Award nomination. A constant stream of well-wishers stopped by our table. Back then I didn't know many people in Los Angeles, except for the transplanted New York actors who relocated out there with the hope of getting work.

For all their smiles and back-slaps, I sure as hell knew many of my acquaintances hated the idea of my being nominated. It was as if I could read their minds. *Why couldn't it have been me? Aren't I a much better actor than Danny?* Of course, none of them would have ever come right out and voiced such sentiments. They just let the resentful thoughts marinate in their minds. Many of these actors I considered my friends. That's just the nature of show business. It has a way of turning good people into envious people.

I wish I could paint my time at the Oscars as one of glamorous parties and mingling with superstars. The truth is that I never have possessed the glad-handing gene. I don't make the social rounds. If people come to me, I am happy to speak to them. But I don't go out of my way to impose myself upon them.

I don't know why I am that way, but it's been true for my whole life. In Hollywood that year, when I should have been riding the celebrity express, I reverted to type. I didn't mingle. I didn't attend the Governor's Ball, the academy's official party, thrown for all the nominees.

On the day of the event, Sandy and I had breakfast on the outside terrace of the Polo Lounge. The feeling of unreality had not relented one bit. I was thankful I had my wife at my side to keep it all in perspective. She was what was real, Sandy and my family.

We returned to the hotel room and dove into our preparations for the evening. What's odd about the Oscars is that by all rights it should be a nighttime event, but because of the time difference with the East Coast TV audiences, it's conducted in the bright light of a Los Angeles afternoon.

Debbie began Max Factoring my wife. Without resorting to surgical tools she attempted to make me look good, too. I don't want you to think that Sandy and I travel with our own private makeup artist. By that point, Debbie had worked with me on every movie I did, every stage or television show over the course of the previous five years. She was like family, very close to me and Sandy. She also happens to be one of the best makeup artists in the business. She had to be, since she was somehow able to perform miracles on me.

One last check in the mirror and we were ready to go. The academy assigns a limousine to each nominee. A good three hours before the event, our driver picked us up and we headed through Hollywood toward downtown and the Dorothy Chandler Pavilion. It took a while for us to get there. So many limos were converging that we were put in holding patterns like jets over a busy airport.

The approach took forever. As I sat in the back of the car with Sandy and Jay Schwartz, my mind refused to calm down. I thought of the stagecoaches in the Wild West, General Custer at Little Big Horn and the circling Indians. I couldn't decide if we were the Sioux warriors or the U.S. Cavalry. Just crazy thoughts in a crazy time.

After what seemed like hours, our limousine pulled up in front of the pavilion. As we emerged the cameras began blasting away.

My name was announced by an impersonal voice over a loud-speaker. The fans in the bleachers screamed. Everyone seemed swept up in the excitement of the moment. All this under the brilliant Southern California sun.

An academy functionary directed me to stand in line to be interviewed by the press. The interviewing reporters were not even looking at me half the time. Instead, they glanced constantly over my shoulder to see if the next celebrity might be more important than I was. After my interview, I watched them and saw that they did this to everyone, not just me.

We finally entered the auditorium and got Sandy seated. I was whisked away by Jay to the greenroom, to be given instructions on what I could expect to happen during the awards ceremony.

"If you're a winner, no long speeches," one of the show's assistant producers told me. "Please be brief."

Don't forget Sandy, don't forget Mom, don't forget your sons and daughter, I told myself. *And, oh, yeah, don't forget Spike.*

I was in great company in the best supporting actor category. Denzel Washington was nominated for the Civil War movie *Glory*, Dan Aykroyd for *Driving Miss Daisy*, Martin Landau for Woody Allen's *Crimes and Misdemeanors*. Marlon Brando got nominated for *A Dry White Season*, but as was his custom, the great man didn't show for the Oscars presentation.

The greenroom felt like madness, so it was a relief to be guided back to my seat next to Sandy, led there by a beautiful escort in a designer gown. The Academy Awards ceremony is such a sprawling event that it has to be run with military precision. That night, the nominees for best supporting actor were placed together at the right side of the theater.

I sat there thinking my outsider thoughts. *What am I doing here? This isn't me. I'm not a party guy, a chitchat guy, rubbing shoulders with people I don't really know. Why didn't I do what Brando did and not show up at all?*

No one seemed to care that Brando wasn't present. And if they didn't care about his not showing, they damn sure wouldn't have cared if I wasn't there. I never let Sandy know exactly how I felt about the evening. I didn't want to ruin it for her. She looked beautiful and seemed to be having a wonderful time.

Billy Crystal might have been very funny that night, appearing for the first time as an Academy Awards host. I couldn't tell you anything about it because I was too nervous with all the thoughts buzzing in my head. The best supporting actor award came up early during the evening. Geena Davis, who had won the best supporting actress Oscar the previous year, presented for the category.

"And the winner is . . . ," Geena said, struggling with the envelope. "Denzel Washington, for *Glory*!"

As the applause began, Sandy blurted out the first thing that popped into her head. "It's political," she exclaimed. Many people heard her, including Denzel. He only smiled. I'm sure he thought the same thing I did: *Well, there's a woman sticking up for her man.*

Is it believable when I tell you that I wasn't crushed? I hadn't allowed myself to think I would win. I told myself that I had gone to the Oscars just to see what all the fuss was about. I wanted to experience the whole business at least once in my life. How many guys like me ever get a chance like that?

Denzel was interviewed after the show and asked if he had

thought beforehand that he was going to win. "I thought Danny Aiello would win," he told the reporter.

I thought Danny Aiello would win. Strange as it seems, that statement by Denzel made my entire Oscar experience worthwhile. Denzel thought I was a winner! Me, a winner!

While Sandy and I were leaving the theater, reporters stopped me, too, and asked how it felt to lose.

"What do you mean, 'lose'?" I asked them right back. I had worked out the math in my head. "This is the sixty-second annual Academy Awards. Five actors get nominated in this category, every year for sixty-two years. That's three hundred ten actors in total, pal. And I was one of the three hundred ten! Would you call that being a loser? I wouldn't."

The big winner that night was my wife, Sandy. All her friends back in New Jersey watched her on television, being interviewed and looking beautiful. I went home thinking the same thing I did when Sandy and I first learned that I had been nominated for an Academy Award.

Wouldn't it be great if our mothers had been here to see us?

Chapter Nineteen

The Shutout

Everyone's star rises after an Oscar nomination. I was the same actor before I got nominated for *Do the Right Thing* as I was afterward. But somehow people who had never given me a second thought were now scrambling to get my agent on the phone.

I had a lot more respect for foreign directors, who always seemed to value me for what I really was instead of what some critic or awards committee said I was. A case in point was Lasse Hallström. Working with him on *Once Around* proved to be a learning experience, and a very good one.

In the course of the film, he gave me the opportunity to sing three songs, "Fly Me to the Moon," "The Glory of Love"—both of which made it onto the movie's soundtrack album—and "Mama." What was strange was that Lasse never told me beforehand that I would sing in the movie or even asked me if I could carry a tune.

Lasse was an extremely charming and intelligent guy. Like all the European directors whom I have worked with, he was very good behind the camera. In his movie I play Joe Bella, the father in a family that includes daughter Renata Bella, played by Holly Hunter. Richard Dreyfuss is Renata's new boyfriend, the fast-talking salesman Sam Sharpe, a character who at times could be a gigantic pain in the ass.

In one scene, Sam's limo driver sleeps on a small couch in the hallway outside of Renata's room. It's the middle of the night. Renata and Sam Sharpe are making a lot of noise downstairs. Gena Rowlands plays my wife, and she and I are in our bedroom, listening to our daughter frolic with a man we barely know.

Now, if the same situation were happening in the Aiello household, I would react by throwing the guy out on his ass. Getting mad and losing my temper was my initial interpretation of the scene as an actor. Lasse and I had a powwow. We spoke for a few moments about what was going on in this scene and my reaction to it.

"Maybe you don't be so angry," Lasse suggested. "Maybe you're not reacting the way you usually do."

Never let it be said I can't take direction. Lasse softened my approach. He gave me a whole new handle on the scene.

In character as Joe Bella, I announce that I'm going to put a stop to whatever is going on between Sam and Renata. My wife tells me not to go. I go anyway, finding the noisy couple fully clothed, hugging and kissing and being very playful with each other.

"Your mother can't sleep," I say. "For chrissakes, it's three o'clock in the morning."

The manner in which I pronounce those lines is miles away from anything Danny Aiello would have said. Then I added an action to help shine a light on Joe Bella's personality. After I wish the couple good night and head back to my own room, I see the limousine driver sleeping on the couch in the hallway. I get a blanket and cover him.

That one bit of business—seeing to the comfort of the chauffeur—served as a small character note that told the audience what kind of guy Joe Bella really was. The scene would've been quite different if I played it the way I would have in real life. Lasse is Swedish, and maybe that's how they react in Sweden if a daughter is having a hell of a time at three a.m. with a guy the parents have never met.

The studio made an Oscar push for *Once Around*, initiated by producer and leading man Richard Dreyfuss. Ads were placed in the *Hollywood Reporter* and *Variety*, asking for Academy Award consideration. Two of the categories listed were best actor and best supporting actor. Much to my surprise there was a campaign for me, not Richard Dreyfuss, who had done a superb job as Sam Sharpe and who I felt was more deserving.

The greatest disappointment in my acting career was never being cast in a Martin Scorsese film. As a director, he was making great movies about people I knew well, people I had grown up with. We share a lot of the same background. I'm a New York City guy and so is he.

At a press conference for one of my movies, a reporter asked why I never worked with Scorsese.

"Maybe you should ask him," I said.

"I did," the reporter responded. "He told me you weren't right for what he was doing."

"Are you kidding? I'm the only Italian in America who hasn't been in any of his movies," I said, making a joke out of it.

The single interview I had with Scorsese regarded the non-speaking part in *Raging Bull.* Robert De Niro set up that meeting because of my early involvement in the development of that film. I found the role Scorsese put forward to be unacceptable. I've always felt he made me an offer that he knew I would refuse. It was the closest I came to working with him.

During the early years of my film career, agents submitted my name to Scorsese for roles in movie after movie, but we never received a response. We kept trying because the projects he was mounting were just too enticing to pass up: *Taxi Driver*; *New York, New York*; *The King of Comedy*; *After Hours*; *Goodfellas*; and *Casino*, to list just a few. It is hard for me to believe I was not right for any of these films.

Why had Scorsese not seen fit to work with me? Was it because he thought I was a terrible actor? Maybe it was something I had done or something I said over the years. In press stories, journalists have written about my street past, the fighting, the stealing, the rough-and-tumble neighborhoods in which I grew up, my hatred for drug use.

Maybe Marty thought I was a potentially violent person. I'm sure I've lost many parts as a result of my own actions, and I have to live with that. But I don't have to forgive the man for not giving me the chance to excel in his films.

During Scorsese's most prolific period in the eighties and nineties, I was white-hot on Broadway and in Hollywood, working with some of the greatest American and foreign directors.

I had my name on the marquee for such plays as *Knockout*,

The Floating Light Bulb, House of Blue Leaves, and *Hurlyburly*. I appeared in *Fort Apache, the Bronx*; *Once Upon a Time in America*; *The Purple Rose of Cairo*; *Do the Right Thing*; *Harlem Nights*—as with Marty's list, I'm mentioning just a few. And I had been well honored for my work, receiving an Obie, a Theatre World Award, multiple Emmys, and an Oscar nomination, again, to name only a few.

If Scorsese didn't cast me because he thought I was a terrible actor, I have to be the most successful one who has ever lived.

There's a kicker to all this. In the spring of 1991, the year after my *Do the Right Thing* nomination, I was invited to be part of the ceremonies at the sixty-third Academy Awards. I stepped out onto the stage of the Shrine Civic Auditorium in Los Angeles to introduce a clip of one of that year's best-picture nominees, *Goodfellas*, yet another Martin Scorsese film this Italian-American wasn't in.

As I've said, foreign directors always seemed to "get" my approach to acting more than some of their American counterparts. Beginning with the British director Mike Newell and 1983's *Blood Feud* and continuing through Italy's Sergio Leone and *Once Upon a Time in America*, France's Élie Chouraqui and 1987's *Man on Fire*, and Spain's Fernando Trueba and 1995's *Two Much*, I did a string of projects with directors who had been nominated for and/ or won Oscars, Césars, BAFTAs, or Golden Bears.

I worked with the English director Adrian Lyne on the supernatural thriller *Jacob's Ladder*, a film that starred Tim Robbins and has gone on to achieve a sort of cult status among fans. When I made the movie with him, the Englishman Lyne was coming off three huge hits, *Flashdance*, *9½ Weeks*, and *Fatal Attraction*.

Filmmaking with Lyne (whose last name is pronounced in the British manner, like the word "line") was quite an experience. He is unique in film, almost a hippie type, and was very much into the post-Vietnam theme of *Jacob's Ladder*. His wife, Samantha, was a sweetheart. I recall her hair being dyed a shade of purple. She gave off the same hippie vibe as her husband.

But the couple's outer appearance shouldn't fool anyone. They were two perfectly normal human beings, very much in love with each other. They didn't have to display their affection for everyone on set to know the depth of their relationship. We just knew from the way they treated each other.

Screenwriter Bruce Joel Rubin, who had written the block-buster *Ghost*, created a whole hellish world in *Jacob's Ladder*. The result had to be one of the spookiest films I have ever seen. The critics were blown away by the movie and by Adrian's directing. He was a specialist in the macabre, and paired with Rubin, he had created a strange afterlife world of dark, depressing effects.

Just about every character in *Jacob's Ladder* turns out to be a demonic creature, with one notable exception. That would be yours truly, playing Louis the chiropractor. I had never been to a chiropractor. I didn't know what their procedures entailed. An hour before we were to begin shooting the scene where I adjust Tim Robbins's back, Adrian introduced me to a chiropractor consultant he had brought in to teach me the tricks of the trade.

Needless to say, I was a rookie spine manipulator. It's not as easy as it looks. I was trying to do multiple things at once. Try tapping your head with your right hand while creating little circles on your stomach with your left hand, all the time quoting Nietzsche, and you'll get some idea of the kind of physical juggling act that's involved. Not a very easy task.

Tim Robbins somehow survived my bending and stretching him. Of all the scenes that I had in the film, this was my favorite.

After the movie came out in theaters, chiropractors started coming up to me on the street. They'd tell me how much I advanced the profession as a result of my bedside manner and my "knowing how to manipulate the spine." One of them told me I was an answer on a multiple-choice quiz for a test in chiropractic school.

My son Danny III doubled Tim Robbins in the action scenes (though not on Louis's spine-manipulating table!). The whole experience of *Jacob's Ladder* was a complete joy. My only regret is that so far I have never had the opportunity to work with this great, quirky director again.

It may sound as if I am always working, but the truth is I normally have plenty of time to hang out. New York is the greatest hangout city in the world. Being in a busy restaurant with friends, with the noise of their conversation and laughter ringing in my ears, that's what public life is for me. There's creativity, possibilities, energy to plug into.

It's not as though I glad-hand my way through these places. Far from it. I hang out not to be seen but to see. When I walk into a crowded room at a party, I generally head for the nearest empty corner and take a seat there. At a restaurant I will never approach another table. If someone approaches mine and speaks to me, I'll respond. I enjoy being with a few friends, listening and observing the scene going on around me but not necessarily participating in any of it.

While working on the Broadway stage, I frequented a lot of popular Theater District restaurants, Charley's on West Forty-Fifth Street, Joe Allen's on West Forty-Sixth Street, Jimmy Ray's on Eighth Avenue and Forty-Sixth, Sardi's on West Forty-Fourth Street. Because I had shows to perform, I went to these joints mainly to eat.

Charley's was one of my favorites. I still dream about London broil with brown sauce and mashed potatoes, sort of a throwback to my youth, when I ate mashed potatoes and brown gravy every afternoon at Jack's Restaurant in the Bronx. Only now I could afford the steak to go along with it. The waiters and waitresses at Charley's were some of the most talented people I have ever met. The joint has an old-fashioned jukebox, and the servers break out in song and perform dances at the drop of a hat. You might see a few of the same faces the next year in a Broadway chorus line.

I always loved Sardi's. Like his father, the original owner of Sardi's, Vincent Sardi Jr. knew how to treat his clientele. He was especially kind to out-of-work actors. He created what was well-known as an actor's menu, for those performers who might be "between jobs," as they say, and unable to pay the regular menu price. Vincent might run a tab, too, to be paid when the down-and-outers got back on their feet. If that never happened, he would tear up the tab. That was Mr. Sardi, who was loved by everyone who had the pleasure of meeting him.

To this day I hit Sardi's as often as I can. Once in a while I might check to see if my caricature is still hanging on the wall. It was first placed there after my run in *Lamppost Reunion*. The restaurant continues to be run in the same gracious manner as it was back when I first started my stage career.

The man responsible for that continuity is Max Klimavicius, a young dynamo of Lithuanian heritage who was actually born in Colombia. Max had a minor job at the restaurant when he started, but Vincent Sardi recognized his dedication to the business. He became one of the owners and a trusted friend of mine and of every other actor who came in contact with him. Incidentally, I love the food at Sardi's, a fact that sometimes gets lost in all the showbiz publicity about the place.

Jimmy Ray's was also a Theater District place that served good food, but it was mostly a watering hole for actors. Being that I don't drink, I wasn't there often, but just about every other actor I knew was. During my *Lamppost Reunion* days, we used Jimmy Ray's as an informal rehearsal space for a few days, just before we went to Broadway with the play.

Like Sardi's and Jimmy Ray's, Joe Allen's restaurant was always filled with theater people, from producers to stagehands, choreographers, dancers, set decorators, writers, and everyone else connected to Broadway. The food was good at Joe Allen's and the ambience perfect if I ever wanted to decompress after a show. This was often a very real need, because I usually had a hyper feeling after coming off a performance. A good dinner helped calm me down.

Another place I hit every once in a while was very familiar to me: the Improvisation. When I left the club after becoming an actor, I continued to stop by to see Budd, as well as catch up with all the regulars who helped me along the way with friendship or career advice.

During my days as an Improv bouncer, when celebrities came in, Budd used to announce their presence from the stage. I always wondered how that felt. Now I would be the one sitting there, eating at a table at the club and hearing my own name being announced.

"The only actor who began his career while working at the Improvisation—Danny Aiello!"

The restaurants I came to frequent were different kinds of places, more in the nature of hangouts than the Theater District joints.

From the late seventies through the eighties and into the nineties, there were a couple West Side restaurants actors frequented. One was Café Central on Amsterdam Avenue in the West Seventies, which later moved to Columbus Avenue, in the same neighborhood under the same ownership. The second was the king of the hill and top of the heap for quite some time, Columbus Café on Sixty-Ninth Street and Columbus Avenue. We dropped the word "café" and simply called it "Columbus." Some notable actors had small ownership stakes in the place, which was run by Paul Herman and his brother Charlie. Paul knew everyone and understood everything that was going on in New York. Anything you wanted to know, he could help you with.

We hung out at Columbus day and night. It was the place to be. At any given time the biggest celebrities in the world might be there. The drug scene was raging in every other restaurant in the city, but somehow it seemed to have bypassed Columbus Café. Maybe that's because detectives and federal agents frequented the joint. Or maybe the actors were too busy eyeing the ballet dancers who flocked there. The dancers didn't come only because Columbus Café was right across the street from Lincoln Center, but also because Misha Baryshnikov owned a percentage of the restaurant.

Taken as a whole, the clientele at Columbus was an odd, world-class mix. Opposites attracted. Gangsters were busy trying to rub shoulders with actors. FBI agents and DEA agents were busy watching the gangsters. Chuck Rose, a federal prosecutor friend of mine, once let me in on a little secret.

"I'm probably not the only guy in here carrying a gun tonight," he said. I laughed, but I don't think he meant it as a joke.

Warren Beatty, Jack Nicholson, and I were sitting at a table at Columbus having dinner one night when a note was delivered to me by a waitress.

"This came from over at the bar," the waitress said.

The note read: "Danny, I can't take my eyes off of you! Can we meet later?" I eyeballed the lineup of incredible beauties at the bar, models and ballerinas and actresses, each one more gorgeous than the next. Here I was, sitting with two of the top swordsmen in the world, and the flirtatious message had come not to Jack, not to Warren, but to me!

I read the note out loud. Beatty and Nicholson started laughing their asses off. I immediately guessed the truth.

"Which one of you guys wrote this?" I asked, starting to laugh myself. Warren finally admitted it.

Columbus Café was a show-business beehive. There were always a lot of meetings going on, producers huddling with other producers, directors with actors, agents with anyone they could get to sit with them. I can't imagine how many contracts were consummated there, many of them signed while under the influence of a drink or two.

At least a couple of the Columbus waitresses were lucky enough to get important jobs in the business because of the connections they made at work. Sheila Jaffe became a top casting director for *The Sopranos,* among many other shows and movies. She partnered with Georgianne Walken, who happened to be Chris Walken's wife. I guess it wasn't the first time someone began on the side of a table and ended up on the top of the world.

It wouldn't surprise me if Paul Herman had something to do with Sheila and Georgianne's success. He helped so many others. Presently Paul is one of the owners of the famous Italian restaurant Ago in West Hollywood. Whenever I am out there he has his kitchen whip me up a dish of my favorite gluten-free pasta, done Sorrentino style. Likewise, whenever Paul comes to New York, we still see each other whenever we can. The friends I made at Columbus Café are mine for life.

Chapter Twenty

Hudson Hawk

At the end of the 1980s, a lot of job offers seemed to be coming my way. I had just completed two films, both shot in Italy, Pasquale Squitieri's *Russicum* and *Man on Fire* with Scott Glenn. This last project allowed me to air out my acting chops in a searing scene where my character had to beg an executioner not to kill him.

In Los Angeles around this time, I met with screenwriter George Gallo, who wrote the screenplay for the movie *Midnight Run*, starring Robert De Niro. He was looking to direct his first feature, *29th Street*, an ultimate New York tale of hard luck, a close-knit family, and a winning lottery ticket. Frank Pesce and James Franciscus got a writing credit, while George Gallo did the screenplay of their story.

The film hadn't been cast yet when I met with George. He and

I sat in a restaurant discussing the project. Today a small plaque marks the counter where we ate, with this inscription: "This is where George Gallo wrote *29th Street*."

My film agent Jimmy Cota told me that studio backing for the film depended on my signing on. When I read the script, I immediately responded to the father-and-son relationship that was central to the story. David Permut, the producer of *29th Street*, called Jimmy and a deal was struck. Anthony LaPaglia and I would play Frank Pesce, senior and junior. Frank Pesce himself, upon whose life the movie is based, would play Vito, my character's other son. I personally chose Lainie Kazan to play my wife.

We were already in preproduction on *29th Street* when Jimmy Cota got a call from a producer named Joel Silver. Joel had done multiple blockbusters and was a major force to be reckoned with in Hollywood. Silver wanted to sign me to a film called *Hudson Hawk*, starring Bruce Willis, with a screenplay based on a story by Bruce himself. The only catch was that the movie was to begin shooting in two weeks.

"Danny's not available," Jimmy Cota told Silver. "He's already signed to *29th Street*, and it'll be shooting at the same time."

Joel Silver is not the kind of producer accustomed to hearing the word "no." He's also not exactly a calm and reasonable guy.

"You stupid bastard," Silver yelled at Jimmy. "Consider yourself fired!"

Silver wasn't about to be refused. I was told later that he dialed up Joe Roth, then head of 20th Century Fox, the studio that was backing *29th Street*.

"I'm in preproduction," Joe Roth explained to Silver. "We've already spent four hundred fifty thousand dollars."

"I'll pay you for your preproduction cost," Silver said. "Just give me Danny."

So the two power players, Roth and Silver, made the deal. Roth put *29th Street* on hold. George Gallo's green light turned yellow. That's typical for Hollywood, where there are always a lot of bumps and detours on the road to filming.

When I first met him, Bruce Willis was an actor-bartender working at Central Café. As his star rose, we still spoke on occasion. We agreed that should an opportunity arise we would work together. Actors say this to each other all the time, but in this case the collaboration came to pass on *Hudson Hawk*.

I knew Bruce's brother David, who was one of his producers on *Hudson Hawk*. I also knew his brother Bobby, a beautiful kid who died early on. Bruce's mother, Marlene, and my wife became quite close. The Willis and Aiello clans hung out, mostly when we were on location in Italy. We went swimming together and went out to eat. We resembled an extended family there for a while, which made it all the more difficult later when the shit hit the fan.

Much of my work on *Hudson Hawk* was done in Italy, with small portions in New York City. The project was Bruce's baby all the way. He had conceived the idea of a caper film that would resemble the Bob Hope–Bing Crosby road movies. He would be Bing and I would be Bob, or maybe it was the other way around.

Even though the director of record was Michael Lehmann, just coming off the teen hit *Heathers*, Bruce was very much involved in every aspect of the filmmaking. He had a habit of giving line readings to all the actors involved, including me. A line reading is where a director or some other know-it-all actually recites your line for you, suggesting that you "do it this way." For a professional actor, it can be the equivalent of a slap in the face. Giving line readings is widely considered bad form, which is not to say the practice never happens.

My son Danny III stunt-doubled for me on *Hudson Hawk*, and just like there were good and bad things about working with Bruce as a friend and costar, there were two sides to having Danny on the set. I loved seeing him, of course, but his job always made me nervous. From his first work on *Fort Apache, the Bronx*, Danny had progressed to where he was tops in his field. My pride over that fact battled it out with my anxiety as a father.

I could have listed thousands of jobs that I would have liked my son to choose, and not one of them would have been movie stuntman. The whole idea of my son in a risky situation made me queasy. Of all the times we worked together, there were only a few instances when I witnessed him doing dangerous stunts. A memorable one was on *Hudson Hawk*.

He was shooting a scene on Fifty-Seventh Street in NYC. Danny and his stunt partner were doubling me and Bruce Willis. I stood below peering up at two tall buildings. Twelve floors up was a cable about thirty-five feet long, stretching from one building to the other. I watched the two figures swing out onto the cable, knowing that one of them was my son and not enjoying the fact that I knew he was up there.

Suddenly the cable dropped downward several feet with the two stuntmen attached. I almost had a heart attack right there on the spot. I didn't know that the drop had been thoroughly planned out. You would think someone might have warned me, just to safeguard my cardiac health.

Danny and the other stuntman made it across the cable safely, a hundred feet above the street. To them, it was no big deal, just another day on the job. I swore to myself that the crazy *Hudson Hawk* cable climb would be the last stunt I'd ever watch my son do.

As the shoot progressed, Bruce took over more and more aspects of the filmmaking. He began actually directing scenes. This created a lot of problems for Michael Lehmann, the director of record. I asked Michael why he didn't just quit the shoot.

"Not for the money I'm getting paid," he said.

Joel Silver was on set a lot, huddling with Willis. There wasn't anyone around with the juice to say no to either of them. "Fuck art!" was one of Joel's favorite phrases, which he employed whenever somebody suggested a more nuanced approach to filmmaking.

I had just finished a scene where my character is locked in a limousine, which goes over a cliff, crashes into a ravine, and catches fire. Somehow, I survive the accident—this is a comedy, after all. When I staggered out of the limo, Bruce wanted to have my hair electrified and standing up on end, Don King style, with smoke coming out of it.

"That's comedy time in the Rockies," I said. "I'm not doing it."

I alluded to the fact that Christopher Lloyd had a similar beat in *Back to the Future*. I thought Hollywood comedies had been there and done that.

"I'll tell you what's funny," I said to Bruce. "What's funny is if my hair is well-groomed and perfectly in place, *and* it has smoke coming out of it. That's what's funny."

He got upset. "We're paying you one million dollars to do this movie," he said.

"Not quite true," I said.

Bruce turned his back and walked away. That was that. We finished the film and our friendship at the same time.

I was doing films back-to-back now, packing up on the *Hudson Hawk* set and going directly into *29th Street*. I could not wait to begin shooting what I've always thought to be the ultimate father-and-son film.

I enjoyed working with *29th Street* producer David Permut and I loved the cast. My son Rick had a part and my son Danny was the stunt coordinator on the movie. Even Sandy had a small speaking role, but the scene she was in was left on the cutting room floor.

Initially, Anthony LaPaglia's Australian accent concerned me, since he would be playing a character from Queens. But it was not a problem and he turned out to be terrific.

Generally, I liked the way the shoot was going and I told George Gallo as much. But I also mentioned that there were certain over-the-top comedic beats in the script that were bothering me. To me, the baggy-pants humor detracted from the father-and-son story that was the core of the film.

"Don't worry, Danny, I'll take care of them," George said.

I worked hard fleshing out my character in this film. In one scene, LaPaglia confronts me, his father. "What did you ever do for us?" he demands.

"I stayed, that's what I did! I stayed for thirty-five years and I did whatever the hell I had to do to keep a roof over our heads. That's what the fuck I did."

"Big deal!" LaPaglia responds. "That's what you're supposed to do."

I get right back into the son's face. "You know, we were doing pretty good until you came along. I didn't want you, but your mother did, and your mother almost died giving birth to you. You get this straight, you sorry son of a bitch. I am not a loser! I am not a fucking loser!"

I thought it was probably among the best scenes that I had ever helped write. It came directly from my heart.

The film was screened in Toronto. Sandy and I drove up to see it. Watching the finished cut, I realized that George had not kept his promise to smooth out the broad comedic beats that didn't fit in this wonderful movie. The film turned out to be very good, but I always thought it could have been great.

Producer Robert Evans, famous for making *The Godfather* and so many other films, called me at home in New Jersey one evening. He told me that he and Jack Nicholson had screened *29th Street* in his home and they both loved it.

"If the curse words weren't used, it would have been better than *It's a Wonderful Life*," Evans said.

From *29th Street* I went almost to the opposite end of the film-making spectrum, playing the lead in a sprawling historical biopic. In 1991 I met with director John Mackenzie and writer Stephen Davis for a film project on the life of Jack Ruby, the Dallas night-club owner who killed Lee Harvey Oswald.

We all had dinner together at Columbus Café. John was yet one more of those foreign directors with an intuitive feel for my work. He had directed a BAFTA-nominated cult thriller called *The Long Good Friday*. John, Steve, and I talked late into the night, discussing the concept of the Jack Ruby project. They never took the position that the film would be a true description of the Kennedy assassination.

"Whenever there are known facts," John said, "those facts will be used, and when there are not, then we'll employ theatrical license."

JFK was being shot at the same time, and Oliver Stone was all over the talk shows claiming that his film would reveal what actually happened in Dallas on November 22, 1963. In contrast, *Ruby* would come out with a disclaimer about its being a work of drama. I much preferred the John Mackenzie approach to Stone's.

A few months after our first meeting, we were in Los Angeles to begin shooting the film. *Ruby* turned out to be a great shoot. I was very excited about working with Mackenzie, one of the UK's best film directors.

I did my own research on Jack Ruby by talking to people who knew him and had appeared in his clubs, comics such as Milton Berle and Jerry Vale. They gave me telling details of Jack's personality. He would give comics silk shirts that he kept in the trunk of his car, usually for the purpose of selling them, but free for the celebrities who worked his clubs. Ruby packed a gun everywhere he went, because he didn't believe in banks and carried a lot of money around with him.

One note that came up in my research was the fact that Jack Ruby sat shiva with his sister in her home when John Kennedy was assassinated. Ruby loved President Kennedy, whom he considered the savior of the Jewish people. I set out to learn the prayer for the dead in Hebrew, working very hard at it. We shot the scene, but unfortunately it didn't make the final cut. I was disappointed because I wanted the audience to know how truly grief-stricken Jack Ruby was about President Kennedy's being killed.

Sherilyn Fenn, an excellent actress who at that time I considered to be one of the most beautiful women in movies, played opposite me as Sheryl Ann DuJean, a.k.a. Candy Cane, a dancer in one of Jack Ruby's clubs. She had an elaborate striptease scene. The day it was shot, I consciously chose to absent myself from the set.

"You didn't watch the scene?" Sherilyn asked me afterward.

"I'm sure you were great," I said, smiling. The truth is, I felt too embarrassed to do so. My old-fashioned attitudes often come out when I'm confronted with overt sexuality on the set. The relationship between Ruby and his dancer girlfriend stirred up all my negative feelings surrounding movie romances between older men and younger women.

We wrapped the film just as *JFK* was about to hit the theaters. There was some debate within our production team as to when *Ruby* should open. I felt strongly that the film should debut while *JFK* was still in release. I met with the producers of *Ruby* from Propaganda Films, Michael Kuhn, Steve Golin, Stephen Davis, and Sigurjon Sighvatsson.

"Use the publicity surrounding *JFK* to benefit our film," I argued. But the publicity campaign for *Ruby* had been locked in for spring 1992. We opened at the end of March. It was too late, and we did very little business.

I have occasionally been asked to speak to performing arts classes or groups of young actors. Since I never had any professional training, I can only give them the lessons I've learned from experience.

One bit of wisdom I usually include comes from simple observation, working on film sets and in the theater over the years.

"If you go into the business of acting while doing drugs, you'll never get off them, because you'll need that crutch forever. There can be no greater feeling than performing without the help of anything but your God-given talent."

On the whole, my opinion of performing arts education has been mixed. I remember once being asked by Ed Setrakian to perform a scene at the Actors Studio. Ed was directing me at the time in an off-Broadway play titled *Easy Money*, written by John Kostmayer. As well as being a director, Ed was also a well-respected actor and a member of the Actors Studio.

"Lee Strasberg wants you as a member of the studio," Ed told me. "You can do any scene that you choose."

The Actors Studio is probably the most prestigious venue anywhere in the world for teaching the dramatic arts. It has a celebrated history, with members like Marlon Brando, Sally Field, Al Pacino, Bea Arthur, and Harvey Keitel, to name only a few. Just to walk by the place in Hell's Kitchen (on West Forty-Fourth, down the street from the Improv) means you're entering who's-who territory. Lee Strasberg served as its director. Membership at the studio is considered an honor in the acting community.

I paid a visit to audit an acting class. I was blown away while watching the actors preparing to do a scene. They were extremely intense. I got the idea that they were going to war. It didn't seem like any of them were having much fun.

Even though I probably could not have fully articulated my philosophy of performing, I knew that what I was seeing at the studio was foreign to me. Acting is hard enough already. I wasn't looking to make it any harder. I decided to take a pass on appearing in Ed's scene at the studio.

I think about this experience whenever I recall working with director Paul Mazursky, who always managed to find the joy and fun in the craft of acting. Throughout my career I've had the opportunity to work with some of the world's greatest film directors, foreign and homegrown. Paul Mazursky was my favorite.

Coincidentally, Mazursky was also responsible for my biggest movie payday. His film *The Pickle* was loosely based on Paul's life as a maverick director, producer, and actor in the wilds of Hollywood. Paul wanted me to play the character of Harry Stone, who was essentially his alter ego. In the film, Stone is a once-famous director on his way out.

Contract negotiations went on for a couple of months. I remember my agent Jimmy Cota telling me how Sam Cohn, Paul Mazursky's agent, responded.

"What the hell is a Danny Aiello?" Cohn demanded. "Doesn't he realize he's working with a great director?"

"That's why he thinks he should get paid the greatest money, because he's working with the greatest," Cota responded.

My agent got what we asked for because of one reason and one reason only: Paul wanted me in the film. His daughter, Meg Mazursky, saw me in *The House of Blue Leaves* at Lincoln Center and convinced her father that I was the one who should play Harry Stone.

Paul surrounded me with a wonderful cast of people: Jerry Stiller, Dyan Cannon, Barry Miller, Chris Penn, Ally Sheedy, Griffin Dunne, Shelley Winters, Little Richard, and so many more.

The director himself acted in his film, playing the projectionist-friend of my character.

Dyan Cannon, the ex-wife of Cary Grant and a wonderful actress, played my wife. The two of us were expected to do love scenes in the movie, which must have felt like combat duty to her. But she never made me feel that way. She was accustomed to doing movie love scenes and tried to make me feel comfortable. I was an amateur at best and I'm sure Paul was aware of that. It was hard for me. Sandy was on the set during most of the shoot.

What I was doing with Dyan Cannon was just moviemaking, but I was afraid it might not look that way to my wife. I thought I would hear about it when we got back home. It turned out that Sandy wasn't at all upset about my scenes with Dyan.

"After being with Cary Grant, what the hell would she want with you?" Sandy said.

Dyan and I talked quite a bit about her ex-husband. I told her I had received my first acting award from Cary. I related the anecdote of my telling him I was nervous, and how Cary had responded with his gracious "So am I!"

Just before beginning *The Pickle*'s love scene with Dyan, I whispered into her ear how nervous I was, expecting her to respond as her ex had.

"Don't worry, I'm not!" she said. I laughed, and the whole exchange helped loosen me up.

My scene with Dyan was light duty compared to what I had to do next, which was make love in a limousine to a twenty-two-year-old Parisian beauty by the name of Clotilde Courau. She and I also had a bedroom scene at the Plaza Hotel. Hard as it is for anyone to believe, this was truly difficult. To say I was apprehensive before my scenes with Clotilde would be an understatement.

"For the sake of the film, I will get through it," I said, putting on a long-suffering face for Sandy. Of course, she wanted to punch me right in the mouth.

Since *The Pickle* was made, we've lost some very special people who were involved in it, Paul himself first and foremost. I always adored Meg Mazursky, Paul's daughter, who passed away. Chris Penn, who played my son in the film, died much too young. Off the set, Chris was truly like a son to me. Shelley Winters, who played my mother, is also gone. I remember telling Shelley that she was too young to be my mother in *The Pickle*.

"Danny, I want this role," she said. "Please, don't say anything to Paul." It's probably the first time that an actress wanted to play older than she actually was.

Whenever I have the opportunity to see *The Pickle*, I am always reminded that there are not many of my films that I enjoy as much. But it's an enjoyment that's tinged with sadness, since I also recall all the great people who are gone.

Chapter Twenty-One

Ready to Wear

The French director Luc Besson is well-known, but back when I first met him, I hadn't seen his action film *La Femme Nikita*, which was being remade in America as *Point of No Return*, starring Bridget Fonda. I connected up with Luc because he had an interesting project to propose, a movie that eventually came to be called *Léon: The Professional*. I had already taken a look at the script and realized that there was something missing.

Whenever I read a screenplay, I always look for the ways in which my character contributes to pushing the dramatic action forward. Whatever role I play, the character has to be somehow involved in turns of the plot. That sounds obvious, but you'd be surprised how many parts are written where the character resembles an inert piece of furniture.

"If you want me to do the film," I told him, "my character would need to have a little larger presence than what's there now."

Like I said, I wasn't really familiar with Luc Besson's work. Only later did I find out what an important director he was. Luc promised to rework the script and I agreed to do the movie. But our agreement coincided with probably one of the oddest things that ever happened in a filmmaker's meeting.

Luc and I were sitting in an outdoor café at Fifty-Ninth Street and Columbus Circle when a man I had never seen before approached me.

"Hey, Danny," he said, lacing his words with a dose of attitude. "I just saw one of your fucking movies and just about everyone in the theater walked out." He had a *What are you going to do about it?* expression on his face.

"Why don't you take a walk?" I replied.

But it didn't stop there. He proceeded to needle me at the top of his lungs, as though he were just begging me to kick his ass. So I got up, walked toward him, and raised my arm as if to take a swing at him. I didn't even come close to connecting, but he must have thought it was real, because he went down like a sack of shit, then got up and ran off. The whole incident was witnessed by everyone present at the café. Some people were laughing, while others looked alarmed.

I returned to the table, wondering what the hell the incident had been all about. Maybe it wasn't the best kind of thing that could happen at a meeting with a director who was about to offer me a film. Then again, the part I eventually played, Tony, was a heavy, so it could also have been the finest sort of audition I could have possibly given.

"Danny, look!" Luc said. He pointed to a building across the street.

In a window on the second floor, I saw a video camera poking out. We figured it had to be the trash talker's accomplice. They had likely been trying to set me up for a lawsuit, knowing that I frequented this café and lying in wait for me. If I really had hit the guy, if I had given him all I had, he probably would have ended up owning my house.

Unlike a lot of American directors who leave the actual shooting to their camera operators (union rules sometimes require this), Luc Besson loved to shoot film himself. He treated the camera as a great big toy, and he had a kidlike smile on his face whenever he was shooting. Behind the camera, he would goof on me every so often while I was in character.

"Danny, give me a smile! Danny, get mad!" Of course, this totally threw off my concentration, and I would want to murder the guy, but Luc was too playful for me to get truly angry.

Besson had discovered some great talent on *Léon: The Professional*. Natalie Portman was all of twelve when we worked together. The camera already loved her. She reminded me of another Natalie, one of my all-time favorites, Natalie Wood. Her mother and father came with her on set, and she resembled her mother to an uncanny degree. You could see the grown-up woman just by looking at her mom.

"Stay just as nice as you are," I told Natalie. "Because this business can make a wreck out of you." From all the evidence, Natalie Portman is one young actor who has remained a genuinely sweet person throughout her years of stardom.

Besson and my costar Jean Reno were great food friends, always dining together, indulging in long, multihour meals in the European style. In Paris, our restaurant of choice was the Italian classic Bice. In New York, we went to the Supreme Macaroni Co. at Ninth Avenue and Thirty-Ninth Street, where you walked through a grocery to get to a restaurant behind. A scene in *Léon* is set in this now-closed eatery, the kind of great place that always seems to vanish from the city, leaving behind only nostalgia for what is lost.

I learned a good lesson about working with foreign film companies on *Léon*. Hollywood is infamous for withholding negotiated payments on so-called back-end percentages, monies paid to actors as a cut of the box office. With foreign film companies, it's different. *Léon* played for twenty-four hours a day in one theater on the Champs-Élyseés in Paris. In a single month after its opening, I got a $25,000 check for my back-end fee. I'm still waiting for my back end on some Hollywood films that were released years ago.

In the mid-1990s, both Robert Altman and I were riding high. My Oscar nomination ensured that a lot of job offers were coming my way. Altman was just coming off directing *The Player*. The movie was a poison-pen letter to Hollywood that starred Tim Robbins. *The Player* sold a lot of tickets. Bob had his first success after a series of duds.

When word got around that Altman was casting for a film about the French fashion industry, A-list actors started banging down his door. He conceived of the project as a *Nashville*-style ensemble piece. The cast would be bursting with big names.

Everyone wanted in. Altman titled the movie *Prêt-à-Porter*, which is how the French refer to ready-to-wear fashion lines, as opposed to custom-made clothes. In America, the title would be *Ready to Wear*.

I was elated when Altman called me. He wanted me for the part of an American fashion buyer, he said. My character would be a fish out of water among all the snooty Parisians. Then Bob dropped a bomb.

"He's a cross-dresser," Altman said. "I want to put you in a nice Chanel gown."

"No way," I said immediately. Me, a cross-dresser? That was so far from my personality that Bob might as well have been asking me to play a Martian.

I'd seen everything in the world on the streets of New York City. I wasn't exactly a babe in the woods. At Toy Top, the after-hours club that I used to manage in the Village, drag queens came by all the time. But I just couldn't picture myself running around wearing a frock and high heels.

"Come on," he said. "Get in touch with your inner woman."

"I don't have an inner woman!" I told him. "I'm all man."

Altman didn't give up. He kept calling, wheedling and begging and telling me how great I would be in the part.

Bob Altman had a highly personal style of directing. He threw a lot of shit at the wall and if it stuck, it stuck. In Bob's world, following a script word-for-word was for wimps. Scenes changed drastically during shooting all the time. It was off-the-cuff movie-making on a multimillion-dollar budget. Get everyone in costume and in character, aim a camera at them, and see what develops.

Did I want to sign on to a Robert Altman film? Did I want to squeeze my six-foot-three frame into a dress? I finally decided that I did. Working with Bob was just too great an opportunity to pass up. In spring 1995 I said good-bye to Sandy and reported to Paris for a ten-week shoot.

I entered into a movie-set minefield. My character, Major Hamilton, was supposed to be a boorish American, a buyer for the Marshall Field's department store in Chicago. He stood out among all the sophisticated fashion designers. Major Hamilton charged around like the bull in the china closet, always butting into people's conversations, saying the wrong thing, behaving in an awkward manner. It didn't take long for my fellow cast members to respond to me as if I really were the boorish Major Hamilton.

The number of world-class names on the set was phenomenal: Sophia Loren, Marcello Mastroianni, Anouk Aimée, Jean-Pierre Cassel, Julia Roberts, Tim Robbins, Lauren Bacall, Kim Basinger, Linda Hunt, and Harry Belafonte.

The cast separated along battle lines. The Americans were in the minority. Altman had stacked the deck with European actors. Brits like Tracey Ullman, Rupert Everett, and Stephen Rea hung out together. Sophia Loren and Marcello Mastroianni were old friends who had costarred in more than a dozen movies over the years. They were pros who treated me with warmth and respect, but many times the only friendly face I saw was Teri Garr, who played the wife of my character.

Julia Roberts and Tim Robbins were closeted away elsewhere. They were working differently and we never saw them. Most of the fashion models in the cast were acting in their first movie. They reminded me of skittish gazelles. They were beautiful and I guess they liked me well enough, but I remained on my best behavior.

From the start, Altman had the harried look of a man who had bitten off more than he could chew. Barbara Shulgasser, the journalist who had cowritten the screenplay with Altman, often stayed by my side, I think because she saw me as an island of normalcy in a sea of divas. I didn't know it at the time, but she was picking my brain for the *Vanity Fair* article that she would eventually write about the experience of doing the movie.

The screenplay that she and Altman wrote was a mystery. We didn't operate with a normal shooting script. We didn't even have pages. I wasn't rehearsing lines, because I didn't know what my lines were or if they even existed. There wasn't a script. There were "situations."

We shot the American contingent's arrival at Charles de Gaulle Airport in Paris. While Kim Basinger and Linda Hunt improvised their lines as they waited for their luggage, I interrupted them with inane questions.

I despise rude people. The character I was playing represented everything I hate about a person. It wasn't me. You would think that professional actors would be experienced enough to separate the actor from the role. But some of my fellow actors interpreted Major Hamilton as Danny Aiello. I guess circumstances made it easier for them to get confused, because I'm an Italian-American, I'm a big guy, and I'm physical. In their minds, that meant I had to be rude.

A few weeks into the shoot, at the end of March, things came to a head. We were filming at a gorgeous château outside Paris. In the scene, my character and most of the other cast members are in the audience to watch a runway show.

When I rehearse, I go off by myself. I don't bother anyone. That morning while we all waited, remaining in character, I sat off to the side mumbling the improvised lines I planned to say. I tried them one way, then shifted the emphasis, changed the wording slightly, and tried them again.

"Why don't you shut up!" Lauren Bacall called over to me.

I was stunned. I hadn't been speaking that loudly. I felt hurt and humiliated in front of all my fellow actors. Suddenly I was back on the street in the Bronx, reacting without thinking.

"Go fuck yourself," I answered, quickly and with passion. "Who in the fuck do you think you are?"

Well, she was Lauren Bacall, that's who she was. Bogart's babe. The queen diva on the set. The European actors on *Prêt-à-Porter* all buzzed around her as if they were bees and Bacall's ass were honey. Meanwhile, she had come at me out of nowhere. She was lucky that I hadn't ripped her fucking head off.

Rupert Everett moved between Bacall and me as if he were heroically preventing an attack on her.

A brief face-off on a film set, the most natural occurrence in the world. But there was a repercussion. I did a scene only a few hours later with Rupert Everett and the other cast members. Sophia Loren, playing Isabella, was supposed to make an entry and collapse upon seeing her long-lost husband, played by Marcello Mastroianni.

Sophia fell to the floor in a classic movie faint. The rest of us gathered around her in character. We played the scene again and again, improvising our reactions.

"How about if I offer to give her mouth-to-mouth resuscitation?" I asked Altman. "Something like, 'Stand back, I'm going to perform mouth-to-mouth!'"

"That would only make her sicker," Everett said. I knew his comment arose from our dustup earlier in the day.

Bob ignored Rupert's comment and agreed to my suggestion. When we did a take of the fainting scene, I was just about to say my improvised line when suddenly Rupert Everett said it before me. He took the mouth-to-mouth line right out of my mouth.

I couldn't believe it. After Altman called out, "Cut!" I confronted Everett.

"Do that again and I'll break your fucking head," I said to him.

"Don't look at me with those Mafia eyes," he said.

"I'm not Italian, I'm Jewish," I said. "And this Jewish guy is gonna kick your fucking ass." In a sense, this was true. I was in character. Major Hamilton was Jewish. Therefore at the moment I was Jewish.

Rupert Everett and I didn't have a chance to come to blows, because Stephen Rea stepped between us. I was so steamed that I lashed out at Rea, too.

"Why don't you go bomb a supermarket with the fucking IRA?" I said. He let go of me immediately.

"I'm gonna see you downstairs later," I told Rupert Everett.

I never got the chance to follow up. Rupert Everett split the scene. He totally disappeared from the set for a full two weeks.

After all that, I felt terrible. I went back to the hotel room, packed my bags, and called Sandy.

"I'm coming home," I said. I told her about what had happened with Bacall.

I didn't care so much that I had almost punched Rupert Everett's lights out or called Stephen Rea a terrorist. But I was miserable over what I had said to Bacall. I thought I knew her. I had met her son Sam Robards, who was also acting in *Prêt-à-Porter*.

I always liked Sam. He was such a great kid. But if he had stepped forward and socked me for what I had said to his mother, I would have accepted the blow as a proper response to my behavior.

I have a salty vocabulary, but if there is a woman present and I happen to use bad language, I seriously apologize. It was how I was raised. Now I had publicly told Betty Bacall to go fuck herself. I had gone right back to the street.

On the phone from the States, Sandy tried to soothe me. She told me that it would be all right, that I shouldn't leave the movie.

I ran my mind over what I might have done to Bacall to warrant her calling me out the way she did. I had first met her many years before doing *Prêt-à-Porter*, when I was starring in a play called *Light Up the Sky* at the John Drew Theater in East Hampton. Phyllis Newman acted as my character's wife in the show. Lauren Bacall was friendly with Phyllis, so I saw the two of them fairly often.

Nothing could be more charming and genteel than East Hampton in the summertime. I was living out there during *Light Up the Sky*. Lauren had a house in the neighborhood, as did Phyllis. Phyllis Newman was a wonderful person, and Bacall had been friendly and open with me.

I encountered her again in New York City after the pleasant times we spent in the Hamptons. She was in town doing a Broadway show, *Woman of the Year*.

"How's Harry Guardino?" I asked.

In the newspaper gossip columns and in casual conversation among my friends, the actor Harry Guardino had been romantically linked with Bacall. I knew Harry from working with him on a road-company production of a play called *Breaking Legs*. Thinking we had Harry as a friend in common, I asked Bacall the question and got what I thought was a rude reply.

"You mean the goombah?" she said.

Not a very polite thing to say to an Italian-American, sort of a derogatory thing, in fact, but I let it pass as a joke.

"I'm sorry," I said. "I thought you two were an item."

"He likes to think so," Bacall responded.

I thought about the exchange while nursing my wounded feelings over the *Prêt-à-Porter* incident. Did Bacall carry some grudge against me from way back when, for bringing up her relationship with Harry Guardino? Of course the two of them were going out. Word of it was all over town. They were in *Woman of the Year* together.

Later on, in her *Vanity Fair* article, Barbara Shulgasser quoted Bacall referring to me as "macho." "I know those Italian guys," Bacall said. "I've been through that war." She was referring to her time with Harry Guardino. It must have represented a sore subject with her, an old injury now made fresh. The memory came back to me when I mulled over her high-handed behavior toward me on the set of *Prêt-à-Porter*.

The Concorde back to New York was fully booked. I couldn't get a flight home. I remained marooned in the hotel. In the middle of my misery, Kim Basinger called me.

"We all like what you did," she said, speaking about Bacall. "She acts so high and mighty to everyone. She was trying to set you up, Danny."

Joe Amiel has been a close friend of mine for over forty years, a restaurateur who owned Symphony Café in New York City and the Old Mill Inn in Spring Lake Heights, New Jersey, and now operates Sallee Tee's in Monmouth Beach. Joe heard from Sandy that I was thinking of leaving Paris and coming home. Soon after Kim's call, the phone rang again in my Paris hotel room. I heard the welcome sound of Joe Amiel's voice.

"Don't leave," he said. "I'm on my way over to keep you company."

The calls from Kim and Joe helped clear my head. Soon enough, gifts started to pour in from other cast members. With champagne, flowers, and chocolates, everyone congratulated me for what I did. And here I thought I was hated.

Marcello Mastroianni tut-tutted sympathetically. "Danny, you must be a paci-feest," he said. "No telling people to please go fuck themselves. Be a paci-feest."

"Fuck that," I said. "I'm no fucking pacifist." Marcello just laughed.

Having Joe Amiel by my side made remaining in Paris palatable. He might have been a lifesaver for me, but he sure had a hell of a time himself when he flew over to serve as my wingman. His lifetime dream had been to meet Marcello Mastroianni, and he wound up having dinner with the man.

Joe laughed his ass off when he witnessed me try to walk around in high heels, stuffed into a bogus Chanel suit with a falsie-filled bra. I wore a wig that made me look like an unpretty Barbra Streisand. Truth be told, I was the ugliest woman I ever saw.

Joe and I were good buddies having a good time hanging out together. At this point I got a call from Cher. She was in Paris and wanted to have dinner. Joe was supposed to take me out on the town that evening. I called him up.

"I've got good news and bad news," I said. "The good news is that Cher is in town and wants to come out with us. Is that okay with you?"

"Are you kidding?" Joe said. "Of course!"

"The bad news is that she'll have six people with her," I said. I wanted him to know, since he would be the one who was picking up the check.

We all rendezvoused at a famous rib joint, David's, pronounced, in the French style, "Daveed's." David greeted his fellow restaurateur Joe Amiel with particular enthusiasm, rubbing his shoulders, hugging him, and practically humping his thigh. The situation amused the whole group as we enjoyed the best ribs I have ever tasted.

Cher's crew were all songwriters who met up every year at a sort of writers' retreat, to socialize and perform songs for one another that they had just composed. I was seated near an unassuming guy in the party who said he was a fan of mine.

"Would I know you?" I asked him.

"Well, I wrote some songs," he said.

I asked him if any of them had been recorded. His name was Jeff Silber, and he mentioned a little number called "The Wind Beneath My Wings."

I practically fell off my chair. "That is one of my all-time favorites!" I said. "I sing it all the time." Whenever I did, I always had my two favorite ladies in mind, my mother and my wife.

Cher offered to pick up the tab for dinner, but Joe insisted on paying for the whole group. Afterward, she invited us along to a party. Johnny Depp showed up. Cher danced like a madwoman. All told, my friend Joe had a great time. He should have, because the grand total for this night of fun and fame came to $2,000.

"Joe," I said as Amiel shelled out for it, "you're being punished, you prick, for the way you laughed at me when I was wearing my Chanel."

There's nothing like a night out in Paris, hanging with Cher and Johnny and Joe, to put other matters into perspective. Joe Amiel's presence and the positive phone call from Kim Basinger kept me from leaving France and going back home. When I returned to the *Prêt-à-Porter* set, tempers had cooled.

I was surprised to be treated as something of a hero for telling off Bacall. Several models in the cast told me tales of her behavior in the screening room. A former model herself, Lauren would criticize the performances of models who had never acted before.

I finally decided that the whole incident was for the best. It was good to have the tension out in the open. Now at least we knew that we hated each other's guts. Since catty infighting was the nature of the French fashion world, it all made sense.

A few years later I was sitting in Columbus Café with Sean Penn. We were catching up with each other over a bite. I hadn't seen him since we were doing *Hurlyburly* together in L.A. He had starred in the movie version. I hadn't been invited to reprise my stage role in the film as the frantic addict Phil.

I didn't think getting shut out from the movie of *Hurlyburly* was all that surprising. These things happen in Hollywood. I had won the Los Angeles Drama Critics Circle Award for best lead performance in the stage play. But that kind of thing evidently didn't carry much weight in the suites of studio execs.

That afternoon at Columbus Café, I got the sense that Sean was uncomfortable talking about why I hadn't been asked to be in the movie version.

"That's okay," I said. "I saw the film."

Nuff said. Just my little dig at how the movie version came out. It had bombed.

Sean laughed knowingly. He searched for something that he could come back at me with.

"Hey," he said. "A friend of yours from L.A. told me to say hello."

"Who?"

"Rupert Everett."

Now it was my turn to give a knowing laugh.

"He did a book," Sean said. "He wrote that you tried to kill him."

Not quite. If I had ever actually raised my hand to the guy, he probably would have fainted. Rupert used hurtful words to insult people and expected never to have to pay the price for those words.

He came close to paying the price with me. He chose a two-week vanishing act instead. I never read his book. I doubt if he'll read mine. But I've been told how he described what took place that day, including the part played by Her Majesty, Lauren Bacall. Everett didn't actually state that I wanted to kill him, but rather that I looked as if I would head-butt him.

Rupert has his version and I have mine. Let's leave it at that.

Chapter Twenty-Two

Dizzy Gillespie's Horn

In 1994 the actress Christine Lahti brought a project to me, a short film called *Lieberman in Love*. She would direct and play the female lead.

"It'll be great," Christine told me in a phone call, trying to entice me to join the cast. "We're going to take it around to all the festivals to try to qualify for the Academy Awards."

That sounded to me like a pipe dream, since it was a television production for Showtime, and the Oscars didn't deal with TV. But I signed on because the script was cute and the shoot would be quick. The final product would be only thirty-nine minutes long.

Christine plays Shaleen, a hooker on the prowl for customers. I play the title character, Joe Lieberman, who has just lost his wife and is at a resort, feeling lonely and looking for companionship. Shaleen's kind of companionship costs money, but Lieberman is agreeable. The two of them embark on a relationship that goes much deeper than the usual prostitute-and-john quickie. They fall in love.

One of the scenes in the short had Christine and me making love in bed, stark naked. It was shot to appear as if we were, anyway, but we were actually pretty well covered. While directing the scene, Lahti jokingly cautioned me.

"Don't get too excited," she said. "You're a married man."

"How can I get excited?" I said. "You remind me of my sister Rosebud!" All we did was laugh our asses off while shooting the entire love scene.

The shoot for *Lieberman* was short and sweet. I moved on. I didn't think too much about it afterward. Christine never called me to say her little movie had been nominated for an Academy Award in the live-action short category. So it was something of a shock when I sat at home watching the Oscars in 1996 and saw my face filling the TV screen. The award was announced and *Lieberman* won.

Throughout the 1990s, I saw myself cast again and again in roles that required me to act in love scenes with some of the world's most alluring actresses. I think Hollywood might have lost its collective mind in this respect. One or two love scenes featuring Danny Aiello, that I could understand. But they kept on happening. I had romantic scenes with Melanie Griffith, Anne Archer, Dyan Cannon, Angelina Jolie, Cathy Moriarty, Sherilyn Fenn, and Cher, to name a few.

As I indicated about my scenes with Clotilde Courau, one of

the lovely young actresses with whom I was paired in *The Pickle*, I have a very strong, very negative reaction to men my age making love to young women in movies. Strong and negative, as in "getting sick and leaving the theater." I probably could find legions of people who feel exactly as I do.

Soon after *Lieberman*, in 1995, Fernando Trueba directed me in *Two Much*, a movie that also starred Antonio Banderas and Melanie Griffith. This was the film where Antonio and Melanie fell in love.

We were shooting a scene where Melanie's character is supposed to get married to Antonio's character. In response to the priest's "speak now or forever hold your peace" question, Melanie's character has second thoughts. She decides she does not want to go through with the marriage. Instead, she walks over to me, hits me with her bridal bouquet, sits on my lap, and begins to kiss me.

Before the shoot began that day, Melanie told me she had a sore throat. We had to shoot and shoot, repeating the action more than a dozen times. "Forever hold your peace," hit me with the flowers, plop onto my lap, kiss. Over and over.

I told the director that I wanted to speak to him in my camper.

"Fernando," I said, "I just cannot kiss Melanie anymore!"

He asked me what the difficulty was. "Well, she has a sore throat," I said. "All I can think about is getting sick. Please, I can't do it anymore."

In his wonderful Spanish accent, Fernando responded with a line that sent us both into gales of laughter. "Imagine how she feels," he said.

We finished the scene.

But all this movie lovemaking caused problems at home with Stacey and Sandy. Not severe problems, more like joke problems. My wife and daughter refuse to go to a theater and watch any movie with a love scene involving myself. They don't want to be there with their friends while Daddy (or Hubby) is in a hot embrace up on-screen. Instead, the two of them torture me by renting my videos and forcing me to watch them at home.

They fast-forward the action, slow it down, fast-forward, slow it down. They make me watch it over and over again, scrutinizing each kiss numerous times. They both have to be satisfied that I never opened my mouth or seemed to be enjoying myself. The pair of them are like the moral guardians of the Aiello household.

Probably the most challenging movie in this respect was *Mojave Moon*, with a lovely twenty-year-old named Angelina Jolie playing one of my romantic interests. This was long before Angie became one of the superstars of the silver screen. I knew her only as her father's daughter, since actor Jon Voight and I had long been friends.

The script demanded that Angie come on to me in an aggressive, over-the-top manner. The first thing she does upon encountering me is greet me with a long, deep kiss. Then we repair to a hotel room. While we were filming, I felt a huge amount of embarrassment. All I could think about was that this beautiful young actress was my friend's daughter.

Angelina didn't care. She threw herself into the role. During film shoots there are always a lot of back-and-forth camera setups called reverses, where two characters exchange dialogue and the camera shoots back and forth, back and forth. At times the other actor in the scene isn't even present while I am shooting my half of the reverse, and I am forced to say my lines to the empty air. It is a great courtesy if actors make it a point to be there for the other character's reverses. When they are, I always think it makes the dialogue feel more realistic on the screen.

Angie and I had a scene in a hotel room where my character, Al McCord, sits on a bed and happens to get a glimpse of her character, Elie, nude after a bath. There was no reason in the world for Angie to be present when director Kevin Dowling shot me reacting to what I was seeing. In the usual course of filmmaking, the person I was supposed to be looking at in the scene would be elsewhere, perhaps relaxing in her trailer.

Angie sprang a surprise on me. She insisted to Kevin that I should respond to actually seeing her, and seeing her totally nude. She thought this would make it easier for the director to get a proper reaction shot.

No one told me and I had no idea that Angie was even on set that day. I looked up, expecting to see an empty room, and instead saw a fully nude Angelina Jolie. She had been only too right about my reaction. I choked, practically swallowing my own tongue, and then broke into laughter. We had to redo the reaction shot several times, and Angie stuck around for each take.

In the mid-nineties, my agent Richard Astor received a phone call from a casting director, asking about my availability for a film with Al Pacino. I was excited, to say the least. Even though we were both Bronx boys from the same neighborhood, we had never worked with each other before.

For a long time after that first query as to my availability, I heard nothing. There seemed to be total radio silence on the part of the production company behind the film, which was an insider take on New York City politics called *City Hall*. I did other projects, wondering what the hell was up with Al and his movie. I had to wait for it to come to me.

Eventually it did. Almost half a year later, I was called in to meet the director, Harold Becker. He had worked with Pacino before on a police potboiler called *Sea of Love*. Becker explained why the process of casting *City Hall* had taken so long.

"Well, Danny, to tell you the truth, Marlon Brando was our first choice to play the part," he told me.

The *City Hall* character of Frank Anselmo was written as an Italian-American Democratic district leader from Brooklyn who loved Broadway musicals. Becker confided that Brando had seen the role differently.

"He wanted to do it as a Mexican-American who loved singing, playing a banjo and/or a bongo," Becker told me, shaking his head in wonderment. "After lengthy discussions with Marlon, I decided that wasn't the way I wanted to go."

We both had a good laugh over Marlon Brando's late-career antics. Becker offered me the role and it didn't take me long to say yes. I didn't suggest anything about banjos or bongos. Becker called a production meeting for the following day.

Al was at the meeting with the other principal cast members: John Cusack, Martin Landau, and Bridget Fonda. Also present were a whole host of A-list screenwriters, including Bo Goldman, Ken Lipper, Nicholas Pileggi, and Paul Schrader. Pacino and I had never formally met. We spoke about the happenstance of our never working together, about our experiences in Pop Bennett's poolroom, name-checking Bronx locales such as Vyse Avenue, Southern Boulevard, and the Dover movie house on Boston Road.

We were of slightly different generations (he was seven years younger), but he and I knew some of the same people, and we made that the basis of our shared Bronx experience. Working together on this film with Al was as easy as sitting at home on a Sunday afternoon having an early dinner with my family.

While shooting a pivotal scene with me, the late Anthony Franciosa, playing a Mafia boss, kept forgetting his lines. This sometimes happens to all actors. The more Anthony forgot, the more embarrassed he became. There were dozens of extras on the set watching all this happen. The number of onlookers seemed to make it much more difficult for Anthony. He was a friend and a fellow New York native, and I felt for him.

Harold Becker took me aside and apologized. "I think I'm going to have to fire Anthony," he said.

"Don't do that!" I said, pleading for him to give Franciosa another chance.

Anthony finally turned in one of the best performances in the film. Later I came to believe that Becker never had any intention of firing him. He just wanted to make sure that I was all right and not getting frustrated doing the scene with Anthony. I would have waited if it had taken Tony twenty-four hours to get a take.

John Herzfeld, with whom I worked after my great experience on *City Hall*, is probably among the most underrated directors in movies. We did several projects together, and John became my close friend.

We first met when we both received daytime Emmy awards in

1981, he for a TV movie titled *Stoned*, me for the blended-family drama *A Family of Strangers*. For some reason we connected right away. We did a television movie together with Patricia Arquette called *Daddy*, and another one on the Robert Chambers case called *The Preppie Murder*.

There's a quality that sets John apart from other directors, some of whom might be more well-known than him. He would rather do nothing than do shit. Every movie he gets involved in is done on his terms or he simply won't do it. This is an attitude that studios usually afford only the most famous directors.

John is uncompromising in his choice of movies. He is a very selective director. He will not and cannot work just for money. He has got to love the specific project. For the most part, he also has to write it himself. John's belief in his idiosyncratic personal vision has attracted A-list stars to his films.

Check out his movies and you will see the amazing line-up of talent he has managed to cast in each one of them. At times he works with tight budgets and is able to offer only very little money. But the stars work with him anyway. Not too many directors enjoy the luxury of not having to pay seven- or eight-figure salaries.

John was a demon in his control over the soundtracks for his films. The music is always his baby, and the results are spectacular. More than that, John has an unerring eye for fresh, undiscovered talent. On 1989's *The Preppie Murder*, for example, he used a young artist by the name of Chris Isaak. John had discovered him, and Chris's song "Wicked Game" on the *Preppie Murder* soundtrack was a hit. Herzfeld's track record in this respect is amazing.

In the present case, John wanted me to play a hit man named Dosmo Pizzo in a black comedy called *2 Days in the Valley*. A lot of people compare this film to *Pulp Fiction*, but I think it's even better, or at least funnier. Once again, John was able to put together a typical stellar cast, including James Spader, Charlize Theron, Eric Stoltz, Jeff Daniels, Teri Hatcher, Marsha Mason, and Glenne Headly.

Also in the cast was my old friend from *The Pickle*, Paul Mazursky. In *2 Days*, Paul was playing his own version of *The Pickle*'s Harry Stone, a formerly famous director on his way out. He was wonderful in the role of Teddy Peppers. I did the character in Paul's movie, and he did the same character in John's film.

The beautiful Charlize Theron and I shared some scenes together, and we developed a sort of game comparing the softness of each other's lips. Every day before a shoot we'd try out the game. We did it as a joke, and it worked to keep us both relaxed.

My character was a very odd sort of hit man. He sported a toupee that was always giving him trouble. During the shoot, I wore a prosthetic pate to make me appear bald on top. One day it was so hot that the pate began shrinking. It almost gave me a face-lift. I felt my eyebrows forced up, inch by inch, toward my hairline. By the end of the scene I looked like a surprised nineteen-year-old. After my experience doing the film, I had to go around assuring reporters that my hair was my own and that I had no need personally to wear a rug.

Glenne Headly and I used to break each other up all the time during the *2 Days in the Valley* shoot. Doing publicity afterward on CNN, Glenne did a very funny take on my habit of always apologizing after cursing in front of women. She explained to the interviewer that she had been present when John Herzfeld had asked me to shave my head for the role.

>   Glenne (doing John): Danny, please, if you could just shave this part up here. [Tapping the top of my head]
>   Glenne (doing me): Give me a fucking break! [Pretending to apologize] Sweetheart, I'm sorry. You forgive me? I didn't mean to curse in front of you. [Back on me ranting] Are you fucking serious? Why the fuck would I want to shave my head? [Apologizing again] I'm sorry, honey. [Ranting again] Are you fucking nuts?

Glenne is one of the funniest women I have ever met. She used to make me hysterical whenever we went out to dinner during the shoot. I reminded John of our chemistry together recently.

"We scored so big on *2 Days in the Valley,* Glenne and I," I told Herzfeld. "Why don't you do a movie with us together as stars?"

John had other plans for me, and more on that later. But I still think a project pairing Glenne Headly and Danny Aiello would be a great idea.

A lot of my preparation work is done in my car. That practice began back when Madonna previewed her *Like a Prayer* album for me in her garage in Malibu.

Driving from my home in New Jersey five hours north to Toronto for a shoot on a CBS television miniseries called *The Last Don,* I was unsure how I would proceed with the character. I was under the gun. We would begin shooting in two days, and I still had not found the key to portraying the title character, Domenico Clericuzio.

It was a difficult task. In the sprawling tale, Clericuzio transforms from being relatively young to being very old. I had no idea how I was going to play an eighty-five-year-old man. Should I change my voice? Should I use prosthetics? Desperate and out of ideas, I had the panicked thought of asking the producers to hire an older version of me as a double.

Dizzy Gillespie was playing on the car radio. Inspiration can strike from any direction. Dizzy's music was like a sign from heaven. Listening to him in my car with the Adirondack Mountains flashing by next to the highway, I recalled an interview I had heard with the great jazz trumpeter many years earlier.

The interviewer asked Dizzy why he played with his famous bent horn, which has an end that crooks upward.

"It sounds better," Dizzy responded. "It's vintage, and it's bent. I busted one many years ago, and I dug how it sounded. It's like now it has lived a life. It has something to say."

Bingo! I thought. Still driving in the car, I stiffened my back and bent my body just like Dizzy's horn. When I spoke in this posture, I realized my voice sounded different, tired, old, and more interesting. I spent the rest of the trip to Toronto happy and energized. I had found the key that unlocked the Last Don's character.

Mario Puzo wrote *The Last Don,* and the series inevitably invites a contrast to the *Godfather* movies, which I think is comparing apples and oranges. They are entirely different animals. During my performance, I always reminded the director, Graeme Clifford, and my fellow cast members to stop me if I ever sounded as though

I were riffing on Marlon Brando's portrayal of Don Corleone. In the end, I think I successfully made Clericuzio my own.

I wanted the Last Don to be a man who was preparing his people for a better life outside of the rackets. Even in regard to my costume for the role, I sought to look like a legitimate businessman. Personally, in real life, I'm a hugger. But Don Clericuzio was not capable of that. I had to portray an educated Italian-American who was not very warm.

More than anything, I wanted to avoid the prejudiced movie clichés of Italian-Americans, who in films usually have an aspect of the coarse *ginzo* to them. I like to see characters with Italian heritage who don't *sound* Italian but *are* Italian. They are thoroughly assimilated Americans.

The producers made it possible for me to speak with Mario Puzo, who called me on the phone. I was beside myself. I had never met the author of one of the bestselling books of all time.

"Mario, if you don't mind, can I ask you a question?" I said. "It's the single thing that I'm most interested in finding out from you."

"What is that?" he asked.

"How the fuck do you pronounce these names?"

Puzo laughed. Beginning with Clericuzio itself, weird names are all over *The Last Don*. Pippi De Lena. Dita Tommey. Virginio Ballazzo. Boz Skannet. Bobby Bantz. Luckily, I had the man himself, Mario Puzo, telling me how to pronounce them all.

"Danny, you're going to be great," Mario said after he schooled me in pronunciation.

"You're not getting Brando," I told him.

"We don't need Brando," he said. "We need you and you're going to be great."

Chapter Twenty-Three

Dellaventura

The Last Don premiered to a fantastic response, becoming CBS's highest-rated miniseries. I got a lot of personal love from viewers, including what amounts to a fan letter from a gentleman whose name you might recognize. It was hand-delivered to me at Carnegie Hall during a CBS affiliates meeting, where the stations would be told of the upcoming season's schedule.

Although we have never met, the letter read, *I much appreciated watching you in most of the things you've done, beginning with* Once Upon a Time in America. *In any event, I saw all the episodes of* The Last Don *and I just thought that you gave an extraordinary performance and deserving of every bit of praise that comes your way. The make-up was a knockout. I wish I had enough sense to use prosthetics the way you did. Anyway done's done and gone's gone and my congratulations. It was wonderful watching you.*

The letter was signed, *Warmest regards, Marlon Brando.*

From one don to another. I'll never be as good as you were, Marlon. I feel sad that I never met the man. I think he and I would have liked each other.

When you have a success of the magnitude of *The Last Don*, the network's first thought will always be to repeat it, which CBS did with *The Last Don II*. That, too, got stratospheric numbers. I was essentially adopted by the network and by its long-serving president, Les Moonves. After the success of *The Last Don*, I think if I had suggested reading the phone book on national television they would have at least given me a pilot for it. It was nice to be wanted.

In 1997 I found myself in Los Angeles sitting around a conference table the size of an aircraft carrier with Moonves, some of the other network brass, and a few of my own representatives. I definitely felt out of my league. I did very little talking. Mostly I listened, mostly to Les. He was saying what he had planned for me in television. He wanted me to do a TV series.

Les Moonves is probably the greatest TV executive in the history of the medium. The proof is in the pudding. He's lasted longer than anyone else in a job that usually is a revolving door for one executive after another. He's guided the network through the most tumultuous years in media, witnessing the rise of cable and the dawn of the Internet. Under his leadership much of the time CBS has been on top.

I was flattered, of course, when Les told me about a possible TV series centered around me as the main character. I was somewhat apprehensive at the same time, given my longtime ambivalence about acting on television. But I didn't leave the room and I continued to listen. Les was very easy to listen to, and he knew the secret of all great communicators, which is the ability to make people believe you're listening to them. He looked at me when he spoke, which I've found to be a rare practice among people whenever I am in Los Angeles.

I decided that if I was going to be in television, then Les was my guy. I left that conference room with a warm, positive feeling. My agent and the producers I was working with later talked over the three properties that had been submitted to me that day.

I chose *Dellaventura*, a private-eye series. I liked the lead character, based on the real-life Anthony Dellaventura, a former cop who was now a private detective, one whose specialty was helping people when the law had let them down.

"I have one concern," I told Les. "I don't like to fly and I don't want to be away from my family. I want *Dellaventura* to be shot in New York."

Without hesitation, Les said yes. This is the kind of executive decision that takes guts. Almost all TV series nowadays are based in Los Angeles. Shooting in New York would cost CBS a bundle. But having the show in my city, on my turf, gave the whole thing a level of reality that I could never get on a fake "New York" block on some Hollywood back lot.

So we shot the exteriors on the familiar streets of the greatest city in the world. My favorite part of the show was a voice-over monologue that closed each episode, showing me walking the neighborhoods of New York. We filmed in real locations, real storefronts, real interiors. This was the best TV experience I could possibly imagine.

Dellaventura drew approximately nine million viewers every week and was nominated for a People's Choice Award for best new television series. But we were scheduled opposite shows that were drawing twenty million viewers.

Any series that hits nine million viewers in today's fragmented media landscape is guaranteed to run for another fifteen years. *Dellaventura* closed after sixteen episodes. Les tried to keep us going, but it just didn't work.

Bob Giraldi is probably one of the greatest director-producers of commercials ever, and he's expanded his career with films and music videos. He did some of Michael Jackson's most famous music videos, including "Beat It," and he was directing the infamous Pepsi commercial when Michael's hair caught on fire.

We met in 1978 when Bob gave me my first commercial, for Löwenbräu beer. The job made me and my family $25,000 and paid my rent for an entire year. I felt forever in debt to him. In later days, I did ads for Miller Lite beer and other commercials with Bob, and voice-overs as well.

Bob grew to love the restaurant scene in New York City, backing a couple of joints on his own and frequenting others with a connoisseur's eye. A good restaurant can be a kind of performance art. He became fascinated with the whole frantic experience of plating a hundred-plus dinners a night from a kitchen the size of a studio apartment. Out of Giraldi's fascination came a film project, *Dinner Rush*, that would be shot in his own restaurant, Gigino Trattoria, on Greenwich Street in Tribeca.

Bob would direct, and he wanted me to do the lead. He had a

terrific script and I knew he would be great at the helm. The budget was small, but because Bob was involved, I would have done the movie for nothing.

I played Louis Cropa, a restaurateur in business with his son, a chef who's a pain in the ass but a great cook. The Mafia is trying to take over the business, and the gangsters fail in their attempt. The film was probably one of the best in its genre, the restaurant film. The critics loved the movie, but it was released in September 2001 and of course disappeared amid the 9/11 tragedy. No one saw it.

A month before 9/11, right in the middle of publicizing the upcoming release of *Dinner Rush,* the office of Mayor Rudolph Giuliani contacted my agent John Planco of William Morris. The mayor wished to speak to me regarding a proposed movie studio to be built on Staten Island.

I was quite surprised. The only time Mayor Giuliani and I had anything to do with each other was when he presented me with a Crystal Apple Award in 1997. The award recognizes citizens who perform some service to the city. It cited my work in making sure *Dellaventura* would shoot in New York. That brought more than $2 million a week into the local economy, more than $30 million over the course of its run.

Now, in the fall of 2001, when Mayor Giuliani sought a working film actor to become involved in the movie studio project, he reached out to me. He simply wanted my advice during the process. I was an actor, and at times a producer, but was by no means an expert on what it took to create a movie studio.

We met at Giuliani's office in Gracie Mansion. I expected to see many Hollywood executives there, but not one was present. The mayor spelled out the scope of the project. If we could put all the pieces in place, he said, a massive studio would rise on thirty-nine acres of property at Staten Island's decommissioned Stapleton Navy Homeport. At the end of the presentation, Mayor Giuliani officially tasked me with going out to the site in order to see if such a studio was feasible.

Okay, I thought, *I can do this. I might not know exactly what I'm doing, but I'll do my due diligence and give him my opinion, for whatever it's worth.*

I went to the Stapleton site. I've long known that Staten Island is the poor relation among the five New York City boroughs. Of course, sometimes it's better to be ignored by government, but in this case, the neglect over the years has been criminal. Stapleton Studios represented a chance to give the Staten Island economy a gigantic boost.

I reported back to Giuliani that I thought the proposed studio would be second only to some of the long-established Hollywood facilities. The site was fantastic, with plenty of room for sound-stages, prop warehouses, and additional offices. I thought a studio hub such as Stapleton would be a shot in the arm for filmmaking in New York, which was rapidly losing ground to places like North Carolina and other right-to-work states.

The mayor received my favorable report and set up a meeting for investors. The property was actually owned by the city and only leased to the U.S. Navy. I agreed to become involved for purely altruistic reasons. A small voice was telling me that working with bureaucrats might be maddening, but a louder voice drowned it out, reminding me that I wanted to do a good deed.

In a huge building on the Stapleton site that formerly housed Arnie's Bagelicious Bakery, our group created a beautiful world-class soundstage. We had a film project, *Max and Grace*, scheduled as the facility's first production, and we had entered into negotiations with Paramount about using the studio for its big-budget feature *School of Rock*.

The tragedy of 9/11 intervened. In the wake of the terrorist attacks, all city projects such as Stapleton Studios were put on hold. In January 2002, the new administration under Michael Bloomberg came into office. From January on, our group had frequent meetings with the city's Economic Development Corporation (EDC), but it soon became apparent to me that the Bloomberg administration had no intention of allowing the studio to happen.

The team promoting Stapleton was dragged through the mud. We were made to look like gangsters, attempting to rip off the city of New York.

If the project had been allowed to proceed, Staten Island would be a thriving mecca of the film business right now. Stapleton Studios would have been a good thing for New York City and a great thing for Staten Island. Our projections showed that it would have provided approximately ten thousand jobs and been a revenue windfall for the city of New York. The citizens of the Stapleton neighborhood were overwhelmingly in favor of the project. Instead, Staten Island, the always-a-bridesmaid-never-a-bride borough, was left at the altar once again.

I felt as though I were reliving my part in the film *City Hall*. In the three years our group was involved, we asked Mayor Bloomberg to meet with us at the Stapleton property numerous times. We got together with officials of the Economic Development Corporation at their offices on William Street, only a short distance from City Hall, but the mayor did not once attend.

I attempted one last time to have a meeting at City Hall with the mayor. A date was set. He canceled. Why? He had a lunch date with the cast of *The Sopranos*. So much for Hollywood-on-the-Hudson. The Stapleton Studios project was declared officially dead.

My takeaway from the whole frustrating experience was that Michael Bloomberg never intended to move on something that was suggested by the previous administration. I can't understand this kind of attitude on the part of politicians. It didn't matter who first proposed it. It was good for New York City under Rudolph Giuliani, and it was good for it under Bloomberg.

Reluctantly, our group sued the city, with our attorney Dan Marotta representing us in New York Supreme Court. We lost the initial round, a development that was well covered in the media. But no journalist bothered to write about our appeal, which we won and which awarded our group a seven-figure settlement. Of course, this was nowhere near the amount of money that was spent in the three years we had been trying to turn Stapleton into a Hollywood-level studio.

The judge who ruled for us on the appeal, Emily Jane Goodman, issued a blistering statement on the case. "I don't know how the city can expect to do business with private parties if this is the way it acts," she said.

As the Stapleton mess was winding down, I lost a longtime friend whose passing had me reassessing my whole career. Louis LaRusso II died on February 22, 2003. At that point, we had known each other for more than three decades. Together, we had worked on a film and four plays, *Lamppost Reunion, Wheelbar-*

row Closers, Knockout, and, in 1999, a limited-run production of his drama *The December Song.*

It is difficult for me to fully grasp the impact Lou had on my life. If not for him, I don't know where I would have ended up—surely not on the Broadway stage. He and I hung out together often and never had a disagreement worth mentioning. How many of our friends can we say that about?

A few months after Lou's death, I was acting in a play called *Adult Entertainment* at the Variety Arts Theater on Third Avenue and Thirteenth Street in New York. I got a visit in my dressing room after the show one night from a young film director. Kevin Jordan had studied at NYU and was now aiming to make his second feature. His first, *Smiling Fish & Goat on Fire*, won a new director award at the Toronto International Film Festival.

Kevin asked if I would be interested in reading a script that he intended to shoot over the course of the next few months.

"It's called *Brooklyn Lobster*," he said.

"I hate seafood," I responded jokingly.

It turned out the Jordan family owned a lobster farm and restaurant in Sheepshead Bay, which was in the process of being taken away by the IRS. Naturally, on an independent movie such as this one, there was hardly any money involved. But his project was at least partially financed by Kevin's father, Bill, and he seemed like a nice enough kid. In his enthusiasm for his work, he brought to mind Lou LaRusso in a lot of ways.

I read the *Brooklyn Lobster* script and called Kevin at two o'clock in the morning. I can be very impulsive sometimes. When I want to do something, I have to do it immediately.

Kevin answered the phone. At first he refused to believe it was me.

"Yeah, Darren, sure, you're Danny Aiello," he said, thinking it was his brother Darren calling. Finally I persuaded him that I was Danny Aiello and I had decided to do his film.

I played Jane Curtin's husband in the movie, and the two of us had a great time with the project. During the shoot I fell in love with lobsters. Not to eat—never!—but just to play around with. I even kissed one on-screen. The lobster seemed to like it. I guess it was trying to tell me it held no hard feelings that I refused to eat it.

Brooklyn Lobster was released in 2005 to great reviews, many of which highlighted my performance in particular. *Variety* wrote that the film "comes across primarily as a showcase for Danny Aiello in a powerhouse performance as a Sheepshead Bay lobster wholesaler."

The kid who had first visited me in my *Adult Entertainment* dressing room turned out to be a very good director. Kevin's entire family and mine remain close: Bill, his father, whom I essentially played in the movie; his mother, Eileen; and his brothers, Michael, Darren, and Brian.

There was a little sting attached to *Brooklyn Lobster*. When I saw it in the theater, the first words that popped up on-screen were "Presented by Martin Scorsese."

Why would Marty, who never had any use for me, put his name on the movie? He didn't produce it, he didn't finance it, and I never once saw the man on set. It turned out that Kevin had connected with Scorsese through their shared alma mater, NYU. That explanation didn't help to take the sting away.

Well, I thought ruefully, *at last I am in a Martin Scorsese film.*

Chapter Twenty-Four

I Just Want to Hear the Words

When I began to have some success in movies and onstage, my mother never stopped encouraging me to pursue singing as a career. "Danny, you're a good actor," she said, "but I hear you sing all the time at home and I want you to be a singer."

It was silly, really, the shyness that kept me from letting everyone in my professional life, including my agents, know that I could sing. For a long time, the situation was just fine with me.

But around the turn of the millennium, I began to question my own behavior. My acting career had matured. I felt a need to step back and take stock. This wasn't a midlife crisis, more like a coming home to myself after years of denial. A question occurred to me: How much time have I wasted not doing something I would have really loved to do, if only I had the guts?

I thought back and realized that for my whole life I had been a singer. I sang as a kid with my friends on street corners and in backyards in my old neighborhood. I sang at family weddings and birthdays. I sang at the Improvisation, belting it out to the tables and chairs in an empty club. My first appearance on the screen, in *Bang the Drum Slowly*, showed me singing the national anthem. I had already notched a couple songs on the *Once Around* soundtrack album. Taken all together, that was farther than many singers get in their entire careers.

I also recalled that around the time I worked with Madonna on "Papa Don't Preach," I had a conversation with a major music executive. Seymour Stein headed up Sire Records, which was Madonna's label. Stein saw the video for my answer song, "Papa Wants the Best for You."

"You should do an album," he said.

My shyness about singing immediately kicked in. "Me?" I said. "What the hell kind of songs would I do?"

"Well, you should do an album of Italian music," Stein said. "You would be a natural."

Here was one of the most successful entrepreneurs in the music industry, with people lining up trying to get a word with him, and I turned him down flat.

"I don't do Italian songs," I said. That was the end of the conversation.

Twenty years later, I felt the same way about doing Italian songs but differently about singing. A friend of mine, Paul De-Angelo, is one of those highly energized, multitalented people who wear a lot of different hats: he was a producer, writer, director, actor, and entrepreneur. He was shooting a film of his in New

Jersey, *Destination Fame*, with my son Rick in a featured role. While visiting the set I met a friend of Paul's, Thomas E. van Dell, president of IN2N Recording Company (the name is pronounced "in tune").

Previously Tommy had been vice president at Motown Records, which was a division of Universal Music Group, one of the biggest record conglomerates in the world. Now he was out on his own with the IN2N label. He asked me the magical question.

"Are you signed musically to anyone?"

My first response was, "Not interested." I told Tom about Seymour Stein's disappointing pitch about my doing Italian music. I reminded him that throughout my years of doing Broadway shows, I had never once done a musical.

In response, Tommy said all the right things. He didn't mention doing Italian songs. "I saw you in *Hudson Hawk*," he recalled. "You sang a couple songs, 'Swinging on a Star' and 'Side by Side.' Then in *Once Around* you did three: 'Fly Me to the Moon,' 'Glory of Love,' and 'Mama.'"

I'll admit I was flattered that this music industry honcho had been following my movie career so closely. Tom was a pretty good bullshit artist. How else can you get to be a vice president of a big record company? Bullshit is a required part of the job.

"What songs would I sing?" I asked him, intrigued now.

"Think about the songs you remember hearing throughout your life," he said. "Write down about fifty of them, then out of those fifty choose fifteen that will be on your album."

He made it sound clear-cut and straightforward. I realized I was ready to take the leap. I signed with IN2N records under the tutelage of Tommy van Dell. My publicity agent was Tracey Miller, the rep for such acts as Michael McDonald, 3 Doors Down, Amy Winehouse, and Run-DMC.

Tracey's husband Joe Geary became my bandleader. Our group consisted of eight people and was called Joe Geary and the Guys. In 2003 we recorded our first album, *I Just Want to Hear the Words*. Released in April 2004, the record hit number four on *Billboard's* traditional jazz chart. I was stunned. Just ahead of me on the chart were Tony Bennett, Diana Krall, and Wynton Marsalis. Pretty good company.

We toured behind the album, mostly in New York venues—the Rainbow Room, the Blue Note, and the Apollo—as well as casinos in Connecticut and Niagara Falls. We hit Atlantic City, appearing at the Tropicana and the Sands Casino Hotel. One of the tour's highlights was an appearance with the Boston Pops Orchestra in Boston.

It was inevitable that I had to come down to earth. The *New York Times* shot me out of the sky. After I appeared at the Regency Hotel in New York City, the newspaper printed a negative review of the show.

"When Danny Aiello sings," the *Times* critic stated, "he likes to point . . . aggressively thrusting out his arm and pointing at various audience members as though delegating a posse or ticking off a hit list."

Hit list? I guess the critic got me mixed up with some Mafia guy of his own imagining. But I took the shot and kept on going. We headed to the West Coast, where we played House of Blues venues in both Los Angeles and Anaheim. The *Los Angeles Times* was kinder: "His voice is warm and amiable, his phrasing easygoing and conversational, his singing revealed influences from his numerous idols."

So I was launched as a singer, and it could not have happened without Paul DeAngelo, Tracey Miller, Joe Geary, and Tommy van Dell. I felt terrific. What was the song that kicked off my debut album? None other than "All of Me," the same number I choked on during my aborted *Arthur Godfrey's Talent Scouts* audition way back in 1946.

Somewhere up there, I knew Mom was smiling.

The 2000s were turning into my musical decade. But I didn't just sit behind a mike and sing. I was busy doing a lot of other things, too. I ran a comedy club in Hoboken, New Jersey, at the Tutta Pasta restaurant called Danny's Upstairs. I did a couple plays, some radio shows, and lots of voice-over work, and kept my hand in with movies, doing *Zeyda and the Hitman* in 2004, *Lucky Number Slevin* in 2006, and *Stiffs* in 2010.

My professional career took a forced detour at this time, when I almost died on the operating table during surgery. A close call like that can put a lot of things in perspective. I decided more than anything that I wanted to continue doing what I loved with music. I also wanted to spend as much time as I could with my children and my grandchildren. I have always been a homebody, happiest when I am with Sandy and my family.

In 2005, I appeared with Joe Geary and the band in Atlantic City at the famed Copa Room of the Sands Casino Hotel. This was the same stage where Frank Sinatra performed his final public U.S. concert in 1994, with me and Sandy watching from the audience. I felt the history of the place tingling in my bones when we recorded one of our shows at the Copa Room.

No one had a thought of releasing the recording of our set as a CD. It was just a way for me and the band to preserve a little history ourselves. But listening to it, we liked what we heard, and that live concert turned into my second CD release, 2008's *Live from Atlantic City*. I hoped it wasn't going to be an omen, but they demolished the Sands hotel immediately after we recorded there.

My Christmas Song for You became my third album in 2011. I worked with an ace keyboard man named Conal Fowkes, who with Joe Geary helped me choose the songs. Conal happens to be Woody Allen's piano player, and in all of Woody's recent movies Conal's exquisite keyboard work can be heard on the soundtracks. He sings, too, and provided the Cole Porter vocals in *Midnight in Paris*.

Conal specializes in a great dry brand of humor. He took the brunt of many of the jokes during the *Christmas Song* sessions. Mostly, we marveled at the shape of his home in Nyack, New York, where we did a lot of our rehearsals. Inside, it is as comfortable as it is beautiful. Outside, it looks as if it's about to slide into the Hudson River at any minute. If you saw *Popeye* with Robin Williams and remember the houses in the movie, you will know the style of rickety grandeur that I'm talking about.

"Get the place insulated in rubber, Conal," Joe Geary told him. "That way, when it collapses, your home will just bounce around a bit, and you and your wife will be safe."

When I could not think of a name for the album, Conal saved the day. He suggested we do an obscure Hoagy Carmichael tune called "My Christmas Song for You." It's a fine song and served as a great record title. For the cover, I used an oil painting by an artist named Jimmy Dellesio, depicting my home block on the West Side when I was growing up. Joe Spano contributed his art direction and graphic expertise on this album, as he did on the previous two.

I always imagined my grandchildren listening while I was working on the record. I included them on the project in a quite delightful way. I did "Pocketful of Miracles" with five of my children's children singing together on background vocals. Conal helped rehearse them and the results were sensational. There's a slight possibility that I am biased, but I believe my grandchildren are all very talented.

We recorded the album at "the Barber Shop" in Hopatcong, New Jersey, otherwise known as the Dream Makers recording studio. Located on the shore of beautiful Lake Hopatcong, the studio was owner-operator Scott Barber's home away from home, and it was one of the prettiest places that you would ever want to see.

It was a time I won't soon forget. I loved working there, with the whole team hanging out with Scott and his beautiful wife Tracey for lunches during sunny afternoons on the deck of the studio, watching boats float by. Scott and Tracey were so positive, so enthusiastic, that they contributed greatly to the success of the project. They've passed their energetic approach to music to their son, Ryan, who has taken over leadership of the Dream Makers team.

I had a problem deciding on the album's opener. I was thinking of narrating the poem " 'Twas the Night Before Christmas" (a.k.a. "A Visit from St. Nicholas"). But those verses had been done so many times that it felt a little stale.

"Why don't you come up with your own version?" Conal suggested. He had heard many tales about my West Side childhood and thought they would make a good holiday story. "Base it on the first Christmas you can remember as a child," he said.

It was many, many years ago that I was a child—probably too many, I thought. Would my first Christmas be impossible to recall?

I lost myself in memory, scribbling out lines. Tears welled in my eyes. It all came flooding back. My first Christmas, our family trying to put together a suitable celebration for the smaller children, me included. The basement apartment; the tree my sister stole, strung with shoestrings and bottle caps; the boxing gloves that were my first Christmas present: I relived it all like it was yesterday.

In a sense, the work I did on that album track, "Danny's Night Before Christmas," was the first step in writing this book. I realized that I had memories that I desperately did not want to lose. Good times, bad times, the whole parade of my life rolling past me like a grand spectacle. The Bronx and the army, the Big Grey Dog and the Improv, Broadway and Hollywood. I saw it all vanishing like a smoke ring floating up toward the ceiling. I resolved to get it down on paper before it was gone forever.

Soon after *My Christmas Song* was released, a singer-songwriter and close friend of mine named Charles Lallo told me he had written a song called "Home America." While sitting in my car in Hoboken, New Jersey, Charles played a demo of the tune. He knew I was getting ready to do another album. I didn't know if his song would fit. As a matter of fact, at that point in time I had no idea what my next album would be. I decided to do "Home America" as a single and see what would happen.

While recording the song at Chung King Studios, then on Varick Street in New York City, a young man approached me and said that he liked what I did in *Do the Right Thing*. I thanked him and was about to leave. He didn't seem to want to let me go, asking what I was up to at the studio.

"I'm actually recording a single," I said. "It's called 'Home America,' and it's sort of a patriotic song."

"Are you producing it?" the young man asked.

"No, I'm singing it," I said.

The young man told me his name was Damon Johnson, but the music industry knew him by another name, Hasan. I was impressed when he listed some of his credits. Working with Sony's Tommy Mottola and Cory Rooney, his brother-in-law, Hasan had produced some outstanding talent in the world of rhythm and blues and rap, including Jennifer Lopez, Marc Anthony, Mary J. Blige, and Mariah Carey. He was recording his own project at Chung King.

I played my single for him and he was actually blown away. He played me what he had just recorded, a rap track laid over a John Mayer song called "Waiting on the World to Change." The original did not have rap on it, but this was Hasan's remix, not for general release but for a charity benefit.

Hasan's track sounded great. We met again the next day in Hoboken. We sat together in my car. He had listened to my first album the night before. We talked about teaming up. I was hesitant because of my negative feelings about rap in general, but I decided to be at least open-minded to the idea.

For a trial run, Hasan selected one of the songs from *Live from Atlantic City*, "Bésame Mucho." We sat together in the car, listening to the rough track of what he had put together. He rapped over my song and the results weren't like anything I had ever heard before. Somehow, two ends of the musical spectrum came together and we wound up with some wonderful songs.

Hasan and I created an album called *Bridges*, released in 2012 and mixed and mastered by Jason Corsaro at Dream Makers Music. The title refers to bridging the gap between two genres, rap and standards. The album features several originals. Charles Lallo's "Home America" is on the record. Up-and-coming singer-songwriter Davido contributed "Running Every Red Light," while "City of Light" was written by Mare Maisano, a brilliant singer-songwriter.

We had a great group of people collaborating to make *Bridges*. Mark Eddinger, with his beloved wife, Lena, by his side, helped produce the album and arranged and played keyboards on the opening cut, "Save the Last Dance for Me." ASCAP's John Titta, also often accompanied by his wife, Lana, helped me understand the maze of music publishing. Vincent Favale, who was my CBS liaison on *Dellaventura* and is now one of David Letterman's producers, gave me his song "Talk to Me," which came from his play *Hereafter*.

Hasan and I went on to do live performances together. We also completed videos for three songs off the album, "Bésame Mucho," "Save the Last Dance," and "City of Light." The *Bridges* videos were created from my original concepts, produced by Jules Nasso, and directed by Frank Nasso, with my friend Paul DeAngelo deeply involved.

My project manager in making all three videos was Louie Baldonieri, who created, produced, and directed the platinum recording artists Dream Street in 2001. In addition to being a producer, Louie was a longtime tap teacher and hoofer. The magnificent choreography in all three videos and for Dream Street was done by his wife, Claudia Swan.

The music video of the *Bridges* cut "Bésame Mucho" has compiled over one million hits on the Internet, over five hundred thousand on YouTube alone. Hasan and I were the first artists ever to do classic standards remixed with rap.

My life during this period was centered on friends and family as much as on my career. In 1999, we had left Ramsey and moved to Saddle River, New Jersey. We loved our home in Ramsey, but it was a corner property. The yard was small in size and not large enough for a swimming pool, which as everyone knows is an asset if you are going to be entertaining grandchildren.

Our new home was a raised ranch of ten thousand square feet, set on two acres of land. Sandy has always loved to swim. I love water when drinking it or washing with it. Otherwise, not so much. Fish swim in it, and I've already made my feelings about those little fuckers clear enough. Besides, I can't swim to save my life.

What better way to see your grandchildren as often as you would like than by simply building a pool? We built one in our backyard in Saddle River, and it worked, at least during the summer. It failed us in the winter, since our pool wasn't big enough to hold an ice-skating rink. But with the seasonal holidays, Thanksgiving and Christmas, Sandy and I see the brood often throughout the year.

Right now we have ten wonderful grandchildren: Dawn, Allison, Brielle, Ricky Jr., Victoria, Sydney, Gabrielle, Zack, Jake, and Willie. I always have a simple bit of advice for my grandchildren, which actually holds true for everyone. If you decide to go into show business, I tell them, make sure you don't do it the way I did.

Rick continues his successful acting career. Jaime became one of the top headhunters in the profession, recruiting executives for financial companies. Stacey and her husband, Will, are busy running after my grandson Little Willie D.

Sandy and I share our home with the most beautiful little girl you've ever seen, Sofi Belle, our tiny Maltese. She weighs in at slightly less than four pounds and has dark eyes and hair the color of snow. She sleeps with me every night, always in the same spot: under my left arm, right near my heart. The whole time I was writing this book, she was sitting on my lap. Sofi remains in my arms no matter what's going on, even while I'm yelling and cheering while watching football.

Sandy presented me with Sofi Belle twelve years ago. My wife chose her because she was the runt of the litter and looked lonely. She has come to mean so much to me. My only regret is we didn't adopt her brother and sisters, because Sofi has lived her whole life without other animals around. She will not coexist with other dogs. She only barks at them.

As a matter of fact, she barks at everything and everyone. Her intention, of course, is to protect us. She never leaves our house, not because she doesn't want to, but because I've been told that there are coyotes in the area that feast on little pets. That's not going to happen to Sofi. I wouldn't know what to do if this little one wasn't in my life.

These years marked the passing of my sister Helen, my sister Gloria, and my brother Joseph. My sister Rosebud passed away from Alzheimer's disease in 2006. Rose's son, my nephew, the New York Yankees announcer Michael Kay, organizes an annual charity dinner that benefits the Alzheimer's Association, in memory of his mother.

In the mid-1990s I had partnered with a group called Heart-Share Human Services to create the Frances Aiello Day Habilitation Program, a treatment center in Brooklyn. This is a day-care place for adults with developmental disabilities, including those with mental retardation, cerebral palsy, epilepsy, autism spectrum disorders, and neurological impairments.

For a long time, I had a deep abiding desire, a feeling that occurred to me again and again. I wanted people to know my mother's name, that she had lived, that she had once laughed and loved and existed on this earth. I usually hate public tears, but when I think that the people at the Day Habilitation Program are being helped in my mother's name, well, it just breaks me up crying.

Chapter Twenty-Five

Danny, My Son, My Son

I can't conclude this book without a dedication to the memory of my son Daniel Aiello III, who passed away in 2010 and left a terrible hole in my life that I'm still struggling to fill.

I didn't see Danny as often as I would have liked after he made it big as one of Hollywood's premier stuntmen. When we did spend time with each other in the last few years of his life, he seemed troubled and was reluctant to talk. It was as though he just wanted to keep busy and not give himself time to think. I knew it had something to do with his relationship with his family, which wasn't the greatest.

In the early 1990s, I got a call from North Carolina, where Danny was working on the film *Ricochet*, starring Denzel Washington and John Lithgow. Danny was doubling Lithgow in a scene that required him to fight Denzel's stunt double on a two-hundred-fifty-foot tower.

Danny and the other stuntman were on the tower, preparing for the scene, and my son just couldn't do it.

"I froze, Dad," Danny said when he called me. "I've never felt so vulnerable, not since Lauren passed away." His infant daughter had died when she was two days old. Now further troubles at home were bearing down on him.

He was not living with his family at the time. Divorce proceedings had been going on for years. When he tried to make the situation easier, it only seemed to get worse. The difficulties at home, plus Danny III's feelings of guilt over the passing of his baby Lauren, became too much for him to bear. He found himself unable to do his job.

Film work can be relentless. Whenever a stunt person cannot perform a stunt, it's immediately assigned to someone else. If it ever became known that a stuntman froze up during a stunt, it could damage his whole career in the business.

I felt bad about that, but I was much more concerned about my son's health. I related to how he was feeling. I recalled when the pressure had become too much for me to take as a young man, when my anxieties put me in the hospital.

"Forget the stunt and come home," I said.

Charlie Picerni, his stunt coordinator on *Ricochet*, told Danny to take a few days off. My son rested, recuperated, and returned to the *Ricochet* set four days later. Normally by that time, the stunt would have been done by someone else. But Charlie had held it for Danny, who then completed the stunt. I will never forget what Charlie did for my kid.

Later that year, the divorce finally happened, but Danny III's relationship with his ex-wife never really recovered. Each of them got remarried. My son always thought his connection with his children could have been better. He felt that way until his passing.

In the summer of 2009, I was at our new home in Saddle River rehearsing a stage play called *Capone: The Musical*. Robert Mitchell was there with me, the author of the work that we were hoping to bring to Broadway. My son Rick walked in. "I have to talk to you, Dad," he said.

"Can I just finish the song?" I responded.

"I have to talk to you!" Rick repeated. Something about the urgency in his voice made me break off from what I was doing.

"Danny was just diagnosed with pancreatic cancer," Rick said.

I went numb. All I could think about was that the next thing I had to do was tell my wife. I just couldn't do it. My son went into the bedroom to talk to his mother. I heard Sandy scream from the next room, then her sobs.

Mechanically, I turned to Robert Mitchell. "I'm sorry," I said, "but we have to cancel the rehearsal."

Eleven months after my son's diagnosis, the whole Aiello family sat together in the living room of Danny's home in Hillsdale, New Jersey. I went into his bedroom, where he was resting. He seemed to be in terrible pain, but he was trying to say something. His strength almost gone, Danny extended his arms awkwardly toward me.

I got down on my knees beside his bed and placed myself close, my face touching his face, his arms holding me tightly. At that moment Sandy walked into the room, saw what was happening, and began to cry softly.

Danny whispered into my ear. The words were faint.

I looked up at my wife, my voice choking with emotion. "I think he said he loves me."

A few hours later he had passed. Afterward, the moment brought to mind that day in church when Danny was a little boy. He had passed out in my arms and I thought he had died.

Only this time, he really was gone.

How do you come back after something like that? I dedicated my Christmas album to the memory of my son. It was a paralyzing time for me and my family, and for the musicians working on the record with me as well. But somehow we got through it.

If you are in the midst of deep sorrow, then you probably shouldn't be singing a lot of holiday music. Christmas songs tend toward the sentimental, which leads to nostalgia, which in turn leads you into sadness for the loss of days gone past. At the end of that path lies bitterness, and I thought if I entered into that, I might not ever get out. For the sake of Danny III's wonderful life, I resolved to emphasize all the good times we had together.

I have the same feeling about my son as I have about my late mother. I want everyone to know him, to remember him, to realize he lived. The outpouring of support and remembrance from his colleagues in the film industry was incredible. Episodes of TV shows that he had worked on were dedicated to him. It all served to recall that Danny was well loved by all who knew him.

There's a simple line that I always remember from the bleak Irish playwright Samuel Beckett. "You must go on . . . I can't go on . . . I'll go on." Somehow the rhythm of those words marks my days and ways ever since I lost my son.

I can't go on. I'll go on.

Chapter Twenty-Six

Searching for Me (Reprise)

In the months after Danny III's passing, I embarked upon a desperate search for distractions, good ones, things that would keep me from going out of my mind. I felt as though I was in the grip of a paradox. I wanted not to dwell on my son's death, but somehow that made me think I was attempting to forget about his life.

I threw myself into a couple of theater projects because I thought they might distract me from my grief. We did a staged reading of *Capone: The Musical*, with me singing the lead. The whole time I felt the process to be a little unreal, as though I were sleepwalking through it. Nothing made sense to me. I wasn't myself.

In 2011, I partnered with a writer and producer named Susan Charlotte on her two-act play *The Shoemaker*. In July we opened for an off-Broadway run at the Acorn Theater in

New York City. We did twenty-seven performances and sold out every one. For a brief moment that summer, we were the hottest ticket in town.

During my appearances in *The Shoemaker*, I continued to have a sense of confusion and unreality. The play revolves around the aftermath of the 9/11 attacks, and a couple scenes required me to cry onstage. I recall asking myself whether I was really crying because I was in character or if the tears were over my own terrible loss.

In 2012, the director John Herzfeld called me at home. By that time we were going on forty years of friendship, and I think he felt for me. We reminisced about my son. John knew Danny almost as long as he had known me. My son had stunt-doubled me on John's film *The Preppie Murder*. He and I had many good memories to share.

Attempting to make me feel better, John gently tried to prod me out of my funk. "It's been two years," he said. He asked if I would do his next film, *Reach Me*.

But when he e-mailed me the script with the suggestion I play the role of a gangster, I turned him down. "John, I've done mobsters before, plenty of times. I'm just not interested in playing another tough guy."

I thought that would be the end of it. I had done the unimaginable and turned down a John Herzfeld movie.

John called me back. "Pick out any role you want, then," he said.

I thought about it for a moment. John's script *did* have a character that had struck a small spark in me. "Okay. The only part I'm interested in is the priest. But it's underwritten."

"I'll expand it," he said immediately.

"I want to play the kind of priest that has never been seen on the screen before," I said.

Working together, we came up with the character of Father Paul, an individual who put on the collar for all the wrong reasons. The role exactly fit my mood. I was dwelling on spiritual matters and asking myself the big questions.

As we shot the film I gradually felt myself returning to life. I recognized that I would never be the same person now and that I would carry grief with me wherever I went. But I didn't obsess over my son's death as much as I celebrated his life. Being with my old friend John, who knew Danny III well, helped in the process.

Musically, I began to push forward, too. I'm currently working on a blues album. Meanwhile, I keep on doing gigs, maybe a half dozen per year. Appearing in front of a crowd always gives me a shot of energy.

I can't go on. I'll go on.

So, yes, I'm working, acting onstage and in films, singing and doing albums. But I'm also thinking about my life. Those meditations led to the creation of this book. I've tried to come to terms with what my chosen profession really entails, what it really means to be an actor.

I understand that what I do onstage and on the screen has been around for a very long time. I'm just one guy at the end of a long line of performers, actors, comedians, minstrels, jesters, and stars. I've tried to do honor to a job I backed into almost by mistake, but one that raised my life to unthinkable heights.

I think about taking my place in the endless parade when I recall a story about the fine actor James Gandolfini.

I met him only a couple of times. The first was at the West Bank Café on West Forty-Second Street near Ninth Avenue. It was

September 2000, and the cast and crew of *The Sopranos* were cel-ebrating the debut season of the HBO series and the Emmy award given to Gandolfini as outstanding lead actor in a drama series.

I was at the party with my cousin Anthony, who acted under the name of Tony Ray Rossi and had appeared in "College," per-haps the most memorable episode of the series.

James Gandolfini came to our table. He put his two hands to-gether as if in prayer, bent at the waist, and said, "I honor you."

I was confused. I thought Jimmy might be putting me on. My cousin whispered in my ear: "That's just the way he is. He's a real sweetheart, a real nice guy." So I thanked Jimmy for his strange three-word tribute. He said, "You're welcome," and walked away.

Then it happened again, years later. Tony Darrow, a cast member from *The Sopranos*, holds an annual golf outing to benefit children with catastrophic diseases, and I make it a point to attend every year. As I sat in the clubhouse with my buddy Louie, I noticed James Gan-dolfini on the other side of the room. Once again he walked over to my table, placed his two hands together, bent at the waist, and said, "I honor you." This time he added, "I'm glad to see you here."

"Thank you," I replied.

"You're welcome," Jimmy said, and returned to his table.

Once again, I felt a little mystified. "Louie, is this guy putting me on? He told me the very same thing about twelve years ago at the West Bank Café."

When Jimmy passed away in June 2013, I began receiving phone queries from the media, asking if I would like to make a comment.

"I'm sorry, but I really didn't know him," I said to the reporters. "But everything I heard about him makes me wish I did."

I asked them not to print any of my remarks. I didn't want to be one of those people who claimed to be great friends of James Gandolfini, saying how their lives would never be the same because of his death, writing articles about their relationship.

Then, a day after his passing, I received a phone call from a *New York Post* reporter, who said that, many years ago, a fourteen-year-old boy had approached the stage after a Broadway show one evening, clearly starstruck. He spoke to one of the lead actors.

Apparently, the *Post* reporter had talked to a Broadway producer, who had told her about the youngster at the play.

"The producer was Joe Garafola, the play was *Lamppost Reunion,* the kid was James Gandolfini, and the actor he spoke with was you."

I was stunned and really didn't know how to answer that one. "Well . . . I always had a lot of people coming up to me after a show," I finally told the reporter. "That was a long time ago."

All those years, I had been wondering why Jimmy would approach me twice with the same message: *I honor you.* Now it might somehow make sense. Is it possible that I was the guy who helped inspire James Gandolfini to find his calling? I was humbled and prayed that it was true, because he turned out to be one hell of an actor.

I'll always link this story to being on the Broadway stage doing *Knockout.* That was when the doomed young actor Jimmy Hayden came to me. Like Gandolfini, that Jimmy is gone now, too. But taken together, the incidents remind me of the great tradition of actors down through the years, taking hope, encouragement, and inspiration from each other in what is, after all, an impossible profession.

I think of it as something like the Olympic torch. People like

Carmine Caridi and Vincent Gardenia passed it on to me, and maybe I passed it on to a fourteen-year-old kid. Reading about my struggles and triumphs in this book just might inspire some young actor-to-be, and the torch might be passed on once again.

Even outside the game of acting, in the game of life, we can help each other, motivate each other, serve as models for one another. That's one of the greatest things about being on the planet, the fact that we share in that long human process of encouragement and love.

About twenty-five years ago, I gave an interview to the *New York Times Magazine*. The story included a quote that dogged me for a long time afterward. "I want to be loved," I told the *Times* interviewer. "In fact, I want to be loved by the greatest number of people it is humanly possible to be loved by."

A lot of my friends laughed over that quote and used to tease me with it. But I stand by it even today. And you know what the great thing is? I'm still in the running to realize my goal.

If you ever encounter me on the stage, on the screen, or on the street, a little love would be nice.

Acknowledgments

I could not have completed this book without the help and support of a number of wonderful people, and I would like to express my gratitude for them here. The staff at Gallery Books guided me throughout the process, including Jennifer Bergstrom, Louise Burke, Jennifer Robinson, and Ed Schlesinger. My agent, Jennifer De Chiara, helped make this dream come true, and was always a sweet and positive presence. Gil Reavill helped me shape my words into a story and then helped make the story into a book. By my side every step of the way was Louie Baldonieri, the best friend and ally that anyone could have.

Also deserving thanks are the dear friends and associates who have lighted my way, lightened the load with laughter, or just shared the journey over the years, including Bill Alexander, Joe Amiel,

Linda Amiel, Pete Antico, Richard Astor, Joseph Avallone, Father Tom Baldonieri, Dominick Barbara, Scott Barbarino, Scott and Tracey Barber, J. J. Barry, Mikhail Baryshnikov, Jill Bauer, Richard Baum, Susan Benkel, Herb Benkel, Joe Berger, Nicky Blair, Herb Blodgett, Frank Bongiorno, Phil Carlo, Buddy Casano, Pamela Casano, Connie Casio, Dominick Casio, Frankie Casio, Joe Castellano, Chacha, Rebekah Chaney, Susan Charlotte, Rob Cioffi, Al Cohen, Madeline Cohen, Harold Cohen, Luigi Comandatore, Anthony Conforti, Mark Cooper, Alex Corrado, Jason Corsaro, Joe Cortese, Jimmy Cota, Vince Cupone, Charina D'Aiuto, Carol D'Angelo, Paul D'Angelo, Dennis D'Mico, Brendan "Spookie" Daly, Davido, Nilda Delarosa, Jimmy Delessio, Carlo DeRosa, Donna DeSeta, Bill DeSeta, Lou Digiaimo, Fortunato DiNatale, Alex Dinerlaris, everyone at DreamMakers Music, Mike Drescher, Mark Eddinger, Judith R. Ehrlich, Harry Ehrlich, Barrett Esposito, Larry Fallon, Laurie Fasinski, Vinnie Favale, Jules Feiler, Jerry Ferentinos, the staff at Five Napkins, including Eric and Nikki, Jerry Foley, Conal Fowkes, all the fine folks at the Friars Club, Mike Furno, George Gallo, Ray Garvey, Joe Geary, Frank Gigante, Bob Giraldi, Rudolph Giuliani, Lula Grant, Jerry Green, Danny Grimaldi, Ulu Grosbard, Bill Guarinello, Joe Guarinello, Mike Guccione, Jeff Hackworth, Dennis Hamill, Brian Hamill, Pete Hamill, Melody Hand, Ray Hand, Glenne Headley, Charlie Herman, Paul Herman, John Herzfeld, Larry Holmes, Chris Hower, Damond Hasan Johnson, Kathleen Johnson, Bill Jordan, Kevin Jordan, Pat Jude, Lou Katz, Drew Katz, Michael Kay, Jodi Kay, Jon Kilik, Peter King, Anna Kirshner, R.J Konner, Robert Koren, Deena Koren, John LaBarbera, Angelica LaBarbera, Michel La Barbiera, Vincent Labarbiera, Charles Lallo, Frank Langella, Don Lass, Elaine Legaro, Brian Leland,

Barbara Ligeti, Sam Linofski, Mark Lipsky, Mike Livingston, Tony Lo Bianco, Lucy Luckinbill, Gene Lutz, Vince Maggio, Debbie Maglio, Steve Maglio, Mare Maisano, Buddy Mantia, Marty Markinson, Dan Marotta, Melinda Martinez, Lisa Mateo, Peter Max, Paul Mazursky, Chris Mazzilli, Anne Meara, Tracey Miller, Barbara Miller, Robert Mitchell, Anthony Monte, Lisa Monte, Bobby Mussina, Ray Negron, Drew Nieporent, Rick Newman, Lois Nicotra, Rich Nicotra, Laura Nikiforchuck, Steve Olsen, Bob Orsini, Renee Pallonpelli, John Palumbo, Artie Pasqual, my friends at Patsy's, Joe Peck, Frank Pellegrino, David Permut, Lou Perry, Charlie Picerni, Johnny Planco, George Pollock, Jimmy Prav, Ed Pressman, Frank Rainone, Eddie Rambolla, Ricardo Razuri, Lynn Reich, Les Rogers, Anthony Rossi, Marie Rossi, Anthony Rossi Jr., John Rothman, Aris Sakellaridis, Sue Schacter, Sal Scognamillo, Ronnie Seidenberg, Stanley Seidenberg, Ray Serra, Mark Settembre, Marcie Siciliano, Nick Siciliano, Ron Silver, Joel Silver, Mark Simone, Eddie Somerfeld, Maryann Spano, Joe Spano, Nicole Spano, Dennis Squitieri, Gary Stein, Jerry Stiller, Claudia Swan, Lenny Termo, Todd Thaler, Roz Tisch, Irv Tisch, John Titta, Lana Titta, Jim Toback, Mike Tyson, Tom Van Dell, Guy Daniel Vastola, Spyros Venduras, Vinnie Viola, Nick Vitagliano, Giustina Vitagliano, Richie Vitieri, Norby Walters, Bronx Wanderers, Irv Welzer, Ira Yohalem, Joe Zappala, Debbie Zoeller, and Fred Zollo.

PHOTO CREDITS

Dedication Page:
Photo by Brian Hamill. Used with permission.
Photo Insert:
Page 1
Photo 1: Courtesy of the author's personal collection.
Photo 2: Courtesy of the author's personal collection.
Photo 3: Courtesy of the author's personal collection.
Page 2
Photo 1: Courtesy of the author's personal collection.
Photo 2: Courtesy of the author's personal collection.
Photo 3: Courtesy of the author's personal collection.
Page 3
Photo 1: Courtesy of the author's personal collection.
Photo 2: Courtesy of the author's personal collection.
Photo 3: Courtesy of the author's personal collection.
Photo 4: Courtesy of the author's personal collection.
Page 4
Photo 1: Courtesy of the author's personal collection.
Photo 2: Courtesy of the author's personal collection.
Photo 3: Courtesy of the author's personal collection.
Photo 4: Courtesy of the author's personal collection.
Page 5
Photo 1: Courtesy of the author's personal collection.
Photo 2: Photo by Joseph De Maria. Used with permission.
Photo 3: Photo by Joseph De Maria. Used with permission.
Page 6
Photo 1: Courtesy of the author's personal collection.
Photo 2: Courtesy of the author's personal collection.
Photo 3: Photo by Brian Hamill. Used with permission.
Page 7
Photo 1: Courtesy of the author's personal collection.
Photo 2: Courtesy of the author's personal collection.
Photo 3: Courtesy of the author's personal collection.
Photo 4: Courtesy of the author's personal collection.
Page 8
Photo 1: Photo by Herb Benkel. Used with permission.
Photo 2: Photo by Herb Benkel. Used with permission.